GOOD GOVERNANCE
Modern Global and Regional Perspectives

GOOD GOVERNANCE
Modern Global and Regional Perspectives

M.G. RAMAKANT RAO

KANISHKA PUBLISHERS, DISTRIBUTORS
NEW DELHI-110 002

KANISHKA PUBLISHERS, DISTRIBUTORS
4697/5-21A, Ansari Road, Daryaganj
New Delhi-110 002
Phones : 2327 0497, 2328 8285
Fax : 011-2328 8285
e-mail: kanishka_publishing@yahoo.co.in

First Published 2008

ISBN 978-81-8457-021-2

PRINTED IN INDIA

Published by Madan Sachdeva for Kanishka Publishers, Distributors, 4697/5-21A, Ansari Road, Daryaganj, New Delhi-110 002; Typeset by Sunshine Graphics, Delhi, and Printed at Nice Printing Press, Delhi.

Preface

This publication entitled "Good Governance: Modern Global and Regional Perspectives" can be considered as an introductory textbook on the subject of "good governance". Besides providing an introductory overview of the subject area in question, this book reflects briefly on major components, such as, participatory democracy, e-democracy, rule of law, consensus, economic efficiency, etc. The Declaration of Delhi on good governance is also presented. Issue, such as, transparency, the core factor as far as good governance is concerned, is discussed in detail, including the theme of media transparency.

The subject areas of corruption, public contracting and monitoring are also covered. The global priorities in these aforementioned areas are highlighted. The initiatives undertaken by the Transparency International and the Transparent Society, besides that of Extractive Industries Transparency Initiative are covered in detail.

Global and regional legal instrument and non-legal actions are discussed. Full list of anti-corruption conventions and related instruments are presented with requisite details and information. Regional initiatives, particularly, that of Africa, America, Asia-Pacific, Europe and Middle East are 'documented' in detail.

A report on the follow-up actions of the United Nations Convention Against Corruption is given, so as to aquaint readers with contemporary developments in this area of global priority for action. Also the Convention Against Transnational Organized Crime is presented in brief along with the review of its reports and notes. The Expert Group Report on Other Monitoring Programmes has been given as an appendix. The book is user friendly and is equipped with a detailed glossary of terms, acronyms/abbreviations and brief bibliography and index.

M.G. Ramakant Rao

Contents

Glossary of Terms

Accountability
The justification of expenditure and decisions made by an institution through financial and administrative reports to an independent person or organisation appointed to represent the interests of those who are affected by its decisions.

Capacity Building
A programme or project designed to increase an institution's ability to carry out its work effectively, for example, staff training, implementing better management procedures or making better use of technology.

Civil Society
Various groups of people come together and organize themselves around common interests. This might be informally at public meetings, or it might be more formally through community groups, non-government organisations, professional associations, sporting clubs and special interest groups. Civil society organisations can influence government policy, are a way of people gaining access to public resources and can build a sense of community based on trust and mutual respect.

Class Action
A legal device that enables one or more persons to sue or be sued as representatives of a large group of people interested in the same author.

Consensus Oriented
A decision process which seeks agreement and resolution of objections to achieve the most agreeable decision. It requires a broad and long-term perspective on what is needed for sustainable human development and how to achieve the goals of such development. This can only result from an understanding of the

historical, cultural and social contexts of a given society or community.

Constitution
A set of rules governing the politics of a nation.

Corruption
The abuse of one's official position for personal gain.

Democracy
Government by the people, exercised either directly or through elected representatives.

Disempower
To take away someone's power. This can be done in a concrete sense by taking away someone's rights but it can also be done in a psychological sense by creating situations where people feel helpless and lose confidence and self-esteem.

Effectiveness and Efficiency
Good governance means that processes and institutions produce results that meet the needs of society while making the best use of resources at their disposal. The concept of efficiency in the context of good governance also covers the sustainable use of natural resources and the protection of the environment.

Empower
To build a person's confidence and belief in their ability to do things. To provide concrete rights and facilities which enable them to accomplish things.

Equity and Inclusiveness
A society's well-being depends on ensuring that all its members feel that they have a stake in it and do not feel excluded from the mainstream of society. This requires that all groups, but particularly the most vulnerable, have opportunities to improve or maintain their well-being.

Good Governance
Good governance has eight major characteristics. It is *participatory, consensus oriented, accountable, transparent, responsive, effective* and *efficient, equitable* and *inclusive* and follows the *rule of law*. It ensures that corruption is minimized, the views of minorities are taken into account and that the voices of the most vulnerable in society

are heard in decision-making. It is also responsive to the present and future needs of society.

Governance
The political, economic and administrative processes carried out by government, business and the civil society sectors.

Infrastructure
The basic facilities, services, and installations needed for the functioning of a community or society, such as transportation and communications systems, water and power lines, and public institutions including schools, post offices, and prisons. It includes physical infrastructure (roads, bridges, buildings, plumbing, wiring and transport facilities) administrative infrastructure (trained staff, established procedures and appropriate equipment) social infrastructure (family and community networks) and political infrastructure (political parties, legislative bodies, electoral commission, judiciary and legal systems).

Judiciary
The system of courts that administers justice and provides a mechanism for the resolution of disputes. The term is also used to refer collectively to the judges, magistrates and other personnel who make decisions on disputed areas of law.

Legislative Body
The group which make the laws.

Non-Government Organizations (NGOs)
Organizations which are not run for profit and committed to improving the physical, social, economic and/or political environments in which people live. They are generally self-funding through donations and various fundraising events but sometimes receive funds from governments to undertake particular activities.

Participation
The ways people, both men and women are involved in political, economic and management decisions. Participation can either be direct or through legitimate intermediate institutions or representatives. It does not necessarily mean that the concerns of the most vulnerable in society are taken into consideration in decision-making. Participation needs to be informed and organized. This means freedom of association and expression on the one hand and an organized civil society on the other.

Political Process
The wide range of matters involved in the government of a country. On a formal level this might mean being a member of a party, voting in an election or being a formal member of government. On an informal level, it can refer to involvement with civil society organisations which might make representations to government. It can also mean being free to go to public meetings on important political and social issues, or having access to information.

Responsiveness
Good governance requires that institutions and processes try to serve all stakeholders within a reasonable timeframe.

Rule of Law
The fair legal framework which is enforced impartially and protects human rights, particularly those of minorities. Impartial enforcement of laws requires an independent judiciary and an impartial and incorruptible police force.

Social Capital
The relationships between people, based on shared values of equality, mutual respect and mutual assistance which enable them to cooperate for enjoyment or to achieve specific goals.

Transparency
An institution is transparent when its activities are open to public examination and accountable.

United Nations (UN)
An international organization of 191 countries (almost every country in the world) who have committed themselves to the UN Charter: to maintain international peace and security; to develop friendly relations among nations; to cooperate in solving international economic, social, cultural and humanitarian problems and in promoting respect for human rights and fundamental freedoms; and to be a centre for harmonizing the actions of nations in attaining these ends. The United Nations is not a world government and it does not make laws but it provides the means to help resolve international conflicts and formulate policies on matters affecting everyone.

Acronyms

ADB	African Development Bank
AFR	Afro-barometer
ASD	Asian Development Bank
BEEPS	Business Environment & Enterprise Performance Survey
BRI, QLM	Business Environment Risk Intelligence
BTI	Bertelsmann Foundation
CCR, FRH, FNT	Freedom House
CPIA	Country Policy & Institutional Assessment
CUD	Columbia University's State Capacity Survey
DRI	Global Insight's Global Risk Service
EBR	European Bank for Reconstruction and Development
EGV	Global E-Government Index
EIU	Economist Intelligence Unit
GAL	Gallup International
GCS, GCSA	World Economic Forum
HER	Heritage Foundation
HUM	State Department / Amnesty International
IJT	IJET Country Security Ratings
LOB	Latino-Barometer

MIG	Merchant International Group
MSI	Media Sustainability Index
PRC	Political Economic Risk Consultancy
PRS	Political Risk Services
RSF	Reporters without Borders
TPR	State Department's Trafficking in People Report
WBS, WDR	World Business Environment Survey
WCY	Institute for Management Development
WMO	Global Insight's Business Conditions and Risk Indicators

1

Good Governance: An Introductory Overview

Governance (in business) is the action of developing and managing consistent, cohesive policies, processes and decision rights for a given area of responsibility. For example, managing at a corporate level: privacy, internal investment, the use of data.

Governance is that separate process or certain part of management or leadership processes that makes decisions that define expectations, grant power, or verify performance. Frequently a government is established to administer these processes and systems.

The word derives from Latin origins that suggest the notion of 'steering'. This sense of 'steering' a society can be contrasted with the traditional 'top-down' approach of governments 'driving' society or the distinction between 'power to' in contrast to governments 'power over'.

As a process, governance may be carried out for any size organisation from a single human being to all of humanity, and it may be carried out for any purpose, good or evil, for profit or not. A reasonable or rational purpose of governance is to see to it (assure), sometimes on behalf of others, that the organisation produces a worthwhile pattern of good results while avoiding an undesirable pattern of bad circumstances.

Perhaps the most moral or natural purpose of governance is to assure, on behalf of those governed, a worthy pattern of good while avoiding a truly undesirable patttern of bad. The ideal purpose, obviously, would assure a perfect pattern of good with no bad. A government, then, is a set of inter-related positions that govern and use or exercise power, particularly coercive power. It may be purposeful or purposeless, its purpose for the good of all, some, one or none.

A good government, following this line, could be a set of interrelated positions exercising coercive power that assures, on behalf of those governed, a worthwhile pattern of good results while avoiding an undesirable pattern of bad circumstances, by making decisions that define expectations grant power and verify performance.

Various systems (i.e., designed or discovered collections of elements that produce a pattern of results) have been used and could be used to govern. Sometimes these could be referred to as models or forms, depending on the completeness of the system.

Politics is a means by which the governance process operates. For example, expectations may be chosen by way of political activity, power may be granted through political action, and performance may be judged through political behaviour.

Conceiving of governance in this way, one can apply the concept to as large a nation state as desired, to corporations, to non-profits or NGOs, to partnerships and other associations, to project teams, and to any number of humans engaged in some purposeful activity.

Meanings

The World Bank defines governance as

> *the exercise of political authority and the use of institutional resources to manage society's problems and affairs.*

An alternate definition suggests that governance is

> *the use of institutions, structures of authority and even collaboration to allocate resources and coordinate or control activity in society or the economy.*

English-speakers sometimes erroneously confuse the term *governance* with the term *government*.

According to the UNDP's Regional Project on Local Governance for Latin America: "Governance has been defined as the rules of the political system to solve conflicts between actors and adopt decision (legality). It has also been used to describe the 'proper functioning of institutions and their acceptance by the public' (legitimacy). And it has been used to invoke the efficacy of government and the achievement of consensus by democratic means (participation)."

The State and Politics

Some suggest that there should be a clear distinction between the concepts of governance and politics. Politics involves processes by which a group of people with initially divergent opinions or interests reach collective decisions generally regarded as binding on the group, and enforced as common policy. Governance, on the other hand, conveys the administrative and process-oriented elements of governing rather than its antagonistic ones. Such an argument continues to assume the possibility of the traditional separation between 'politics' and 'administration'. This distinction is sometimes questioned in contemporary governance practice and theory, under the premise that both 'governance' and 'politics' involve aspects of power.

In general terms governance occurs in three broad ways:

1. through top-down methods that primarily involve governments and the state bureaucracy,
2. the use of market mechanisms where market principles of competition are employed to allocate resources while operating under government regulation, and
3. through networks involving Public-private Partnerships (PPP) or with the collaboration of community organisations.

These modes of governance are often presented in terms of hierarchy, markets and networks.

Corporate Organisations

Corporate organisations often use the word *governance* to describe the manner in which boards or their like direct a corporation, and laws and customs applying to that direction.

Industry

The term *governance* also occurs in industry—especially in the Information Technology (IT) sector—to describe the processes to follow in a successful department, team or project. (See project governance)

Fair Governance

A fair governance implies that these mechanisms function in a way that allows the executives (the "agents") to respect the rights and interests of the stakeholders (the "principals"), in a spirit of democracy.

Global Governance

Global governance refers to a system-wide structure that both allows and constrains the behaviour of actors in interdependent relationships in the absence of an overarching political authority. The global international system offers the best example of this.

Corporate Governance

The fundamental concerns of corporate governance include:

- ensuring that conditions apply whereby a firm's directors and managers act in the interests of the firm and of its shareholders and even of its workers.
- ensuring the means exist to hold managers accountable to investors and employees for the use of assets.

Corporate governance specifies the relationships between, and the distribution of rights and responsibilities among, the main groups of participants:

- the board of directors
- the managers (if any)
- the workers
- the shareholders or owners
- the regulators
- the customers
- the community (people affected by the actions of the organisation)
- the suppliers.

The individuals within the above groups transact with the firm for their own individual purposes, so as the entire group can achieve more mutual benefit than any individual can alone. For instance, directors, workers and management receive salaries, benefits and reputation; whilst shareholders receive capital return. Customers receive goods and services; and suppliers receive compensation for their goods or services. In return, these individuals provide the time, labour, expertise, capital, goods, services, consent, etc., required for the organisation to pursue its purpose.

The edifice of corporate governance includes:

- the national/regional laws governing the formation of corporate bodies.
- the bye-laws established by the corporate body itself.
- the organisational structure of the corporate body.

Corporate governance aims to:

- align the actions of the individual parts of an organisation toward aggregate mutual benefit.
- provide the means by which each individual part of the organisation can trust that the other parts each make their contribution to the mutual benefit of the organisation and that none gain unfairly at the expense of others.
- provide a means by which information can quickly flow between the various stakeholders to ensure that the changing nature of both the stakeholder needs and desires and the environment in which the organisation operates get effectively factored into decision processes.

Project Governance

The term *governance* as used in industry [especially in the Information Technology (IT) sector] describes the processes that need to exist for a successful project.

Global Governance

In contrast to the traditional meaning of governance some authors like James Rosenau have used "global governance" to denote the regulation of interdependent relations in the absence of an overarching political authority. The best example of this in the international system or relationships between independent states. The term can however be applied wherever a group of free equals need to form a regular relationship.

INTRODUCTION TO GOOD GOVERNANCE

Recently the terms "governance" and "good governance" are being increasingly used in development literature. Bad governance is being increasingly regarded as one of the root causes of all evil within our societies. Major donors and international financial institutions are increasingly basing their aid and loans on the condition that reforms that ensure "good governance" are undertaken.

This article tries to explain, as simply as possible, what "governance" and "good governance" means.

Governance

The concept of "governance" is not new. It is as old as human civilization. Simply put "governance" means: **the process of decision-making and the process by which decisions are implemented (or not implemented).** Governance can be used in several contexts such as corporate governance, international governance, national governance and local governance.

Since governance is the process of decision-making and the process by which decisions are implemented, an analysis of governance focuses on the formal and informal actors involved in decision-making and implementing the decisions made and the formal and informal structures that have been set in place to arrive at and implement the decision.

Government is one of the actors in governance. Other actors involved in governance vary depending on the level of government that is under discussion. In rural areas, for example, other actors may include influential landlords, associations of peasant farmers, cooperatives, NGOs, research institutes, religious leaders, finance institutions, political parties and the military etc. The situation in urban areas is much more complex. Figure 1.1 provides the interconnections between actors involved in urban governance. At the national level, in addition to the above actors, media, lobbyists, international donors, multi-national corporations, etc., may play a role in decision-making or in influencing the decision-making process.

All actors other than government and the military are grouped together as part of the "civil society." In some countries in addition to the civil society, organized crime syndicates also influence decision-making, particularly in urban areas and at the national level.

Similarly formal government structures are one means by which decisions are arrived at and implemented. At the national level, informal decision-making structures, such as "kitchen cabinets" or informal advisors may exist. In urban areas, organized crime syndicates such as the "Land Mafia" may influence decision-making. In some rural areas locally powerful families may make or influence decision-making. Such, informal decision-making is often the result of corrupt practices or leads to corrupt practices.

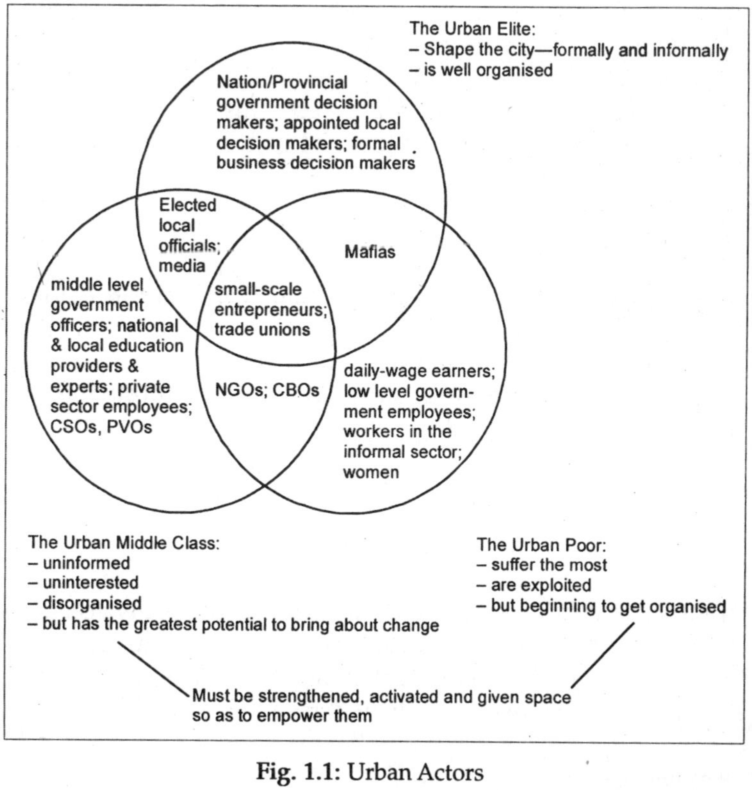

Fig. 1.1: Urban Actors

Good Governance

Good governance has 8 major characteristics. It is participatory, consensus oriented, accountable, transparent, responsive, effective and efficient, equitable and inclusive and follows the rule of law. It assures that corruption is minimized, the views of minorities are taken into account and that the voices of the most vulnerable in society are heard in decision-making. It is also responsive to the present and future needs of society.

Participation

Participation by both men and women is a key cornerstone of good governance. Participation could be either direct or through legitimate intermediate institutions or representatives. It is important to point out that representative democracy does not necessarily mean that the concerns of the most vulnerable in society would be taken into consideration in decision-making. Participation needs to be informed and organized. This means freedom of association and expression on the one hand and an organized civil society on the other hand.

Rule of Law

Good governance requires fair legal frameworks that are enforced impartially. It also requires full protection of human rights, particularly those of minorities. Impartial enforcement of laws requires an independent judiciary and an impartial and incorruptible police force.

Transparency

Transparency means that decisions taken and their enforcement are done in a manner that follows rules and regulations. It also means that information is freely available and directly accessible to those who will be affected by such decisions and their enforcement. It also means that enough information is provided and that it is provided in easily understandable forms and media.

Responsiveness

Good governance requires that institutions and processes try to serve all stakeholders within a reasonable timeframe.

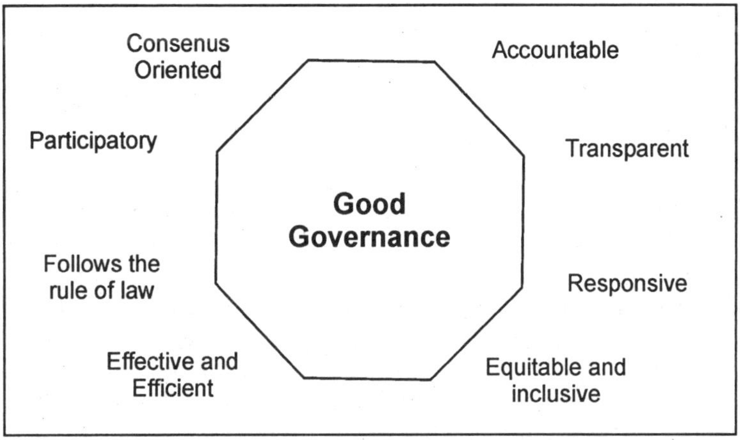

Fig. 1.2: Characteristics of Good Governance

Consensus Oriented

There are several actors and as many view points in a given society. Good governance requires mediation of the different interests in society to reach a broad consensus in society on what is in the best interest of the whole community and how this can be achieved. It also requires a broad and long-term perspective on what is needed for sustainable human development and how to achieve the goals of such development. This can only result from an understanding of the historical, cultural and social contexts of a given society or community.

Equity and Inclusiveness

A society's well-being depends on ensuring that all its members feel that they have a stake in it and do not feel excluded from the mainstream of society. This requires all groups, but particularly the most vulnerable, have opportunities to improve or maintain their well-being.

Effectiveness and Efficiency

Good governance means that processes and institutions produce results that meet the needs of society while making the best use of resources at their disposal. The concept of efficiency in the context of good governance also covers the sustainable use of natural resources and the protection of the environment.

Accountability

Accountability is a key requirement of good governance. Not only governmental institutions but also the private sector and civil society organisations must be accountable to the public and to their institutional stakeholders. Who is accountable to whom varies depending on whether decisions or actions taken are internal or external to an organization or institution. In general an organisation or an institution is accountable to those who will be affected by its decisions or actions. Accountability cannot be enforced without transparency and the rule of law.

Conclusions

From the above discussion it should be clear that good governance is an ideal which is difficult to achieve in its totality. Very few countries and societies have come close to achieving good governance in its totality. However, to ensure sustainable human development, actions must be taken to work towards this ideal with the aim of making it a reality.

GOOD GOVERNANCE: AN OVERVIEW

The terms governance and **good governance** are being increasingly used in development literature. Governance describes the process of decision-making and the process by which decisions are implemented (or not implemented). Hereby, public institutions conduct public affairs, manage public resources, and guarantee the realization of human rights. **Good governance** accomplishes this in a manner essentially free of abuse and corruption, and with due regard for the rule of law.

Good governance defines an ideal which is difficult to achieve in its totality. However, to ensure sustainable human development, actions must be taken to work towards this ideal. Major donors and international financial institutions, like the IMF or World Bank, are increasingly basing their aid and loans on the condition that reforms ensuring **good governance** are undertaken.

Good governance can be understood as a set of 8 major characteristics:

- participation,
- rule of law,
- transparency,
- responsiveness,
- consensus orientation,
- equity and inclusiveness,
- effectiveness and efficiency, and
- accountability.

These characteristics assure that

- corruption is minimized,
- the views of minorities are taken into account, and
- that the voices of the most vulnerable in society are heard in decision-making.

Participation

- Participation by both men and women.
- Participation could be either direct or through legitimate intermediate institutions or representatives.
- Participation also means freedom of association and expression on the one hand and an organized civil society on the other hand.

Rule of Law

- Good governance requires fair legal frameworks that are enforced impartially.
- Full sprotection of human rights, particularly those of minorities.
- It also means independent judiciary and an impartial and incorrsuptible police force.

Transparency

- Decisions taken and their enforcement are done in a manner that follows rules and regulations.
- Information is freely available and directly accessible to

those who will be affected by such decisions and their enforcement.

Responsiveness

- Institutions and processes try to serve all stakeholders within a reasonable timeframe.

Consensus Orientation

- Need of mediation of the different interests in society to reach a broad consensus in society on what is in the best interest of the whole community and how this can be achieved.
- It also requires a long-term perspective for sustainable human development and how to achieve the goals of such development.

Equity and Inclusiveness

- Ensuring that all members of society feel that they have a stake in it and do not feel excluded from the mainstream.
- This requires all groups, and especially the most vulnerable to have opportunities to maintain or improve their well-being.

Effectiveness and Efficiency

- Processes and institutions produce results that meet the needs of society while making the best use of resources at their disposal.
- It also means sustainable use of natural resources and the protection of the environment.

Accountability

- Governmental institutions as well as the private sector and civil society organisations must be accountable to the public and to their institutional stakeholders.
- In general organisations and institutions are accountable to those who will bess affected by decisions or actions.

A Basic Practical Example of Good Governanance would be where a member of a committee, with a vested interest in a topic being discussed at committee, would absent themselves from the discussion and not attempt to exert influence.

PARTICIPATORY DEMOCRACY

Participatory democracy is a process emphasizing the broad involvement of constituents in the direction and operation of political systems. While etymological roots imply that all governments deserving the name "democracy" would rely on the participation of their citizens (the Greek *demos* and *kratos* combine to suggest that "the people rule"), traditional representative democracies tend to limit citizen participation to voting, leaving the main work of governance to a professional political elite. Participatory democracy strives to create opportunities for all members of a political group to make meaningful contributions to decision-making, and seeks to broaden the range of people who have access to such opportunities.

Some scholars argue for refocusing the term 'participatory democracy' on community-based activity within the domain of civil society, based on the belief that a strong non-governmental public sphere is a precondition for the emergence of a strong liberal democracy. These scholars tend to stress the value of separation between the realm of civil society and the formal political realm.

Political Variantss

Its political variants include:

- Anticipatory democracy,
- Consensus democracy,
- Deliberative democracy,
- Direct democracy, and
- Non-partisan democracy.

Representative democracy is not generally considered participatory. Bioregional democracy often is, but that is not necessary to its definition. Grassroots democracy is an alternative term that has actually been used to imply almost any combination of the above.

Participatory politics or Parpolity is a long-range political theory that also incorporates many of the above and strives to create a political system that will allow people to participate in politics, as much as possible in a face-to-face manner.

Panocracy also has similarities with participatory democracy. However, it avoids the concept of *demos* or the people having a single view with the inevitable limitations that come from trying to agree what that view is. It also avoids the expectations that attach to anything called democracy.

Green View

All theories of green politics include some variant of participatory methods. In these theories, of which the best known is the Four Pillars of the Green Party, making consultation on important decisions by those who will carry it out reduces the probability of a decision that seriously disadvantages one group (reducing social justice) or of violent resistance (breaking non-violence). Expressing ecological wisdom in law, for instance, is not likely to be respected unless the persons who live near protected eco-systems help to carry out the decision on a daily basis. Efforts to redefine green politics to exclude the participatory and consensus decision-making methods have historically failed.

Workplace Variants

Workplace democracy is an application of methods generally used in politics in the economic enterprise, including the election or hiring of management by workers. These methods are inherently participatory since the daily work is being carried out by the people who have made the decision, who bear its consequences.

E-DEMOCRACY

E-democracy, a portmanteau of **electronic** and **democracy**, comprises the use of electronic communications technologies, such as the Internet, in enhancing democratic processes within a democratic republic or representative democracy. It is a political development still in its infancy, as well as the subject of much debate and activity within government, civic-oriented groups and societies around the world.

The term is both descriptive and prescriptive. Typically, the kinds of enhancements sought by proponents of e-democracy are framed in terms of making processes more accessible; making citizen participation in public policy decision-making more expansive and direct so as to enable broader influence in policy outcomes as more individuals involved could yield smarter policies; increasing transparency and accountability; and keeping the government closer to the consent of the governed, increasing its political legitimacy. E-democracy includes within its scope *electronic voting*, but has a much wider span than this single aspect of the democratic process.

E-democracy is also sometimes referred to as **cyberdemocracy** or **digital democracy**. Prior to 1994, when the term e-democracy was coined in the midst of on-line civic efforts in Minnesota, the term **teledemocracy** was prevalent. "Teledemocracy", coined by political scientist Ted Becker in 1981, combined elements of e-democracy with those of "deliberative democracy" coined about the same time. "Teledemocracy" then is an umbrella term that includes both "e-democracy", "deliberative democracy" and many types of "direct democracy."

Practical Issues with E-democracy

The challenge for governments and bureaucracies, as well as for individuals and groups, is to develop tools and adapt processes so as to meet the aspirations of e-democracy. There are numerous practical and theoretical issues which have yet to be scoped, understood or solved, and work is underway in many democracies on a wide and diverse set of experiments and trials to test approaches and techniques.

One major problem which needs to be overcome for e-democracy to be a success is that of citizen identification. For secure elections and other secure citizen-to-government transactions, citizens must have some form of identification that preserves privacy and maybe also one which could be used in Internet forums. The need to allow anonymous posting while at the same time giving certain contributors extra status such as biologists can be solved using certain cryptographic methods. In the United Kingdom there is much contention about the introduction of the British national identity card.

Another such problem would be that there are many vested interests that would be harmed by a more direct democracy. Amongst these are politicians, media moguls and some in big business and trade unions. These organisations are likely to oppose meaningful application of e-democracy concepts.

Internet as Political Medium

The Internet is viewed as a platform and delivery medium for tools that help to eliminate some of the distance constraints in direct democracy. Technical media for e-democracy can be expected to extend to mobile technologies such as phones.

There are important differences between previous communication media and the Internet that are relevant to the Internet as a political medium. Most importantly the Internet is a many-to-many communication medium where radio and television, which broadcast few-to-many, and telephones broadcast few-to-few, are not. Also, the Internet has a much greater computational capacity allowing strong encryption and database management, which is important in community information access and sharing, deliberative democracy and electoral fraud prevention. Further, people use the Internet to collaborate or meet in an asynchronous manner—that is, they do not have to be physically gathered at the same moment to get things accomplished. Due to all these factors, the Internet has the potential to take over certain traditional media of political communication such as the telephone, the television, newspapers and the radio.

Benefits and Disadvantages

Some traditional objections to direct democracy are argued to apply to e-democracy, such as the potential for governance to tend towards populism and demagoguery. More practical objections exist, not least in terms of the digital divide between those with access to the media of e-democracy (mobile phones and Internet connections) and those without, as well as the opportunity cost of expenditure on e-democracy innovations.

Contemporary technologies such as electronic mailing lists, peer-to-peer networks, collaborative software, wikis, Internet forums and blogs are clues to and early potential solutions for some aspects of e-democracy; equally, they are bellwethers of some of the issues associated with the territory, such as the inability to sustain new initiatives or protect against identity theft, information overload and vandalism.

Electronic Direct Democracy

Electronic direct democracy is a form of direct democracy in which the Internet and other electronic communications technologies are used to ameliorate the bureaucracy involved with referenda. Many advocates think that also important to this notion are technological enhancements to the deliberative process. Electronic direct democracy is sometimes referred to as EDD (many other names are used for what is essentially the same concept).

EDD requires the ability to register votes on issues electronically. As in a direct democracy, in an EDD citizens would have the right to vote on legislation before parliament, author new legislation and recall representatives at any stage.

Ross Perot was for a time a prominent advocate of EDD when he advocated "electronic town halls" during his 1992 and 1996 Presidential campaigns in the United States.

A contemporary example that takes an evolutionary approach to EDD is where representatives independently conduct referenda on issues using the Internet or other electronic communications technologies. This potential step toward electronic direct democracy does not require any constitutional changes as it simply strengthens the relationship between the constituent and the representative.

EDD as a system is not fully implemented anywhere in the world although Switzerland, already partially governed by direct democracy, is moving towards such a system.

RULE OF LAW

The **rule of law** is the principle that governmental authority is legitimately exercised only in accordance with written, publicly disclosed laws adopted and enforced in accordance with established procedure. The principle is intended to be a safeguard against arbitrary governance.

In continental European legal thinking, rule of law is associated with a *Rechtsstaat*. According to Anglo-American thinking, hallmarks of adherence to the rule of law commonly include a clear separation of powers, legal certainty, the principle of legitimate expectation and equality of all before the law.

Some authors, as J. Shklar, claim that "the phrase 'the Rule of Law' has become meaningless thanks to ideological abuse and general over-use."

Samuel Rutherford was one of the first modern authors to give the principle theoretical foundations in *Lex, Rex* (1644), and later Montesquieu in *The Spirit of the Laws* (1748).

Generalities

Aristotle first defined the contrast between the *rule of men* and the *rule of law*, the latter being seen as separate and stemming from an external and pure authority.

Thomas Aquinas defined a valid law as being one that

- is in keeping with reason,
- was established by a proper authority,
- is for the purpose of achieving good, and
- was properly communicated to all.

In Commonwealth law, the most famous exposition of the concept of rule of law was laid down by Albert Venn Dicey in his *Law of the Constitution.*

> "The rule of law is a political principle the classic exposition of which is in Dicey Law of the Constitution (10th Edn, 1959) p. 187 et seq. Dicey identified three principles which together establish the rule of law: (1) the absolute supremacy or predominance of regular law as opposed to the influence of arbitrary power; (2) equality before the law or the equal subjection of all classes to the ordinary law of the land administered by the ordinary courts; and (3) the law of the constitution is a consequence of the rights of individuals as defined and enforced by the courts."

—*Halsbury's Laws of England,*
Vol: Constitutional Law and Human Rights,
paragraph 6, footnote 1

> ...every official, from the Prime Minister down to a constable or a collector of taxes, is under the same responsibility for every act done without legal justification as any other

> citizen. The Reports abound with cases in which officials have been brought before the courts, and made, in their personal capacity, liable to punishment, or to the payment of damages, for acts done in their official character but in excess of their lawful authority. [Appointed government officials and politicians, alike]... and all subordinates, though carrying out the commands of their official superiors, are as responsible for any act which the law does not authorise as is any private and unofficial person.
>
> —*Law of the Constitution*
> (London: MacMillan, 9th ed., 1950), 194.

Another definition can be found at *Halsbury's Laws of England*, Vol: Constitutional Law and Human Rights, paragraph 6

> The legal basis of government gives rise to the principle of legality, sometimes referred to as the rule of law. This may be expressed as a number of propositions, as described below:
>
> (1) The existence or non-existence of a power or duty is a matter of law and not of fact, and so must be determined by reference either to the nature of the legal personality of the body in question and the capacities that go with it, or to some enactment or reported case. As far as the capacities that go with legal personality are concerned, many public bodies are incorporated by statute and so statutory provisions will define and limit their legal capacities. Individuals who are public office-holders have the capacities that go with the legal personality that they have as natural persons. The Crown is a corporation sole or aggregate and so has general legal capacity, including (subject to some statutory limitations and limitations imposed by European law) the capacity to enter into contracts and to own and dispose of property. The fact of a continued undisputed exercise of a power by a public body is immaterial, unless it points to a customary power exercised from time immemorial. In particular, the existence of a power cannot be proved by the practice of a private office.
>
> (2) The argument of state necessity is not sufficient to establish the existence of a power or duty which would entitle a

public body to act in a way that interferes with the rights or liberties of individuals. However, the common law does recognise that in case of extreme urgency, when the ordinary machinery of the state cannot function, there is a justification for the doing of acts needed to restore the regular functioning of the machinery of government.

(3) If effect is to be given to the doctrine that the existence or non-existence of a power or duty is a matter of law, it should be possible for the courts to determine whether or not a particular power or duty exists, to define its ambit and provide an effective remedy for unlawful action. The independence of the judiciary is essential to the principle of legality. The right of access to the courts can be excluded by statute, but this is not often done in express terms. A person whose civil or political rights and freedoms as guaranteed by the Convention for the Protection of Human Rights and Fundamental Freedoms (the European Convention on Human Rights) have been infringed is entitled under the Convention to an effective right of access to the courts and an effective national remedy. On the other hand, powers are often given to bodies other than the ordinary courts, to decide questions of law without appeal to the ordinary courts, and sometimes in such terms that their freedom from appellate jurisdiction extends to their findings of fact or law on which the existence of their powers depends.

(4) Since the principal elements of the structure of the machinery of government, and the powers and duties which belong to its several parts, are defined by law, its form and course can be altered only by a change of law. Conversely, since the legislative power of Parliament is unrestricted, save where European Community law has primacy, its form and course can at any time be altered by Parliament. Consequently there are no powers or duties inseparably annexed to the executive government.

In American law, the most famous exposition of the same principle was drafted by John Adams for the constitution of the Commonwealth of Massachusetts, in justification of the principle of separation of powers:

> In the government of this commonwealth, the legislative department shall never exercise the executive and judicial powers or either of them: the executive shall never exercise the legislative and judicial powers, or either of them: the judicial shall never exercise the legislative and executive powers, or either of them: to the end it may be a government of laws and not of men.
>
> —*Massachusetts Constitution,*
> Part The First, Article XXX (1780).

The last phrase, "to the end it may be a government of laws and not of men," has been quoted with approval by the U.S. Supreme Court and every state supreme court in the United States.

A similar concept is found in *Common Sense* (1776) by Thomas Paine:

> ... the world may know, that so far as we approve of monarchy, that in America THE LAW IS KING. For as in absolute governments the King is law, so in free countries the law OUGHT to be King; and there ought to be no other.

The concept "rule of law" is generally associated with several other concepts, such as:

- *Nullum crimen, nulla poena sine praevia lege poenali*: No *ex post facto* laws.
- *Presumption of Innocence*: All individuals are "innocent until proven otherwise."
- *Double Jeopardy*: Individuals may only be punished *once* for every specific crime committed. Retrials may or may not be permitted on the grounds of new evidence.
- *Legal Equality*: All individuals are given the same rights without distinction to their social stature, religion, political opinions, etc. That is, as Montesquieu would have it, "law should be like death, which spares no one."
- *Habeas Corpus*: In full *habeas corpus ad subjiciendum*, a Latin term meaning "you must have the body to be subjected (to examination)." A person who is arrested has the right to be told what crimes he or she is accused of, and to request that his or her custody be reviewed by judicial authority. Persons unlawfully imprisoned have to be freed.

The concept of "rule of law" *per se* says nothing of the "justness" of the laws themselves, but simply how the legal system upholds the law. As a consequence of this, a very undemocratic nation or one without respect for human rights can exist with or without a "rule of law", a situation which many argue is applicable to several modern dictatorships. However, the "rule of law" or *Rechtsstaat* is considered a pre-requisite for democracy, and as such, has served as a common basis for human rights discourse between countries such as the People's Republic of China and the West.

The rule of law is an ancient ideal first posited by Aristotle as a system of rules inherent in the natural order. It continues to be important as a normative ideal, even as legal scholars struggle to define it. The concept of impartial rule of law is found in the Chinese political philosophy of legalism, but the totalitarian nature of the regime that this produced had a profound effect on Chinese political thought which at least rhetorically emphasized personal moral relations over impersonal legal ones. Although Chinese emperors were not subject to law, in practice they found it necessary to act according to regular procedures for reasons of statecraft.

In the Anglo-American legal tradition rule of law has been seen as a guard against despotism and as enforcing limitations on the power of the government. In the People's Republic of China the discourse around rule of law centers on the notion that laws ultimately enhance the power of the state and the nation, which is why the Chinese Government adopts the principle of rule *by* law rather than rule *of* law.

Declaration of Delhi

In 1959, an international gathering of over 185 judges, lawyers, and law professors from 53 countries, meeting in New Delhi and speaking as the International Commission of Jurists, made a declaration as to the fundamental principle of the rule of law.

Bingham's Sub-Rules

In his speech on 16 November, 2006, Lord Bingham of Cornhill postulated eight sub-rules of the rule of law:

- the law must be accessible and so far as possible intelligible, clear and predictable,
- questions of legal right and liability should ordinarily be

resolved by application of the law and not the exercise of discretion,

- the laws of the land should apply equally to all, save to the extent that objective differences justify differentiation,
- the law must afford adequate protection of fundamental human rights,
- means must be provided for resolving, without prohibitive cost or inordinate delay, *bona fide* civil disputes which the parties themselves are unable to resolve,
- ministers and public officers at all levels must exercise the powers conferred on them reasonably, in good faith, for the purpose for which the powers were conferred and without exceeding the limits of such powers,
- adjudicative procedures provided by the state should be fair, and
- the state must comply with its obligations in international law, the law which whether deriving from treaty or international custom and practice governs the conduct of nations.

Authoritarianism

Rule of law is opposed by authoritarian and totalitarian states. The explicit policy of those governments, as evidenced in the Night and Fog decrees of Nazi Germany, is that the government possesses the inherent authority to act purely on its own volition and without being subject to any checks or limitations. Dictatorships generally establish secret police forces, which are not accountable to established laws, which can suppress threats to state authority.

Critique

The rule of law, i.e., the application of the body of law to the government, does not restrict the government in any way since any desired government privilege can be made by the government into a legal provision. The rule of law should be seen as a bureaucratic hoop for the government to jump through, rather than as a material restriction on government power. This criticism is although mostly relevant where the principle of the separation of powers is not respected (i.e., where the legislative power and the executive power—the government—are held by the same body).

When the government is not also the legislative body, the principle of the rule of law may hold.

Another critique is that the principle of legal equality can be easily subverted since many laws affect different people in different ways. A law giving the legislators a raise, for example, affects the legislators in a different way than it affects the rest of the public. But since such laws are not necessarily made in accordance with the rule of law, it remains unclear if this criticism is really aimed at the principle of the rule of law itself rather than to actual legislatures.

Marxist theory analyzed the capitalist state as an instrument of oppression of the people at the hands of the bourgeoisie, which set the laws to suit itself. Following this, some critical theorists analyze the "rule of law" as a juridical fiction which aims at disguising the reality of violence and, in Marxist terminology, "class struggle." This theory presumes that the "bourgeoisie" holds the power to set the laws.

The Italian philosopher Giorgio Agamben argues that the state of exception is at the core of the concept of sovereignty, and not the "rule of law" as liberal thinkers have it. While the sovereign claims to follow the "rule of law", any protection the people have, however fundamental, can be jettisoned once the government finds it convenient to do so.

DECLARATION OF DELHI

The New Delhi Congress or Declaration of Delhi was an international gathering of over 185 judges, lawyers and law professors from 53 countries all over the world, united as the International Commission of Jurists that took place in New Delhi, India in 1959. The theme of the New Delhi Congress was "The Rule of Law in a Free Society." The Congress further developed the principles and procedures underlying the Rule of Law as well as defining and clarifying the concept itself.

History

In Anglo-American tradition, the most influential version of the rule of law has been that popularised by British jurist A.V. Dicey in 1885. Dicey's doctrine on the rule of law is a three-fold one:

(*i*) *The absolute supremacy or predominance of 'regular' law* as opposed to the influence of arbitrary power and the absence of discretionary authority on the part of the government. No man is punishable or can be lawfully made to suffer in body or goods except for a distinct breach of law established in the ordinary legal manner before the ordinary courts.

(*ii*) *Equality before the law:* All persons whether high official or ordinary citizen are subject to the same law adminstered by the ordinary courts.

(*iii*) The constitution in the result of the ordinary law of the land **developed by the judges on a case by case basis.** It is thus woven into the very fabric of law and not superimposed from above. This is essentially a defence to the United Kingdom's unwritten constitution.

Modern lawyers would regard the rule of law as essentially a political or moral idea, although none the less important for that, since it affects the way the law is developed and applied. It concerns ideas of regularity, access to the courts, fair procedure and honouring expectations. The 'rule of law' in Dicey's sense was a political factor that led to the enactment of the **Crown Proceedings Act,** 1947 in the United Kingdom. Before that Act the Crown, that is, the Central Government, was immune from liability in the courts for breach of contract or for injuries inflicted by its servants.

Since the Second World War there have been several attempts to draw up Internationally binding codes of basic human rights. The Nurenberg Trials of Nazi war criminals that were organised by the victorious allies were based upon the assumption that some of the laws of Nazi Germany were not valid as they were repugnant to the standards of morality accepted by all civilised nations. This approach to law raises profound philosophical problems, but the role of modern human rights treaties and declarations is a less dramatic one. These include the **United Nations Universal Declaration of Human Rights** (1948), and the **Declaration of Delhi** or **New Delhi Congress** (1959).

The Modern Concept of the Rule of Law

The Delhi Congress gave rise to three important elements in the concept of the Rule of Law:

- First, that the individual is **possessed of certain rights and freedoms** and that he is entitled to protection of these rights and freedoms by the State;
- Second, that there is an absolute need for an **independent judiciary** and bar as well as for effective machinery for the protection of fundamental rights and freedoms; and
- Third, that **the establishment of social, economic and cultural conditions** would permit men to live in dignity and to fulfil their legitimate aspirations.

In preparation of the Congress, the Commission held a preparatory meeting in The Hague, Netherlands on the 7 and 8 July, 1958, where the drafting of the Congress Working Paper on the Rule of Law was mandated to former ICJ Secretary-General, Mr. Norman Marsh. The 134 pages paper were based on information gathered in an international survey of lawyers and legal institutions conducted by the ICJ Secretariat in the course of 1957. The information gathered was divided into the following sections:

1. The Legislative and the Rule of Law.
2. The Executive and the Rule of Law.
3. Criminal Process and the Rule of Law.
4. The Judiciary and Legal Profession under the Rule of Law.

The committees set-up during the Congress were each dedicated to one of the four themes with the Working Paper providing the basis of the discussions. The reports and conclusions of the committees were presented in two plenary sessions and the texts were subsequently referred to a Steering Committee, which issued the conclusions at the closing plenary session.

The Legislative and the Rule of Law

In its conclusions, the committee on the legislative stated that under the Rule of Law, the legislature carried out the function of creating and maintaining conditions that would uphold the dignity of man. This would include recognition of civil and political rights as well as the establishment of the social, economic, educational and cultural conditions, which the committee deemed essential to the full development of the individual's personality.

The committee also stated that minimum standards and principles regulating the individual within society were essential for the Rule of Law. Such standards would, however, imply certain limitations on legislative power. The limitations on the legislative should be enshrined in a constitution and safeguarded by an independent judicial tribunal.

According to the conclusions of the committee, the legislative had the responsibility to: abstain from enacting retroactive penal legislation; not discriminate in its laws between one citizen and another; not interfere with freedom of religious belief; not deny members of society the right to responsible government; not place restrictions on the freedom of speech, assembly or association; not impair the exercise of fundamental rights and freedoms of the individual; and provide the procedural mechanisms to protect the above-mentioned freedoms ("procedure of due process").

The Executive and the Rule of Law

The committee on the executive concluded that the granting of power by the legislative to the executive should be undertaken within the narrowest possible limits and that legislature should define the extent and purpose of such delegated powers, as well as the procedures by which such delegated power was to be brought into effect. An independent judicial body should be given the power to review the legislation passed by the executive (judicial review).

When the executive directly and adversely affected a person or the property rights of an individual, he or she should have the right to present his or her case before a court as well as the right to an adequate remedy. In the absence of a judicial review mechanism, antecedent procedures of hearing, enquiry and consultation should be established, through which parties whose rights or interests would be affected can have an adequate opportunity to make representation.

The committee also concluded that the Rule of Law would be strengthened if the executive were to be required to formulate its reasons when reaching its decisions, and at the request of a concerned party, to communicate them.

Criminal Process and the Rule of Law

The committee considered the practical application of the Rule of Law in the field of criminal process. The committee clarified rules which it regarded as the minimum necessary to ensure the observance of the Rule of Law.

The committee made its conclusions regarding the prohibition of retrospective enactment of penal legislation (certainty of the law) as well as on the principle of presumption of innocence, which in the committee's view required that the burden of proof should only be shifted once facts creating a contrary presumption had been established.

Concerning the arrest of an individual, the power to arrest should be regulated and the arrested person should be told at once the grounds of his or her arrest. He or she should be entitled to a legal adviser and be brought before a judicial authority within a short period of time.

In relation to pre-trial detention, the committee listed the rights of the arrested, including the right to apply for bail.

Conclusions were also made in respect to the preparation and conduct of the defence and the minimum duties of the prosecution. These included the requirement that the prosecution not withhold favourable evidence from the accused.

Regarding the examination of the accused, the committee laid down minimum standards, such as respect for the right not to incriminate oneself and provisions that guarantee the physical and psychological integrity of the accused.

The committee also made conclusions regarding trial in public for criminal cases and the right to appeals and remedies.

Lastly, the committee concluded that the Rule of Law did not require any particular theory regarding punishment, but must necessarily condemn cruel, inhuman or excessive preventive measures or punishments and thus the committee supported the adoption of reformative measures wherever possible.

The Judiciary and Legal Professions under the Rule of Law

The committee on the Judiciary and the Legal Profession emphasised the importance of an independent judiciary in upholding the Rule of Law. The independence of the judiciary would be safeguarded by certain measures, including co-operation between at least two branches of the state (i.e. judiciary and legislative) on the appointment of judges. Furthermore, the committee perceived the "irremovability" of the judiciary as an important safeguard of the Rule of Law.

Regarding the legal profession, the committee deemed an organised legal profession free to manage its own affairs to be essential. While a lawyer should be free to accept any case which is offered to him, he should also in some cases be obliged to defend persons with whom he does not sympathise.

The committee also addressed the issue of equal access to the justice. It was perceived to be the primary obligation of the legal profession to use its best efforts to ensure that adequate legal advice and representation were provided. The state and community would however have the obligation to assist the legal profession in carrying out this responsibility.

The Declaration of Delhi

This International Congress of Jurists, consisting of 185 judges, practising lawyers and teachers of law from 53 countries, assembled in New Delhi in January 1959 under the aegis of the International Commission of Jurists, having discussed freely and frankly the Rule of Law and the administration of justice throughout the world, and having reached conclusions regarding the legislative, the executive, the criminal process, the judiciary and the legal profession, (which conclusions are annexed to this Declaration),

Now solemnly

Reaffirms the principles expressed in the Act of Athens adopted by the International Congress of Jurists in 1955, particularly that independent judiciary and legal profession are essential to the maintenance of the Rule of Law and to the proper administration of justice;

Recognises that the Rule of Law is a dynamic concept for the expansion and fulfillment of which jurists are primarily responsible and which should be employed not only to safeguard and advance the civil and political rights of the individual in a free society, but also to establish social, economic, educational and cultural conditions under which his legitimate aspirations and dignity may be realised;

Calls on the jurists in all countries to give effect in their own communities to the principles expressed in the conclusions of the Congress; and finally

Requests the International Commission of Jurists

1. To employ its full resources to give practical effect throughout the world to the principles expressed in the conclusions of the Congress.

2. To give special attention and assistance to countries now in the process of establishing, reorganising or consolidating their political and legal institutions.
3. To encourage law students and the junior members of the legal profession to support the Rule of Law.
4. To communicate this Declaration and the annexed conclusions to governments, to interested international organisations, and to associations of lawyers throughout the world.

This Declaration shall be known as the Declaration of Delhi.

Done at Delhi this 10th January, 1959.

CONSENSUS

Consensus has two common meanings. One is a general agreement among the members of a given group or community, each of which exercises some discretion in decision-making and follow-up action. The other is as a theory and practice of getting such agreements (for information on the *practice* of achieving formal consensus.

Achieving consensus requires serious treatment of every group member's considered opinion. Once a decision is made it is important to trust in members' discretion in follow-up action. In the ideal case, those who wish to take up some action want to hear those who oppose it, because they count on the fact that the ensuing debate will improve the consensus. In theory, action without resolution of considered opposition will be rare and done with attention to minimize damage to relationships.

Consensus as Collective Thought

A close equivalent phrase might be the "collective opinion" of a group, keeping in mind that a high degree of variation is still possible among individuals, and certainly if there must be individual commitment to follow-up the decision with action, this variation remains important. There is considerable debate and research into both collective intelligence and consensus decision-making.

This article focuses strictly on the idea of consensus in the abstract, not on the implications of consensus for politics or economics, where follow-up action is required.

Consensus usually involves collaboration, rather than compromise. Instead of one opinion being adopted by a plurality, stakeholders are brought together (often with facilitation) until a convergent decision is developed. If this is done in a purely mechanical way it can result in simple trading—we'll sacrifice this if you'll sacrifice that. Genuine consensus typically requires more focus on developing the relationships among stakeholders, so that they work together to achieve agreements based on willing consent.

Models of Consensus

The most common and most successful model of consensus is called the prisoner's dilemma. An introduction and discussion of this concept can be found in any contemporary introduction to Political Science. This approach might be called "algebraic" as opposed to analytic, within mathematics, because it represents an agent by a symbol and then examines the algebraic properties of that symbol. For example, the question, "Can two agents be combined to make a new agent?" sounds like an algebraic question. (More formally, "is the operation of consensus closed in the domain of agents? Is there a larger domain of abstract agents in which this operation is closed?")

In a more analytic style, we might natively start by envisioning the distribution of opinions in a population as a Gaussian distribution in one parameter. We would then say that the initial step in a consensus process would be the written or spoken synthesis that represents the range of opinions within perhaps three standard deviations of the mean opinion. Other standards are possible, e.g. two standard deviations, or one, or a unanimity minus a certain tolerable number of dissenters. The following steps then operate both to check understanding of the different opinions (parameter values), and then to find new parameters in the multi-dimensional parameter space of all possible decisions, through which the consensus failure in one-dimensional parameter space can be replaced by a solution in multi-dimensional parameter space.

An alternative, qualitative, mathematical description is to say that there is an iterative process through (m+n)-dimensional parameter space, starting from initial guesses at a solution in (m)-dimensional parameter space, which tries to converge to find a common solution in (m+n)-dimensional parameter space.

A criticism of such modelling is that the opinions or agreements are only theoretical, and that the strength or degree of conviction as measured is not closely correlated to the willingness of any given individual to take action. In direct action politics, the consensus is constantly tested by asking those who agree to immediately place their own bodies 'on the line' and in harm's way, to actually demonstrate that they are committed to a consensus. The ecology movement, peace movement, and labour movement have historically required such demonstrations of commitment. Some have disdained any attempt at formal models or methods, but others have prepared extensive documentation on both formal and informal consensus decision-making processes.

Typically, the usefulness of formal models of consensus is confined to cases where follow-up action is closely and centrally controlled, e.g., in a military hierarchy or a set of similar computer programmes executing on hardware that it completely controls. The idea of consensus itself is probably quite different when considering action by a group of independent human agents, or considering action by those taking orders and committed to executing them all without question, or suffering great harm or exile for any disobedience.

Consensus upon a particular formal model of consensus can lead to groupthink, by making it harder for those who reject that formal model (and using informal or different models) to be heard. This recursion suggests the extreme complexity of reasoning about consensus in a political context. An example is the peace movement's objection to the game theory logic of mutual assured destruction during the Cold War. Peace activists, objecting to military goals and spending found the formal models of the military to be major obstacles. As they had not mastered game theory models they simply were not heard.

In Democracy

As this example suggests, the concept of consensus is a particularly important one in the context of society and government, and forms a cornerstone of the concept of democracy. Democracy, in its rawest form, direct democracy, has been criticized by a significant number of scholars since the time of Plato as well as adherents to strict republican principles, and is sometimes referred to as the "tyranny of the majority", with the implication that one faction of the society is dominating other factions, possibly repressively.

Others, however, argue that if the democracy adheres to principles of consensus, becoming a deliberative democracy, then party or factional dominance can be minimized and decisions will be more representative of the entire society. This too is discussed in depth in the article on consensus decision-making, with many actual examples of the tradeoffs and different tests for consensus used in actual societies and polities.

A major cornerstone of the Westminster System is Cabinet Government. All Cabinet decisions are consensual collective and inclusive, a vote is never taken in a Cabinet meeting. All ministers, whether senior and in the Cabinet, or junior ministers, must support the policy of the government publicly regardless of any private reservations. If a minister does not agree with a decision he or she, can resign from the government; as did several British ministers over the 2003 invasion of Iraq. This means that in the Westminster System of government the cabinet always collectively decides all decisions and all ministers are responsible for arguing in favour of any decision made by the Cabinet.

Drawbacks

Business and political analysts have pointed out a number of problems with consensus decision-making. A too-strict requirement of consensus may effectively give a small self-interested minority group veto power over decisions. Decision by consensus may take an extremely long time to occur, and thus may be intolerable for urgent matters, e.g., those of executive decisions. In some cases, consensus decision-making may encourage groupthink, a situation in which people modify their opinions to reflect what they believe others want them to think, leading to a situation in which a group makes a decision that none of the members individually think is wise. It can also lead to a few dominant individuals making all decisions. Finally, consensus decision-making may fail in a situation where there simply is no agreement possible, and interests are irreconcilable.

While each of these scenarios can make consensus harder to reach, there are a number of ways to mitigate each of them. For example, concern that consensus takes longer to achieve has, in many cases proven to be a factor that can be overcome through effective facilitation and group process.

Examples within Computing

Within the Internet Engineering Task Force (IETF), the concept of "rough consensus and running code" is the basis for the standardization process. It has proven extremely effective for standardizing protocols for inter-computer communication, particularly during its early years.

In computer science, Consensus is a distributed computing problem in which a group of nodes must reach agreement on a single value. Achieving consensus is a challenging problem in distributed systems, particularly as the number of nodes grows or the reliability of links between nodes decreases.

"Consensus" may also refer to the *Consensus Theorems* in Boolean algebra.

Examples of Non-Consensus

Interestingly, the peer review process in most scientific journals does not use a consensus based process. Referees submit their opinions individually and there is not a strong effort to reach a group opinion.

ECONOMICS EFFICIENCY

Economic efficiency is a general term for the value assigned to a situation by some measure designed to capture the amount of waste or "friction" or other undesirable economic features present. The term micro-economic reform refers to any policy designed to increase economic efficiency.

There are several measures of economic efficiency, including:

- Pareto efficiency,
- Kaldor-Hicks efficiency,
- X-efficiency,
- Allocative efficiency,
- Distributive efficiency,
- Productive efficiency, and
- Optimisation of a social welfare function.

For applications of these principles, see:

- Efficient market hypothesis,
- Welfare economics,
- Production theory basics, and
- Micro-economic reform.

Documentary Films

OPTIMUM—The Crusade for Efficiency, a Film by Henry Colomer, 2000, 55 minutes. This documentary focuses on three crusaders for efficiency, namely Jeremy Bentham, Charles Babbage and Francis Galton.

2

Transparency, Corruption, Public Contracting and Monitoring: Global Priorities

TRANSPARENCY

Transparency (humanities), as used in the humanities, implies openness, communication and accountability. It is a metaphorical extension of the meaning used in the physical sciences: a "transparent" object is one that can be seen through.

When liberal democracies, like USA or Norway, are developing their democracy one step further, transparency is introduced as a means of holding public officials accountable and fighting corruption. When government meetings are open to the press and the public, when budgets and financial statements may be reviewed by anyone, when laws, rules and decisions are open to discussion, they are seen as transparent and there is less opportunity for the authorities to abuse the system in their own interest.

Transparency cannot exist as a purely one-way communication though. If the media and the public knows everything that happens in all authorities and county administrations there will be a lot of questions, protests and suggestions coming from media and the public. People who are interested in a certain issue will try to influence the decisions. Transparency creates an everyday participation in the political processes by media and the public.

Modern democracy builds on such participation of the people and media. There are, for anybody who is interested, many ways to influence the decisions at all levels in society.

The elections and referendums are no longer the prime or only way for the people to rule itself. The democracy is working continuously, and the elections are there just to make major changes in the political course.

While a liberal democracy can be a plutocracy, where decisions are taken behind locked doors and the people have very small possibilities to influence the politics between the elections, a participative democracy is much closer connected to the will of the people.

Participative democracy, built on transparency and everyday participation, has been used officially in northern Europe for decades. (In the northern Europe country Sweden, public access to government documents became a law as early as 1766.) It has officially been adopted as an ideal to strive for by the rest of EU.

Many countries in the world still have older forms of democracy, or other forms of government.

Transparent procedures include open meetings, financial disclosure statements, the freedom of information legislation, budgetary review, audits, etc.

In government, politics, ethics, business, management, law, economics, sociology, etc., **transparency** is the opposite of privacy; an activity is transparent if all information about it is open and freely available. Thus, when courts of law admit the public, when fluctuating prices in financial markets are published in newspapers, those processes are transparent.

When military authorities classify their plans as secret, **transparency** is absent. This can be seen as either positive or negative; positive, because it can increase national security, negative, because it can lead to secrecy, corruption and even a military dictatorship.

Some organisations and networks, for example, Wikipedia, the GNU/Linux community and Indymedia, insist that not only the ordinary information of interest to the community is made freely available, but that all (or nearly all) *meta*-levels of organizing and decision-making are themselves also published. This is known as radical transparency.

- To promote transparency in Politics Hans Peter Martin, Paul van Buitenen (Europa Transparant) and Ashley Mote decided to cooperate under the name Platform for Transparency (PfT) in 2005.
- A similar organisation that promotes transparency is Transparency International.

MEDIA TRANSPARENCY

Media Transparency is the concept of determining how and why information is conveyed through various means.

This is a specific case of the topic, Transparency (humanities). As used in the humanities, it implies openness and accountability. It is a metaphorical extension of the meaning used in the physical sciences: a "transparent" object is one that can be seen through.

In communication studies, Media is transparent when:

- there are many, often competing, sources of information;
- much is known about the method of information delivery; and
- the funding of media production is publicly available.

Aspects of **transparent media** include open source documentation, open meetings, financial disclosure statements, the freedom of information legislation, budgetary review, audit, peer review, etc.

Some organisations and networks insist that not only the ordinary information of interest to the community is made freely available, but that all (or nearly all) meta-levels of organising and decision-making are themselves also published. This is known as radical transparency. These organisations include: Wikipedia, the GNU/Linux community, and Indymedia.

Media Transparency may also refer to the non-profit organisation of the same name which maintains a website at mediatransparency.org devoted to providing information on right-wing funding, especially as it relates to United States media.

Example

When an organisation (corporate, government, non-profit, or other) holds a meeting and the proceedings are open to the public and the press, when the meeting is:

- broadcast over radio,
- reviewed on television,
- reported in newsprint, and
- · journalized on weblogs.

The meeting is more transparent because there is less opportunity for the organisation to abuse the system of information delivery in their own interest. This assumes that the organisation does not own or otherwise affect the media conveying the information.

Related Terms

- *Distortion*: Involves some level of undue or inappropriate interference in the media through funding sources, personal or organisational bias, or some other influences.
- *Privacy*: Obscuring a matter from media attention by anonymity, confidentiality, court order, military classification, or other means. There is value in both privacy and transparency. Privacy can protect a news source from retaliation, increase the number of whistleblowers, improve national security, and the like, but excessive privacy allows for increased corruption, statism and military dictatorship.
- Freedom of speech if a censorship order is blocking the media from publishing.
- Suppression of dissent when a more powerful opponent tries to silence the other.

EXTRACTIVE INDUSTRIES TRANSPARENCY INITIATIVE (EITI)

An Extractive Industries Transparency Initiative (or EITI) announced by UK Prime Minister Tony Blair at the World Summit on Sustainable Development in Johannesburg, September 2002, expressed as its aim to increase transparency over payments by companies to governments and to government-linked entities, as well as transparency over revenues by those host country governments. Ghana, Nigeria and Azerbaijan, piloted the EITI approach. As of September 2006, EITI is being implemented in some twenty resource rich countries around the world. Three countries Azerbaijan, Guinea and Nigeria have produced EITI reports; another five are expected to do so shortly.

Revenues from oil, gas and mining companies, in the form of taxes, royalties, signature bonuses and other payments should be an important engine for economic growth and social development in developing and transition countries. However, the lack of accountability and transparency in these revenues can exacerbate poor governance and lead to corruption, conflict and poverty.

EITI has issued a set of reporting guidelines, a Statement of Principles, available on its official website, and six Criteria which represent the global minum standard for EITI implementation. EITI received official endorsement from the World Bank Group, announced December 9, 2003. The World Bank pioneered pressure for structuring revenue transparency in several high-profile extractive industries projects in the opening years of the 21st century, including the Chad-Cameroon pipeline and the Baku-Tbilisi-Ceyhan pipeline.

In May 2005, an International Advisory Group (IAG) was established under the Chairmanship of Peter Eigen. Members of the IAG included: the Governments of Azerbaijan, France, Nigeria, Norway, Peru and the United States; Anglo-American, BP, Chevron and Petrobras; the Azerbaijan EITI Coalition, Global Witness, Revenue Watch Institute, West African Catholic Bishops Conference; and F&C Assets Management. It was supported by the UK Government, the IMF and the World Bank. It is reporting to the next EITI Conference in Oslo in mid-October 2006.

THE TRANSPARENT SOCIETY

The Transparent Society (1998, ISBN 0-7382-0144-8, ISBN 0-201-32802-X) is a non-fiction book by the science-fiction author David Brin in which he forecasts the erosion of privacy, as it is overtaken by low-cost surveillance, communication and database technology. He argues that true privacy will be lost in the "transparent society"; however, we have the choice between one that offers the illusion of privacy by restricting the power of surveillance to authorities, or one that destroys that illusion by offering everyone access (including the ability to watch the watchers).

He argues that it would be good for society if the surveillance is equal for all, and the public has the same access as those in power. He bases this argument upon the claim that the most dangerous and corrupt abuses of power go hand-in-hand with a lack of accountability and transparency.

Brin also has a novel, Kiln People, placed in a future where cameras are everywhere and everybody can access the public ones and, for a fee, the private ones.

The collation of all publicly and privately available personal data in the United States by the Information Awareness Office is viewed by some as a move towards the more pessimistic of the possible futures envisaged by Brin in his book.

Inverse Transparency and Bi-Directional Transparency

Transparency is sometimes confused with equiveillance (the balance between surveillance and sousveillance). This balance (equilibrium) allows the individual to construct their own case from evidence they gather themselves, rather than merely having access to surveillance data that could possibly incriminate them. Sousveillance therefore, in addition to Transparency, assures contextual integrity of surveillance data (i.e. a lifelong capture of personal experience can provide "best evidence" over surveillance data to prevent the surveillance—only data from being taken out of context).

Recently Brin participated in the opening keynote panel discussion at the 2005 Association for Computing Machinery (ACM) Computers, Freedom, and Privacy Conference, where 500 sousveillance devices were also created to contextualize and explore this debate further. (Each attendee was given a wearable camera-dome bag which created, in effect, an inverse panopticon.)

TRANSPARENCY INTERNATIONAL: A CASE STUDY

Transparency International, the global civil society organisation leading the fight against corruption, brings people together in a powerful worldwide coalition to end the devastating impact of corruption on men, women and children around the world.

TI's mission is to create change towards a world free of corruption.

Transparency International challenges the inevitability of corruption, and offers hope to its victims. TI plays a lead role in improving the lives of millions around the world, by building momentum for the anti-corruption movement, raising awareness and diminishing apathy and tolerance of corruption, as well as devising and implementing practical actions to address it.

Transparency International (TI) is a global network including more than 90 locally established national chapters and chapters-information. These bodies fight corruption in the national arena in a number of ways. They bring together relevant players from government, civil society, business and the media to promote transparency in elections, in public administration, in procurement and in business. TI's global network of chapters and contacts also use advocacy campaigns to lobby governments to implement anti-corruption reforms.

Politically non-partisan, TI does not undertake investigations of alleged corruption or expose individual cases, but at times will work in coalition with organisations that do.

TI has the skills, tools, experience, expertise and broad participation to fight corruption on the ground, as well as through global and regional initiatives.

Now in its second decade, Transparency International is maturing, intensifying and diversifying its fight against corruption.

Corruption

Corruption is the abuse of entrusted power for private gain. It hurts everyone whose life, livelihood or happiness depends on the integrity of people in a position of authority.

Why does fighting corruption matter?

Corruption hurts everyone, and it harms the poor the most. Sometimes its devastating impact is obvious:

- A father who must do without shoes because his meagre wages are used to pay a bribe to get his child into a supposedly free school.
- The unsuspecting sick person who buys useless counterfeit drugs, putting their health in grave danger.
- A small shop owner whose weekly bribe to the local inspector cuts severely into his modest earnings.
- The family trapped for generations in poverty because a corrupt and autocratic leadership has systematically siphoned off a nation's riches.

Other times corruption's impact is less visible:

- The prosperous multi-national corporation that secured a contract by buying an unfair advantage in a competitive market through illegal kickbacks to corrupt government officials, at the expense of the honest companies who didn't.

- Post-disaster donations provided by compassionate people, directly or through their governments, that never reach the victims, callously diverted instead into the bank accounts of criminals.
- The faulty buildings, built to lower safety standards because a bribe passed under the table in the construction process that collapse in an earthquake or hurricane.

Corruption has dire global consequences, trapping millions in poverty and misery and breeding social, economic and political unrest.

Corruption is both a cause of poverty, and a barrier to overcoming it. It is one of the most serious obstacles to reducing poverty.

Corruption denies poor people the basic means of survival, forcing them to spend more of their income on bribes. Human rights are denied where corruption is rife, because a fair trial comes with a hefty price tag where courts are corrupted.

Corruption undermines democracy and the rule of law.

Corruption distorts national and international trade.

Corruption jeopardises sound governance and ethics in the private sector.

Corruption threatens domestic and international security and the sustainability of natural resources.

Those with less power are particularly disadvantaged in corrupt systems, which typically reinforce gender discrimination.

Corruption compounds political exclusion: if votes can be bought, there is little incentive to change the system that sustains poverty.

The conclusion—Corruption hurts everyone.

GLOBAL PRIORITIES OF TRANSPARENCY INTERNATIONAL

Transparency International's thematic webpages include the latest anti-corruption research, tools for fighting corruption and examples of best practice. They also contain information about projects from TI's network of national chapters and contacts around the world, and related links and other resources.

TI has defined five global priorities in the fight against corruption:

- Corruption in politics,
- Corruption in public contracting,
- Corruption in the private sector,
- International anti-corruption conventions, and
- Poverty and development.

TI also continues to focus its attention on the following thematic issues:

- Access to information,
- Education,
- Health, and
- Forest Integrity Network (FIN).

Political Corruption

Political corruption affects us all. We elect politicians and political parties expecting them to act in the public interest. By electing them we give them access to public resources and the power to take decisions that impact on our lives. Given this privileged position, immense damage can be inflicted by politicians or parties acting out of greed, or in the service of those who bankroll their ascent to power. It is not surprising that people the world over are demanding absolute probity of their political leaders: citizens in three out of four countries polled by TI and Gallup International in 2003 and in 2004 singled out political parties as the institution they perceived as most corrupt.

Reflecting this worldwide concern, TI has been working on the issue of political corruption for several years, focusing initially on corruption during the electoral cycle. Subsequently TI also worked on mechanisms that can help prevent corruption by politicians who are in power—such as codes of conduct and post-employment restrictions aimed at closing the "revolving door" between business and politics. As with so many other areas of anti-corruption work, most innovation in this sphere comes from the practitioners in the field who make up the TI network. Several effective tools have been developed, for example to monitor corruption in politics. This has made the problem manifest for policy makers and for the general public, and has provided evidence to underpin recommendations for reform.

At the international level TI has been involved in standard setting, issuing the **TI Standards on Political Finance and Favour** in 2004.

These standards go beyond other international principles and recommendations by insisting on a role for civil society in designing and monitoring political finance regulations. TI recognises a need for strong political systems and political parties. Reform-minded politicians are important agents of change, as is the media as an important opinion former, since the strongest impetus for change in the political sphere comes from the electorate.

This website provides an introduction to political corruption, analysing why the problem is so widespread and looking at what can and has been done to tackle it. The website is not exhaustive, but rather focuses on the ongoing work and concerns of TI's network of national chapters in the areas of:

- campaign and political party finance,
- corrupt money flows from the corporate sector to politicians,
- obstacles to bringing corrupt politicians to justice,
- vote buying,
- parliamentary ethics, and
- electoral fraud and election monitoring.

Enhancing Standards in the Private Sector

Practices that were once seen as an inevitable part of doing business in many parts of the world are becoming increasingly unacceptable. More stringent domestic laws and international conventions such as the 1999 OECD Anti-Bribery Convention and the United Nations Convention against Corruption are compelling companies to develop new anti-bribery policies or to review existing ones. The high-profile corporate scandals of recent years have made companies increasingly aware that corrupt practices pose serious and costly risks to their reputation and sustainability. This understanding, coupled with growing public expectation of accountability and probity in the corporate sector, are putting added pressure on companies to articulate and live up to more ethical business practices.

But in spite of some progress, there are many signs that point to the challenge that remains ahead. The revelation in the report of the Independent Inquiry Committee (IIC) into the Iraq Oil for Food Programme that more than 50 per cent of the 4,500 companies involved were investigated for making illegal payments is an alarming reminder that corrupt practices are alive and well in the business sector.

TI's goal in working with the private sector is to change company behaviour by developing and raising the standards of practice in countering bribery. In an effort to assist this process, we have created tools to help companies develop effective anti-bribery programmes. Foremost among these tools is the **Business Principles for Countering Bribery**, a generic anti-bribery code developed by TI with a group of leading multi-nationals and non-corporate stakeholders. The Business Principles, which have become the cornerstone of TI's private sector activity, provide a model of good practice adaptable to different company sizes and settings.

TI also works with industry sectors, an approach which has proved very helpful in diagnosing industry-specific problems to which tailored approaches and tools can be developed. A number of current TI initiatives are focusing on the defence industry, the engineering and construction industry and the extractive industries.

Public Contracting

Public contracting is one way in which public policy is implemented, and it is an enormous and lucrative area of business. Think of pharmaceutical companies vying to supply a government vaccination programme, the privatisation of a government-owned telecommunications company, or the awarding of contracts to reconstruct destroyed infrastructure in Iraq. Most of these contracts are meant to buy or produce goods or services that should benefit citizens directly, like the construction of a road or a sewage system. Others should benefit citizens indirectly, by contributing to a more efficient or effective delivery of a specific service or good, and prudently investing or increasing public funds. The key question is whether genuine efforts to serve the public interest motivate the contracting decisions being made.

All levels of government perform contracting activities in most countries, from municipalities and towns, to provinces and national or federal governments. While federal or national level contracting can be bigger in terms of value per contract, local government contracting is also significant in terms of the number of processes and their impact.

On the pages devoted to public contracting, you can find useful and in-depth information and links regarding TI's work. TI has strived for concrete guidelines and tools in this area, illustrated by TI's Integrity Pacts (IP) and various other Anti-Corruption Instruments. The section on Key Sectors in Contracting looks at areas in the contracting field which are especially prone to corruption: the arms industry, construction and engineering, oil and development aid.

Under Projects and Activities, the work of TI's National Chapters is presented, as well as some selected global activities and tools. To facilitate better understanding of this topic, we have compiled a Glossary, listing a number of terms used in the field of corruption in public contracting.

We are constantly working towards providing you with the most accurate up-to-date information on corruption in public contracting. However, you should not expect this section to be exhaustive or to have included all relevant material available. We welcome your suggestions and appreciate your sharing of additional documents, information, best practices and links. Please send your input to publiccontracting@transparency.org.

Costs of Corruption in Public Contracting

An avoidable misuse and abuse of public funds results from corruption. Corruption in public contracting leads to a distortion of fair competition, the waste of scare resources and the neglect of basic needs, perpetuating poverty. Massive market inefficiencies can also arise from corruption and, in the extreme, lead to the destruction of development opportunities. If corruption in public contracting is not contained, it will grow. It is estimated that systemic corruption can add 20-25 per cent to the costs of government procurement, and frequently results in inferior quality goods and services and unnecessary purchases.

It is argued that, on average, approximately 70 per cent of Central Government expenditure turns in one way or another into contracts. Contracts are sources of power to those who give them out, and targets of ambition for those who may receive them, making public contracts particularly prone to abuse at the expense of public need. The risk of corruption in public contracting exists even before the contracting process has started, perhaps even at the moment when public budgets are allocated, and it perpetuates beyond the awarding of a contract to its implementation.

For all these reasons TI has been working on alerting governments, the business community and civil society worldwide about the importance of curbing corruption in public contracting and on developing a number of anti-corruption tools. Most importantly, TI has demonstrated that corruption in public contracting can be reduced.

UNPAN Statistical Databases Central Government Expenditures by Type and Function, as percentage of all Central Government expenditure as of 1997. Uses as source: IMF Government Finance Statistics. Calculations by TI-S. Result comes from excluding wages and interest payments.

Monitoring: Checking on Country's Performance

While conventions express important national government commitments, the key to their success is prompt government ratification, implementation, application and enforcement. In order to comply with their obligations under anti-corruption conventions after ratification, national governments frequently need to introduce new legislation, and new or enhanced structures. They also need to ensure that there are adequate resources for the government departments responsible for following up, and that sufficient attention is paid to the new obligations by those departments. None of these steps is a given since governments face many competing priorities, often contend with limited resources and may not take their convention commitments seriously enough.

Experience teaches that in order to ensure that the commitments made are translated into action, a convention needs an inter-governmental monitoring process. Thus, it is increasingly common for international conventions to provide in their text or via subsequent protocols for the requirement or possibility of signatory states participating in a follow-up mechanism involving some form of evaluation of progress. Some of the systems provided for or in operation are described in this section.

Because of the importance of monitoring, TI has been involved for more than five years in promoting the development and effective functioning of monitoring mechanisms for the OECD and OAS Conventions. As of 2004, TI has also been engaged in working with a Study Group to develop proposals for monitoring the UN Convention against Corruption. Furthermore, TI National Chapters have been contributing inputs to the country review processes run by the OECD, Council of Europe/GRECO and OAS to monitor the implementation of the requirements laid down in the anti-corruption conventions and other instruments developed by the members of those institutions.

In the absence of such inter-governmental monitoring, or to supplement it, civil society organisations can make an important contribution by carrying out independent monitoring.

3

Anti-Corruption Instruments: Global and Regional Coverage

INTRODUCTION TO ANTI-CORRUPTION CONVENTIONS AND INSTRUMENTS

International anti-corruption conventions and instruments are increasingly important in a world in which states and private actors are more and more interconnected through travel, communications, trade, investment and financial transactions.

The range of anti-corruption conventions and instruments in existence today are the manifestations of an international consensus that emerged in the early 1990s identifying corruption as an important problem needing to be addressed and in particular requiring internationally agreed solutions.

Anti-Corruption Conventions and Instruments: Meaning, Scope and Evolution

Anti-corruption conventions embody binding agreements between states on standards and requirements in the prevention, detection, investigation, and sanctioning of acts of corruption, including better cross-border cooperation in these areas. They are intended to produce better policies and practices in and among the states that make a binding commitment to apply them (States Parties). Some conventions have a very broad scope; others are narrower and may cover only a limited number of countries or anti-corruption measures. Other international anti-corruption instruments establish non-binding standards.

The adoption of conventions by assemblies of governments, such as the UN General Assembly or regional assemblies, establishes international consensus on the matters covered. This consensus is further strengthened when they are signed by a significant number of the governments in those assemblies. They become binding when a predetermined number of countries ratify them.

Conventions are implemented at national level, with the convention providing the operational framework and standards.

The major anti-corruption conventions and instruments of importance today are global, inter-regional, regional and sub-regional, covering all regions of the world.

The end of the Cold War removed the national security rationale for tolerating and supporting corrupt regimes around the world. At the same time, the Post-Cold War agenda of democratisation, accountability and transparency focused the attention of major international financial and development institutions and others on the corruption problem. Moreover, there was concern in the international community that the corruption problem was growing. Some researchers have claimed that new corruption opportunities had resulted from worldwide initiatives to privatise and deregulate. Other researchers have claimed that reductions in trade barriers in the 1980s and 90s produced not only increased market access but also increased competition among multinationals and—as a by-product—increased corruption in a number of important sectors.

Added to this, multinational companies based in the United States considered themselves disadvantaged in global markets due to the 1977 Foreign Corrupt Practices Act, which imposed criminal penalties for engaging in foreign bribery, and the US Government became a leading sponsor of efforts to find a solution through an international regime to limit cross-border bribery.

Anti-corruption conventions and instruments are especially important in providing a framework for addressing cross-border issues. They also serve to establish valuable common standards for domestic institutions, policies, processes and practices, which are of assistance for anti-corruption efforts at national level. The standards and requirements for governments established by international agreements cannot easily be dismissed given their international backing.

The common frameworks provided by international anti-corruption conventions serve to:

- facilitate international cooperation in the control and

sanctioning of corruption in order to address a cross-border phenomenon.

- provide internationally agreed reference points, useful for reforming governments, citizens and donors.
- create peer pressure on governments, especially when bolstered by an effective review process.
- provide civil society with a tool for holding their governments accountable.
- promote collective pressure on the private sector.
- provide for fora in which governments, and in some cases non-governmental actors, can meet to discuss corruption issues, align concepts and review anti-corruption efforts.

Many anti-corruption conventions contemplate the creation of inter-governmental follow-up mechanisms in order to assure that the States Parties comply with their commitments. These monitoring or review mechanisms are essential for the conventions to be effective.

Bringing a Convention to Life

- *Negotiation*: A convention is negotiated by a group of states, generally within an institutional framework.
- *Adoption*: Once they have reached agreement, the convention is placed before an assembly of the states participating in the treaty-making process for a formal act through which they express their consent and the form and content of the proposed treaty are established. Treaties negotiated within an international organisation whose membership corresponds to the potential participation in the treaty will usually be adopted by resolution of a representative organ.
- *Signature*: After a convention is adopted it is then opened for signature by states. This indicates their intent to become parties.
- *Ratification or Accession*: To become a party to a convention, and thus bound by its requirements when it enters into force, a state must express its consent to be bound by the treaty by ratification or accession to the convention. The procedures for doing so are laid out under national law and often involve approval by a national legislative body. Accession is the act whereby a state accepts the offer or the

opportunity to become a party to a treaty already negotiated and signed by other states. It usually occurs after the treaty has entered into force.

- *Deposit of Instrument of Ratification or Accession*: The final step in the ratification and accession processes is generally for the government of the ratifying or acceding country to deposit an instrument of ratification or accession with an institution or office designated in the treaty.
- *Entry into Force*: A convention applies to states that have ratified it only once it enters into force, which usually depends on ratification by a minimum number of states. The convention will specify how many ratifications must be deposited for entry into force. It will also fix an amount of time between the deposit of the threshold instrument and the actual entry into force. For additional countries ratifying, the convention may also fix an amount of time to elapse before entry into force in those countries.
- *Conference of States Parties*: One or more meetings may be convened of all the parties to a convention or, on occasion, of all the signatories, to establish rules of procedure and follow-up and review the status of a convention.
- *Implementation into Law*: After ratifying, States Parties must review whether their national legislation is consistent with convention requirements and make any necessary changes in law implied by the convention. In case of self-executing convention provisions, implementation into law is not required.
- *Implementation into Institutional Policy and Practice, Application and Enforcement*: Apart from changing the legislative framework where necessary, states must review and make changes to the policies and practices of state institutions to bring them into line with convention requirements. This will include ensuring that legal prohibitions are actually enforced. Governments must provide funding and staffing for organisations administering anti-corruption programmes.

Activities or Behaviour Addressed by Anti-Corruption Conventions

The conventions cover a range of corrupt activities with the main focus on preventing and punishing the bribery of public sector officials, including payment and receipt of bribes, as well as diversion of property by public officials. Some conventions also cover the bribery of private sector employees and embezzlement by them. Apart from these criminal offences, corruption addressed by conventions includes nepotism and favouritism in public sector recruitment and promotion. Related offences covered by the conventions include laundering the proceeds of corruption, aiding and abetting corruption and obstruction of justice.

The following corrupt activities are identified as criminal offences in the UN Convention Against Corruption (UNCAC) and some or all of this behaviour is also covered by other anti-corruption conventions:

- Bribery of national public sector officials.
- Bribery of foreign public sector officials.
- Bribery of officials of public international organisations.
- Illicit enrichment by a public official, defined as "a significant increase in the assets of a public official that he or she cannot reasonably explain in relation to his or her lawful income" (UNCAC Art. 20).
- Embezzlement, misappropriation or other diversion of property by a public official.
- Trading in influence.
- Abuse of functions.
- Bribery of private sector decision-makers.
- Embezzlement by persons working in private sector entities.

Corruption is also understood under UNCAC and some other conventions to cover

- nepotism and favouritism in public sector recruitment and promotion.

In addition, associated criminal offences under the UNCAC and other conventions include

- laundering the proceeds of corruption—a key part of the corruption equation.
- concealment or continued retention of the proceeds of crime.

- Aiding and abetting corruption.
- Obstruction of justice.

Measures Provided for Under Anti-Corruption Conventions and Instruments

Several anti-corruption instruments take a comprehensive approach to the problem, as a basis for effectively preventing and combating corruption. They set standards in the area of preventive measures, punitive measures and international cooperation. This is the case for the UNCAC, AU Convention, OAS Convention and ADB-OECD Action Plan.

Other conventions take a more selective approach to the corruption problem. The OECD Convention, Council of Europe Criminal Law Convention and EU instruments focus primarily on criminalisation of bribery. In the case of the OECD Convention the focus is even narrower—the criminalisation of foreign bribery. The Council of Europe Civil Law Convention primarily covers civil remedies. (It should be noted, however, that the collection of Council of Europe instruments that are reviewed by GRECO, when taken together, represent a comprehensive approach.)

Examples of the kinds of measures included in conventions are provided below:

Preventive Measures: These measures covered aim to create conditions that promote good, honest, transparent and efficient public management and high private sector standards of behaviour. These include measures in the area of

- role of preventive body for anti-corruption;
- public sector ethics and procedures;
- public procurement;
- public sector finance,
- public reporting, access to information, whistleblower protection;
- public education;
- private sector standards, including accounting and auditing standards; and
- measures to prevent money laundering.

Punitive Measures: These measures are provided for in most anti-corruption conventions and call for punishment of corrupt actions taken, by means of judicial or administrative organs. They call for governments to establish or consider establishing certain criminal offences. They generally call for

- adoption of the necessary legislation and other measures to establish as criminal offences under their domestic laws the acts of corruption described. The kinds of offences are listed above in the description of kinds of activities covered by anti-corruption conventions.

In addition, the UNCAC and some other conventions provide for such matters as

- liability of legal persons, criminal, civil or administrative;
- long statute of limitations;
- sanctions, immunities, release pending trial, parole;
- suspension or re-assignment of public officials;
- disqualifications of persons from holding public office for a period of time;
- freezing, seizure and confiscation;
- protection of witnesses, experts, victims, reporting persons,
- compensation for damages; and
- requirement of independent specialised anti-corruption authority.

International Cooperation between Law Enforcement Authorities: These measures aim to make cross-border law enforcement efforts more effective. These are some of the most important provisions. They cover topics such as:

- Extradition;
- Mutual legal assistance in investigations, prosecutions and judicial proceedings; and
- Law enforcement cooperation, including joint investigations and special investigative techniques.

Other Measures: The UNCAC and some other conventions also contain important provisions relating to

- asset recovery (also treated in the AU Convention and the OAS Convention),

- technical assistance; and
- mechanisms for implementation.

Note that the complicated process of recovering illegally obtained assets is always preceded by three stages: (1) investigative measures to trace the assets; (2) preventive measures to immobilize the assets (freezing, seizing); and (3) confiscation. Only once these three stages have been completed is the recovery of the proceeds of crime possible.

LIST OF ANTI-CORRUPTION CONVENTIONS AND OTHER RELATED INTERNATIONAL INSTRUMENTS

Anti-corruption conventions and instruments are of key importance in the work of Transparency International (TI) and have been since its inception. These texts, agreed by governments, recognise corruption as a worldwide and cross-border affliction, and express a shared high-level political commitment to addressing this critical problem individually and collectively. Each text establishes an international, regional or sub-regional framework of rules and standards, some of them binding, that promote domestic action and facilitate international cooperation. Some take a selective approach and address some key aspects of the problem. Many of them adopt a comprehensive approach to corruption, calling for a wide range of measures to prevent it, measures to punish it when it occurs, measures to check corruption-related money laundering and facilitate the return of corruptly taken assets; and measures to provide assistance to countries where required. The most comprehensive of them is also the most recent, the landmark UN Convention Against Corruption (2003), global in its reach and with the most extensive approach to addressing the corruption problem.

Important as they are, the adoption of anti-corruption conventions is only a first step and only significant if there is follow-up. The key is sustained national implementation by all participating countries. This calls for action by governments, civil society organisations, private sector, international institutions and others to maintain the political will and momentum reflected in anti-corruption conventions. The more committed governments will need to encourage and support those of their peers who are proceeding slowly, reluctantly or with inadequate resources. Citizens and civil society organisations will need to be active in pressing their governments to make the conventions a priority, by reminding them of convention requirements and holding them accountable to convention standards. International institutions can help keep anti-corruption conventions high on the international agenda and provide fora for discussing progress.

Most of the instruments discussed here provide for review and follow-up processes for the conventions. These are essential. Not only do such processes help maintain the needed pressure on governments to give priority to compliance, but they also provide a setting in which concepts can be aligned, difficulties can be discussed and common approaches developed.

TI and its National Chapters have played an important role in promoting conventions from the negotiation phase through to monitoring their transformation into law, and their application in practice. TI contributed to the negotiations for the UN Convention Against Corruption (UNCAC), the OECD Anti-Bribery Convention and the African Union Convention on Preventing and Combating Corruption. TI has actively promoted ratification, implementation and enforcement of the OECD and OAS Conventions, and is currently promoting ratification and implementation of the AU Convention. TI and its National Chapters have also contributed to the monitoring processes for the OECD, OAS and Council of Europe Conventions, and TI is currently developing proposals for monitoring the UNCAC, which will be followed by a campaign in support of monitoring. All of these activities are discussed in the pages that follow:

A. Global and Inter-regional Level

- UN Convention Against Corruption (UNCAC).
- United Nations Convention Against Transnational Organized Crime (UNTOC).
- OECD Convention on the Bribery of Foreign Public Officials in International Business Transactions (OECD Convention).
- Revised Recommendation of the Council of the OECD on Combating Bribery in International Business Transactions.

B. Africa

- AU Convention on Preventing and Combating Corruption (AU Convention).

- SADC Protocol Against Corruption (SADC Protocol).
- ECOWAS Protocol on the Fight Against Corruption (ECOWAS Protocol).

C. Americas

- The Inter-American Convention Against Corruption (OAS Convention).

D. Asia

- ADB-OECD Action Plan for Asia-Pacific (Action Plan).

E. Europe

- Council of Europe Criminal Law Convention.
- Council of Europe Civil Law Convention.
- Resolution (99) 5 of the Committee of Ministers of the Council of Europe: Agreement Establishing the Group of States against Corruption.
- Resolution (97) 24 of the Committee of Ministers of the Council of Europe: Twenty Guiding Principles for the Fight against Corruption.
- European Union Convention on the Protection of the Communities' Financial Interests and the Fight against Corruption and two Protocols.
- European Union Convention on the Fight against Corruption involving officials of the European Communities or officials of Member States.

Regional Coverage of Conventions

International anti-corruption conventions and other international instruments have been developed at the global, international, regional and sub-regional level, within a range of inter-governmental institutions. In any given region, several different anti-corruption instruments may apply. In this section, information is provided by region about the main inter-governmental anti-corruption agreements that apply, starting with the most global instruments and moving down to the more specifically regional. For each region, an overview table is also provided indicating which countries have signed and ratified the international and regional conventions.

1. Africa
2. Americas
3. Asia and Pacific
4. Europe
5. Middle East.

TI National Chapters in all these regions have given high priority to promoting the signature and ratification of the UN Convention Against Corruption (UNCAC) a high priority in all the above regions. They are also planning a campaign for an effective UNCAC monitoring process. The National Chapters in the industrialised countries of the OECD (Organisation for Economic Cooperation and Development) are now also promoting enforcement of the OECD Anti-Bribery Convention, and contributing to monitoring its enforcement. The signatory countries are in Europe, Asia and the Americas. There is also conventions work in progress on a purely regional basis. In Africa TI National Chapters are actively advocating ratification and implementation of the African Union Convention on Preventing and Combating Corruption. In the Americas they are promoting and contributing to monitoring the implementation of the OAS Convention. In Europe National Chapters regularly contribute to the Council of Europe/GRECO process for monitoring the Council of Europe Conventions and other instruments.

AFRICA

In Africa anti-corruption conventions have been developed at the global, regional and sub-regional level. Each of these conventions has evolved in response to specific demands, pressures and needs at particular points in time. They represent, step-by-step, an evolution in the approach to the corruption problem from the late 1990s through 2003.

The conventions and protocols relevant for Africa take a comprehensive approach to the corruption problem, including preventive and punitive measures, as well as measures relating to international cooperation.

With the resulting multi-layered collection of anti-corruption agreements, it is important that governments and civil society organisations determine where the conventions overlap and where they differ, and also determine in which forums review of implementation is likely to be the most effective.

Conventions Applying in Africa

- United Nations Convention Against Corruption (2003).
- United Nations Convention Against Transnational Organised Crime (2000).
- African Union Convention on Preventing and Combating Corruption (2003).
- SADC Protocol Against Corruption (2001).
- ECOWAS Protocol on the Fight Against Corruption (2001).

AMERICA

The two main anti-corruption conventions to apply in the Americas are the OAS Convention and the UN Convention Against Corruption, both of which take a comprehensive approach to the corruption problem, incorporating preventive and punitive measures, as well as measures relating to international cooperation. The UN Convention on Transnational Organised Crime is also applicable in all countries of the Americas. In addition to these there is a fourth, narrower international convention, the OECD Anti-Bribery Convention with application in only six of the countries in the Americas, namely Argentina, Brazil, Canada, Chile, Mexico and the USA. This fourth convention addresses the supply side of international bribery and covers 35 major exporting countries, in the Americas, Asia and Europe. Finally, two countries in the Americas, the US and Mexico, are subject to two additional conventions (and an associated protocol) primarily targeted at European states, but also open to a few other countries—these are the Council of Europe Criminal and Civil Law Conventions.

Conventions Applying in the Americas

- United Nations Convention Against Corruption (2003).
- United Nations Convention Against Transnational Organised Crime (2000).
- OECD Convention Against Bribery of Foreign Public Officials (only for Argentina, Brazil, Canada, Chile, Mexico, USA) (1997).

- Inter-American Convention Against Corruption (1996).
- Council of Europe Criminal Law Convention (only for USA and Mexico) (1998).

ASIA AND PACIFIC

At the same time, since the end of the 1990s, four leading countries in the region—Australia, Japan, New Zealand and South Korea, have been subject to the OECD Anti-bribery Convention, which addresses the supply side of international bribery and covers 35 major exporting countries. Moreover, since 2001 Asian countries have had the opportunity to adhere to a non-binding instrument applicable in the Asia region, the ADB-OECD Anti-Corruption Action Plan for Asia-Pacific.

Conventions Applying in the Asia-Pacific Region

- United Nations Convention Against Corruption (2003).
- United Nations Convention Against Transnational Organised Crime (2000).
- OECD Convention on Combating Bribery of Foreign Public Officials in International Business Transactions (only for Australia, Japan, New Zealand, South Korea) (1997).
- ADB-OECD Anti-Corruption Action Plan for Asia-Pacific (2001).

EUROPE

The first steps towards a regional approach to the corruption problem were taken in Europe at the level of the European Union, at the same time as the OAS Convention was in development in the Americas. The first EU Convention to touch on the subject in 1995 was followed by a further EU Convention, two Protocols, then in 1997 the OECD Convention applying to 36 major exporting countries, a majority of them in Europe, in 1999 the two Council of Europe Conventions, and, finally, in 2000 and 03, the two UN Conventions adopted. European countries are now covered by many levels of international anti-corruption agreements.

Conventions Applying in Europe

- United Nations Convention Against Corruption (2003).

- United Nations Convention Against Transnational Organised Crime (2000).
- OECD Convention Against Bribery of Foreign Public Officials (1997).
- Council of Europe Criminal Law Convention (1998) and Protocol (2003).
- Council of Europe Civil Law Convention (1999).
- GRECO review process (1999).
- European Union Convention on the protection of the communities' financial interests and the Fight Against Corruption (1996), First Protocol (1996) and Second Protocol (1997).
- European Union Convention on the fight against corruption involving officials of the European Communities or officials of Member States (1997).

MIDDLE EAST

Prior to the adoption of the UN Convention Against Corruption and the UN Convention on Transnational Organised Crime, there was no international anti-corruption convention or regional instrument applicable in the Middle East. Thus, these two global instruments will be of particular importance in the region.

Conventions Applying in the Middle East

- United Nations Convention Against Corruption (2003).
- United Nations Convention Against Transnational Organised Crime (2000).

4

UN Convention Against Corruption: A Report on Follow-up Initiatives

UNITED NATIONS CONVENTION AGAINST CORRUPTION (UNCAC)

Adopted	: 31 October, 2003 by the UN General Assembly.
Signatories	: 140 (as of 30 October, 2006). Opened for signature on 9 December, 2003.
Ratifications	: 70 (as of 30 October, 2006).
Entry into Force	: 14 December, 2005.
Open to	: All countries and regional economic organisations.

In its eight Chapters and 71 Articles, the UNCAC obliges the States Parties to implement a wide and detailed range of anti-corruption measures affecting their laws, institutions and practices. These measures aim to promote the prevention, detection and sanctioning of corruption, as well as the cooperation between State Parties on these matters. The UNCAC is unique as compared to other conventions, not only in its **global coverage** but also in the extensiveness and detail of its provisions.

The UNCAC was negotiated over a two-year period at the United Nations office in Vienna by representatives of more than a hundred countries from all regions. The secretariat for the negotiations was the United Nations Office on Drugs and Crime (UNODC). Representatives of civil society organisations, including Transparency International, also participated in this process. Following the conclusion of the negotiations in October 2003, the text of the Convention was presented for approval by the General Assembly on 31 October, 2003. Once approved, it was opened for the states to sign, starting with a signing conference in Merida, Mexico on 9-10 December, 2003. (International Anti-Corruption Day on 9 December marks the anniversary of this signing conference.)

The UNCAC was initially signed by 111 countries and, by October 2005, the number had risen to 133. The 30 ratifications required for entry into force of the Convention were reached on 15 September, 2005 and the entry into force date is 14 December, 2005.

Obligations of the Parties

The obligations of the parties fall into the following categories:

1. *Preventive Measures*: Of all existing anti-corruption Conventions, the UNCAC has the most extensive provisions on the ways, means and standards for preventive measures in the public and private sectors. However, an important deficiency is that the requirements on transparency in funding of political candidates and of political parties are not mandatory in the UNCAC. For more details on preventive measures.
2. *Criminalisation*: UNCAC calls for criminalisation of a wide range of offences and contains a broad definition of the term public official. Moreover, it includes offences relating both to public sector corruption and private sector (private-to-private) corruption.
3. *International Cooperation*: The UNCAC also provides an international cooperation framework which has the potential to improve mutual law enforcement assistance, notably in extradition and investigations. These provisions are potentially some of the most important in the Convention.
4. *Asset Recovery Framework*: One of its most noteworthy aspects is that it elaborates an asset recovery framework for the first time on a global basis, covering countries in the north and south.
5. *Technical Cooperation and Information Exchange*: In terms of the overall composition and balance of the UNCAC, the provisions on technical cooperation and information exchange are key. These take account of the need for

"enhanced financial and material assistance" to developing countries and technical assistance to developing countries and countries in transition to help them implement the Convention. Without such assistance, some countries will not be in a position to implement UNCAC requirements.

6. *Implementation Mechanism*: UNCAC Chapter VII provides for an implementation mechanism under the auspices of the Conference of States Parties. The first Conference of State Parties to the Convention is to be convened within a year after entry into force of the Convention and regularly thereafter. The responsibilities of the Conference of States Parties include:
   - reviewing periodically the implementation of the Convention by States Parties;
   - making recommendations to improve the Convention and its implementation, including recommendations about technical assistance needs;
   - using relevant information produced by other international and regional mechanisms; and
   - putting into effect supplemental review mechanisms and establishing any review body it deems necessary to assess the measures taken by States Parties (and difficulties encountered) to implement the Convention.

In addition, the States Parties are required to provide information about the measures they have taken to implement the Convention.

Noteworthy Provisions

Some specific noteworthy provisions in the UNCAC are

- requirement of disallowance of tax deductibility of bribes of either foreign or national officials (Article 12);
- requirement of liability of legal persons i.e. companies (Article 26);
- recognition of need for long statutes of limitations (Article 29); and
- recognition of the right of entities or persons who have suffered damages from corruption, to initiate legal proceedings for compensation (Article 35).

United Nations Convention Against Corruption

Preamble

The States Parties to this Convention,

Concerned about the seriousness of problems and threats posed by corruption to the stability and security of societies, undermining the institutions and values of democracy, ethical values and justice and jeopardizing sustainable development and the rule of law,

Concerned also about the links between corruption and other forms of crime, in particular organized crime and economic crime, including money-laundering,

Concerned further about cases of corruption that involve vast quantities of assets, which may constitute a substantial proportion of the resources of States, and that threaten the political stability and sustainable development of those States,

Convinced that corruption is no longer a local matter but a transnational phenomenon that affects all societies and economies, making international cooperation to prevent and control it essential,

Convinced also that a comprehensive and multi-disciplinary approach is required to prevent and combat corruption effectively,

Convinced further that the availability of technical assistance can play an important role in enhancing the ability of States, including by strengthening capacity and by institution-building, to prevent and combat corruption effectively,

Convinced that the illicit acquisition of personal wealth can be particularly damaging to democratic institutions, national economies and the rule of law,

Determined to prevent, detect and deter in a more effective manner international transfers of illicitly acquired assets and to strengthen international cooperation in asset recovery,

Acknowledging the fundamental principles of due process of law in criminal proceedings and in civil or administrative proceedings to adjudicate property rights,

Bearing in mind that the prevention and eradication of corruption is a responsibility of all States and that they must cooperate with one another, with the support and involvement of individuals and groups outside the public sector, such as civil society, non-governmental organisations and community-based organizations, if their efforts in this area are to be effective,

Bearing also in mind the principles of proper management of public affairs and public property, fairness, responsibility and equality before the law and the need to safeguard integrity and to foster a culture of rejection of corruption,

Commending the work of the Commission on Crime Prevention and Criminal Justice and the United Nations Office on Drugs and Crime in preventing and combating corruption,

Recalling the work carried out by other international and regional organisations in this field, including the activities of the African Union, the Council of Europe, the Customs Cooperation Council (also known as the World Customs Organisation), the European Union, the League of Arab States, the Organisation for Economic Cooperation and Development and the Organisation of American States,

Taking note with appreciation of multilateral instruments to prevent and combat corruption, including, *inter alia*, the Inter-American Convention against Corruption, adopted by the Organisation of American States on 29 March, 1996,[1] the Convention on the Fight against Corruption involving Officials of the European Communities or Officials of Member States of the European Union, adopted by the Council of the European Union on 26 May, 1997,[2] the Convention on Combating Bribery of Foreign Public Officials in International Business Transactions, adopted by the Organisation for Economic Cooperation and Development on 21 November, 1997,[3] the Criminal Law Convention on Corruption, adopted by the Committee of Ministers of the Council of Europe on 27 January, 1999,[4] the Civil Law Convention on Corruption, adopted by the Committee of Ministers of the Council of Europe on 4 November, 1999,[5] and the African Union Convention on Preventing and Combating Corruption, adopted by the Heads of State and Government of the African Union on 12 July, 2003,

---

1. See E/1996/99.
2. *Official Journal of the European Communities*, C 195, 25 June, 1997.
3. See *Corruption and Integrity Improvement Initiatives in Developing Countries* (United Nations Publication, Sales No. E.98 III.B.18).
4. Council of Europe, *European Treaty Series*. No. 173.
5. *Ibid.*, 174.

Welcoming the entry into force on 29 September, 2003 of the United Nations Convention against Transnational Organized Crime,[1]

Have agreed as follows:

Chapter I: General Provisions

Article 1: Statement of Purpose

The purposes of this Convention are:

(*a*) to promote and strengthen measures to prevent and combat corruption more efficiently and effectively;
(*b*) to promote, facilitate and support international cooperation and technical assistance in the prevention of and fight against corruption, including in asset recovery;
(*c*) to promote integrity, accountability and proper management of public affairs and public property.

Article 2: Use of Terms

For the purposes of this Convention:

(*a*) "Public official" shall mean: (*i*) any person holding a legislative, executive, administrative or judicial office of a State Party, whether appointed or elected, whether permanent or temporary, whether paid or unpaid, irrespective of that person's seniority; (*ii*) any other person who performs a public function, including for a public agency or public enterprise, or provides a public service, as defined in the domestic law of the State Party and as applied in the pertinent area of law of that State Party; (*iii*) any other person defined as a "public official" in the domestic law of a State Party. However, for the purpose of some specific measures contained in Chapter II of this Convention, "public official" may mean any person who performs a public function or provides a public service as defined in the domestic law of the State Party and as applied in the pertinent area of law of that State Party;

1. General Assembly resolution 55/25, Annex I.

(*b*) "Foreign public official" shall mean any person holding a legislative, executive, administrative or judicial office of a foreign country, whether appointed or elected; and any person exercising a public function for a foreign country, including for a public agency or public enterprise;

(*c*) "Official of a public international organisation" shall mean an international civil servant or any person who is authorized by such an organisation to act on behalf of that organisation;

(*d*) "Property" shall mean assets of every kind, whether corporeal or incorporeal, movable or immovable, tangible or intangible, and legal documents or instruments evidencing title to or interest in such assets;

(*e*) "Proceeds of crime" shall mean any property derived from or obtained, directly or indirectly, through the commission of an offence;

(*f*) "Freezing" or "seizure" shall mean temporarily prohibiting the transfer, conversion, disposition or movement of property or temporarily assuming custody or control of property on the basis of an order issued by a court or other competent authority;

(*g*) "Confiscation", which includes forfeiture where applicable, shall mean the permanent deprivation of property by order of a court or other competent authority;

(*h*) "Predicate offence" shall mean any offence as a result of which proceeds have been generated that may become the subject of an offence as defined in Article 23 of this Convention;

(*i*) "Controlled delivery" shall mean the technique of allowing illicit or suspect consignments to pass out of, through or into the territory of one or more States, with the knowledge and under the supervision of their competent authorities, with a view to the investigation of an offence and the identification of persons involved in the commission of the offence.

Article 3: Scope of Application

1. This Convention shall apply, in accordance with its terms, to the prevention, investigation and prosecution of corruption and to the freezing, seizure, confiscation and

return of the proceeds of offences established in accordance with this Convention.

2. For the purposes of implementing this Convention, it shall not be necessary, except as otherwise stated herein, for the offences set forth in it to result in damage or harm to state properly.

Article 4: Protection of Sovereignty

1. States Parties shall carry out their obligations under this Convention in a manner consistent with the principles of sovereign equality and territorial integrity of States and that of non-intervention in the domestic affairs of other States.
2. Nothing in this Convention shall entitle a State Party to undertake in the territory of another State the exercise of jurisdiction and performance of functions that are reserved exclusively for the authorities of that other State by its domestic law.

Chapter II: *Preventive Measures*

Article 5: Preventive Anti-Corruption Policies and Practices

1. Each State Party shall, in accordance with the fundamental principles of its legal system, develop and implement or maintain effective, coordinated anti-corruption policies that promote the participation of society and reflect the principles of the rule of law, proper management of public affairs and public properly, integrity, transparency and accountability.
2. Each State Party shall endeavour to establish and promote effective practices aimed at the prevention of corruption.
3. Each State Party shall endeavour to periodically evaluate relevant legal instruments and administrative measures with a view to determining their adequacy to prevent and fight corruption.
4. States Parties shall, as appropriate and in accordance with the fundamental principles of their legal system, collaborate with each other and with relevant international and regional organisations in promoting and developing the measures referred to in this article. That collaboration may include participation in international programmes and projects aimed at the prevention of corruption.

Article 6: Preventive Anti-Corruption Body or Bodies

1. Each State Party shall, in accordance with the fundamental principles of its legal system, ensure the existence of a body or bodies, as appropriate, that prevent corruption by such means as:
   (*a*) implementing the policies referred to in Article 5 of this Convention and, where appropriate, overseeing and coordinating the implementation of those policies; and
   (*b*) increasing and disseminating knowledge about the prevention of corruption.
2. Each State Party shall grant the body or bodies referred to in paragraph 1 of this article the necessary independence, in accordance with the fundamental principles of its legal system, to enable the body or bodies to carry out its or their functions effectively and free from any undue influence. The necessary material resources and specialized staff, as well as the training that such staff may require to carry out their functions, should be provided.
3. Each State Party shall inform the Secretary-General of the United Nations of the name and address of the authority or authorities that may assist other States Parties in developing and implementing specific measures for the prevention of corruption.

Article 7: Public Sector

1. Each State Party shall, where appropriate and in accordance with the fundamental principles of its legal system, endeavour to adopt, maintain and strengthen systems for the recruitment, hiring, retention, promotion and retirement of civil servants and, where appropriate, other non-elected public officials:
   (*a*) That are based on principles of efficiency, transparency and objective criteria such as merit, equity and aptitude;
   (*b*) That include adequate procedures for the selection and training of individuals for public positions considered especially vulnerable to corruption and the rotation, where appropriate, of such individuals to other positions;

(*c*) That promote adequate remuneration and equitable pay scales, taking into account the level of economic development of the State Party; and

(*d*) That promote education and training programmes to enable them to meet the requirements for the correct, honourable and proper performance of public functions and that provide them with specialized and appropriate training to enhance their awareness of the risks of corruption inherent in the performance of their functions. Such programmes may make reference to codes or standards of conduct in applicable areas.

2. Each State Party shall also consider adopting appropriate legislative and administrative measures, consistent with the objectives of this Convention and in accordance with the fundamental principles of its domestic law, to prescribe criteria concerning candidature for and election to public office.
3. Each State Party shall also consider taking appropriate legislative and administrative measures, consistent with the objectives of this Convention and in accordance with the fundamental principles of its domestic law, to enhance transparency in the funding of candidatures for elected public office and, where applicable, the funding of political parties.
4. Each State Party shall, in accordance with the fundamental principles of its domestic law, endeavour to adopt, maintain and strengthen systems that promote transparency and prevent conflicts of interest.

Article 8: *Codes of Conduct for Public Officials*

1. In order to fight corruption, each State Party shall promote, *inter alia*, integrity, honesty and responsibility among its public officials, in accordance with the fundamental principles of its legal system.
2. In particular, each State Party shall endeavour to apply, within its own institutional and legal systems, codes or standards of conduct for the correct, honourable and proper performance of public functions.
3. For the purposes of implementing the provisions of this article, each State Party shall, where appropriate and in

accordance with the fundamental principles of its legal system, take note of the relevant initiatives of regional, inter-regional and multi-lateral organisations, such as the International Code of Conduct for Public Officials contained in the annex to General Assembly resolution 51/59 of 12 December, 1996.

4. Each State Party shall also consider, in accordance with the fundamental principles of its domestic law, establishing measures and systems to facilitate the reporting by public officials of acts of corruption to appropriate authorities, when such acts come to their notice in the performance of their functions.
5. Each State Party shall endeavour, where appropriate and in accordance with the fundamental principles of its domestic law, to establish measures and systems requiring public officials to make declarations to appropriate authorities regarding, *inter alia*, their outside activities, employment, investments, assets and substantial gifts or benefits from which a conflict of interest may result with respect to their functions as public officials.
6. Each State Party shall consider taking, in accordance with the fundamental principles of its domestic law, disciplinary or other measures against public officials who violate the codes or standards established in accordance with this article.

Article 9: *Public Procurement and Management of Public Finances*

1. Each State Party shall, in accordance with the fundamental principles of its legal system, take the necessary steps to establish appropriate systems of procurement, based on transparency, competition and objective criteria in decision-making, that are effective, *inter alia*, in preventing corruption. Such systems, which may take into account appropriate threshold values in their application, shall address, *inter alia*:
   (*a*) The public distribution of information relating to procurement procedures and contracts, including information on invitations to tender and relevant or pertinent information on the award of contracts,

allowing potential tenderers sufficient time to prepare and submit their tenders;

(*b*) The establishment, in advance, of conditions for participation, including selection and award criteria and tendering rules, and their publication;

(*c*) The use of objective and predetermined criteria for public procurement decisions, in order to facilitate the subsequent verification of the correct application of the rules or procedures;

(*d*) An effective system of domestic re view, including an effective system of appeal, to ensure legal recourse and remedies in the event that the rules or procedures established pursuant to this paragraph are not followed; and

(*e*) Where appropriate, measures to regulate matters regarding personnel responsible for procurement, such as declaration of interest in particular public procurements, screening procedures and training requirements.

2. Each State Party shall, in accordance with the fundamental principles of its legal system, take appropriate measures to promote transparency and accountability in the management of public finances. Such measures shall encompass, *inter alia*:

(*a*) Procedures for the adoption of the national budget;

(*b*) Timely reporting on revenue and expenditure;

(*c*) A system of accounting and auditing standards and related oversight;

(*d*) Effective and efficient systems of risk management and internal control; and

(*e*) Where appropriate, corrective action in the case of failure to comply with the requirements established in this paragraph.

3. Each State Party shall take such civil and administrative measures as may be necessary, in accordance with the fundamental principles of its domestic law, to preserve the integrity of accounting books, records, financial statements or other documents related to public expenditure and revenue and to prevent the falsification of such documents.

Article 10: *Public Reporting*

Taking into account the need to combat corruption, each State Party shall, in accordance with the fundamental principles of its domestic law, take such measures as may be necessary to enhance transparency in its public administration, including with regard to its organisation, functioning and decision-making processes, where appropriate. Such measures may include, *inter alia*:

(*a*) Adopting procedures or regulations allowing members of the general public to obtain, where appropriate, information on the organisation, functioning and decision-making processes of its public administration and, with due regard for the protection of privacy and personal data, on decisions and legal acts that concern members of the public;

(*b*) Simplifying administrative procedures, where appropriate, in order to facilitate public access to the competent decision-making authorities; and

(*c*) Publishing information, which may include periodic reports on the risks of corruption in its public administration.

Article 11: *Measures Relating to the Judiciary and Prosecution Services*

1. Bearing in mind the independence of the judiciary and its crucial role in combating corruption, each State Party shall, in accordance with the fundamental principles of its legal system and without prejudice to judicial independence, take measures to strengthen integrity and to prevent opportunities for corruption among members of the judiciary. Such measures may include rules with respect to the conduct of members of the judiciary.
2. Measures to the same effect as those taken pursuant to paragraph 1 of this article may be introduced and applied within the prosecution service in those States Parties where it does not form part of the judiciary but enjoys independence similar to that of the judicial service.

Article 12: *Private Sector*

1. Each State Party shall take measures, in accordance with the fundamental principles of its domestic law, to prevent

corruption involving the private sector, enhance accounting and auditing standards in the private sector and, where appropriate, provide effective, proportionate and dissuasive civil, administrative or criminal penalties for failure to comply with such measures.

2. Measures to achieve these ends may include, *inter alia*:
   (*a*) Promoting cooperation between law enforcement agencies and relevant private entities;
   (*b*) Promoting the development of standards and procedures designed to safeguard the integrity of relevant private entities, including codes of conduct for the correct, honourable and proper performance of the activities of business and all relevant professions and the prevention of conflicts of interest, and for the promotion of the use of good commercial practices among businesses and in the contractual relations of businesses with the State;
   (*c*) Promoting transparency among private entities, including, where appropriate, measures regarding the identity of legal and natural persons involved in the establishment and management of corporate entities;
   (*d*) Preventing the misuse of procedures regulating private entities, including procedures regarding subsidies and licences granted by public authorities for commercial activities;
   (*e*) Preventing conflicts of interest by imposing restrictions, as appropriate and for a reasonable period of time, on the professional activities of former public officials or on the employment of public officials by the private sector after their resignation or retirement, where such activities or employment relate directly to the functions held or supervised by those public officials during their tenure;
   (*f*) Ensuring that private enterprises, taking into account their structure and size, have sufficient internal auditing controls to assist in preventing and detecting acts of corruption and that the accounts and required financial statements of such private enterprises are subject to appropriate auditing and certification procedures.

3. In order to prevent corruption, each State Party shall take such measures as may be necessary, in accordance with its domestic laws and regulations regarding the maintenance of books and records, financial statement disclosures and accounting and auditing standards, to prohibit the following acts carried out for the purpose of committing any of the offences established in accordance with this Convention:
   (*a*) The establishment of off-the-books accounts;
   (*b*) The making of off-the-books or inadequately identified transactions;
   (*c*) The recording of non-existent expenditure;
   (*d*) The entry of liabilities with incorrect identification of their objects;
   (*e*) The use of false documents; and
   (*f*) The intentional destruction of book-keeping documents earlier than foreseen by the law.
4. Each State Party shall disallow the tax deductibility of expenses that constitute bribes, the latter being one of the constituent elements of the offences established in accordance with Articles 15 and 16 of this Convention and, where appropriate, other expenses incurred in furtherance of corrupt conduct.

Article 13: *Participation of Society*

1. Each State Party shall take appropriate measures, within its means and in accordance with fundamental principles of its domestic law, to promote the active participation of individuals and groups outside the public sector, such as civil society, non-governmental organisations and community-based organisations, in the prevention of and the fight against corruption and to raise public awareness regarding the existence, causes and gravity of and the threat posed by corruption. This participation should be strengthened by such measures as:
   (*a*) enhancing the transparency of and promoting the contribution of the public to decision-making processes;
   (*b*) ensuring that the public has effective access to information;

(*c*) undertaking public information activities that contribute to non-tolerance of corruption, as well as public education programmes, including school and university curricula; and

(*d*) respecting, promoting and protecting the freedom to seek, receive, publish and disseminate information concerning corruption. That freedom may be subject to certain restrictions, but these shall only be such as are provided for by law and are necessary:

(*i*) for respect of the rights or reputations of others; and

(*ii*) for the protection of national security or *ordre public* or of public health or morals.

2. Each State Party shall take appropriate measures to ensure that the relevant anti-corruption bodies referred to in this Convention are known to the public and shall provide access to such bodies, where appropriate, for the reporting, including anonymously, of any incidents that may be considered to constitute an offence established in accordance with this Convention.

Article 14: *Measures to Prevent Money-laundering*

1. Each State Party shall

(*a*) institute a comprehensive domestic regulatory and supervisory regime for banks and non-bank financial institutions, including natural or legal persons that provide formal or informal services for the transmission of money or value and, where appropriate, other bodies particularly susceptible to money-laundering, within its competence, in order to deter and detect all forms of money-laundering, which regime shall emphasize requirements for customer and, where appropriate, beneficial owner identification, record-keeping and the reporting of suspicious transactions;

(*b*) without prejudice to Article 46 of this Convention, ensure that administrative, regulatory, law enforcement and other authorities dedicated to combating money-laundering (including, where appropriate under domestic law, judicial authorities) have the ability to cooperate and exchange information at the national and international levels within the conditions prescribed by its domestic law and, to that end, shall consider the establishment of a financial intelligence unit to serve as a national centre for the collection, analysis and dissemination of information regarding potential money-laundering.

2. States Parties shall consider implementing feasible measures to detect and monitor the movement of cash and appropriate negotiable instruments across their borders, subject to safeguards to ensure proper use of information and without impeding in any way the movement of legitimate capital. Such measures may include a requirement that individuals and businesses report the cross-border transfer of substantial quantities of cash and appropriate negotiable instruments.
3. States Parties shall consider implementing appropriate and feasible measures to require financial institutions, including money remitters:
   (*a*) to include on forms for the electronic transfer of funds and related messages accurate and meaningful information on the originator;
   (*b*) to maintain such information throughout the payment chain; and
   (*c*) to apply enhanced scrutiny to transfers of funds that do not contain complete information on the originator.
4. In establishing a domestic regulatory and supervisory regime under the terms of this article, and without prejudice to any other article of this Convention, States Parties are called upon to use as a guideline the relevant initiatives of regional, inter-regional and multilateral organisations against money-laundering.
5. States Parties shall endeavour to develop and promote global, regional, sub-regional and bilateral cooperation among judicial, law enforcement and financial regulatory authorities in order to combat money-laundering.

Chapter III: *Criminalization and Law Enforcement*

Article 15: *Bribery of National Public Officials*

Each State Party shall adopt such legislative and other measures as may be necessary to establish as criminal offences, when committed intentionally:

(*a*) The promise, offering or giving, to a public official, directly or indirectly, of an undue advantage, for the official himself or herself or another person or entity, in order that the official act or refrain from acting in the exercise of his or her official duties;

(*b*) The solicitation or acceptance by a public official, directly or indirectly, of an undue advantage, for the official himself or herself or another person or entity, in order that the official act or refrain from acting in the exercise of his or her official duties.

Article 16: *Bribery of Foreign Public Officials and Officials of Public International Organisations*

1. Each State Party shall adopt such legislative and other measures as may be necessary to establish as a criminal offencc, when committed intentionally, the promise, offering or giving to a foreign public official or an official of a public international organisation, directly or indirectly, of an undue advantage, for the official himself or herself or another person or entity, in order that the official act or refrain from acting in the exercise of his or her official duties, in order to obtain or retain business or other undue advantage in relation to the conduct of international business.
2. Each State Party shall consider adopting such legislative and other measures as may be necessary to establish as a criminal offence, when committed intentionally, the solicitation or acceptance by a foreign public official or an official of a public international organisation, directly or indirectly, of an undue advantage, for the official himself or herself or another person or entity, in order that the official act or refrain from acting in the exercise of his or her official duties.

Article 17: *Embezzlement, Misappropriation or Other Diversion of Property by a Public Official*

Each State Party shall adopt such legislative and other measures as may be necessary to establish as criminal offences, when committed intentionally, the embezzlement, misappropriation or other diversion by a public official for his or her benefit or for the benefit of another person or entity, of any property, public or private funds or securities or any other thing of value entrusted to the public official by virtue of his or her position.

Article 18: *Trading in Influence*

Each State Party shall consider adopting such legislative and other measures as may be necessary to establish as criminal offences, when committed intentionally:

(*a*) The promise, offering or giving to a public official or any other person, directly or indirectly, of an undue advantage in order that the public official or the person abuse his or her real or supposed influence with a view to obtaining from an administration or public authority of the State Party an undue advantage for the original instigator of the act or for any other person; and

(*b*) The solicitation or acceptance by a public official or any other person, directly or indirectly, of an undue advantage for himself or herself or for another person in order that the public official or the person abuse his or her real or supposed influence with a view to obtaining from an administration or public authority of the State Party an undue advantage.

Article 19: *Abuse of Functions*

Each State Party shall consider adopting such legislative and other measures as may be necessary to establish as a criminal offence, when committed intentionally, the abuse of functions or position, that is, the performance of or failure to perform an act, in violation of laws, by a public official in the discharge of his or her functions, for the purpose of obtaining an undue advantage for himself or herself or for another person or entity.

Article 20: *Illicit Enrichment*

Subject to its constitution and the fundamental principles of its legal system, each State Party shall consider adopting such legislative and other measures as may be necessary to establish as a criminal offence, when committed intentionally, illicit enrichment, that is, a significant increase in the assets of a public official that he or she cannot reasonably explain in relation to his or her lawful income.

Article 21: *Bribery in the Private Sector*

Each State Party shall consider adopting such legislative and other measures as may be necessary to establish as criminal offences, when committed intentionally in the course of economic, financial or commercial activities:

(*a*) The promise, offering or giving, directly or indirectly, of an undue advantage to any person who directs or works, in any capacity, for a private sector entity, for the person himself or herself or for another person, in order that he or she, in breach of his or her duties, act or refrain from acting;
(*b*) The solicitation or acceptance, directly or indirectly, of an undue advantage by any person who directs or works, in any capacity, for a private sector entity, for the person himself or herself or for another person, in order that he or she, in breach of his or her duties, act or refrain from acting.

Article 22: *Embezzlement of Property in the Private Sector*

Each State Party shall consider adopting such legislative and other measures as may be necessary to establish as a criminal offence, when committed intentionally in the course of economic, financial or commercial activities, embezzlement by a person who directs or works, in any capacity, in a private sector entity of any property, private funds or securities or any other thing of value entrusted to him or her by virtue of his or her position.

Article 23: *Laundering of Proceeds of Crime*

1. Each State Party shall adopt, in accordance with fundamental principles of its domestic law, such legislative and other measures as may be necessary to establish as criminal offences, when committed intentionally:
   (*a*) (*i*) The conversion or transfer of property, knowing that such property is the proceeds of crime, for the

purpose of concealing or disguising the illicit origin of the property or of helping any person who is involved in the commission of the predicate offence to evade the legal consequences of his or her action;

(*ii*) The concealment or disguise of the true nature, source, location, disposition, movement or ownership of or rights with respect to property, knowing that such property is the proceeds of crime;

(*b*) Subject to the basic concepts of its legal system:

(*i*) The acquisition, possession or use of property, knowing, at the time of receipt, that such property is the proceeds of crime;

(*ii*) Participation in, association with or conspiracy to commit, attempts to commit and aiding, abetting, facilitating and counselling the commission of any of the offences established in accordance with this article.

2. For purposes of implementing or applying paragraph 1 of this article:

(*a*) Each State Party shall seek to apply paragraph 1 of this article to the widest range of predicate offences;

(*b*) Each State Party shall include as predicate offences at a minimum a comprehensive range of criminal offences established in accordance with this Convention;

(*c*) For the purposes of sub-paragraph (*b*) above, predicate offences shall include offences committed both within and outside the jurisdiction of the State Party in question. However, offences committed outside the jurisdiction of a State Party shall constitute predicate offences only when the relevant conduct is a criminal offence under the domestic law of the State where it is committed and would be a criminal offence under the domestic law of the State Party implementing or applying this article had it been committed there;

(*d*) Each State Party shall furnish copies of its laws that give effect to this article and of any subsequent changes to such laws or a description thereof to the Secretary-General of the United Nations; and (*e*) If required by fundamental principles of the domestic law of a State Party, it may be provided that the offences set forth in paragraph 1 of this article do not apply to the persons who committed the predicate offence.

Article 24: *Concealment*

Without prejudice to the provisions of Article 23 of this Convention, each State Party shall consider adopting such legislative and other measures as may be necessary to establish as a criminal offence, when committed intentionally after the commission of any of the offences established in accordance with this Convention without having participated in such offences, the concealment or continued retention of property when the person involved knows that such property is the result of any of the offences established in accordance with this Convention.

Article 25: *Obstruction of Justice*

Each State Party shall adopt such legislative and other measures as may be necessary to establish as criminal offences, when committed intentionally:

(*a*) The use of physical force, threats or intimidation or the promise, offering or giving of an undue advantage to induce false testimony or to interfere in the giving of testimony or the production of evidence in a proceeding in relation to the commission of offences established in accordance with this Convention;
(*b*) The use of physical force, threats or intimidation to interfere with the exercise of official duties by a justice or law enforcement official in relation to the commission of offences established in accordance with this Convention. Nothing in this sub-paragraph shall prejudice the right of States Parties to have legislation that protects other categories of public official.

Article 26: *Liability of Legal Persons*

1. Each State Party shall adopt such measures as may be necessary, consistent with its legal principles, to establish

the liability of legal persons for participation in the offences established in accordance with this Convention.

2. Subject to the legal principles of the State Party, the liability of legal persons may be criminal, civil or administrative.
3. Such liability shall be without prejudice to the criminal liability of the natural persons who have committed the offences.
4. Each State Party shall, in particular, ensure that legal persons held liable in accordance with this article are subject to effective, proportionate and dissuasive criminal or non-criminal sanctions, including monetary sanctions.

Article 27: Participation and Attempt

1. Each State Party shall adopt such legislative and other measures as may be necessary to establish as a criminal offence, in accordance with its domestic law, participation in any capacity such as an accomplice, assistant or instigator in an offence established in accordance with this Convention.
2. Each State Party may adopt such legislative and other measures as may be necessary to establish as a criminal offence, in accordance with its domestic law, any attempt to commit an offence established in accordance with this Convention.
3. Each State Party may adopt such legislative and other measures as may be necessary to establish as a criminal offence, in accordance with its domestic law, the preparation for an offence established in accordance with this Convention.

Article 28: Knowledge, Intent and Purpose as Elements of an Offence

Knowledge, intent or purpose required as an element of an offence established in accordance with this Convention may be inferred from objective factual circumstances.

Article 29: Statute of Limitations

Each State Party shall, where appropriate, establish under its domestic law a long statute of limitations period in which to commence proceedings for any offence established in accordance with this Convention and establish a longer statute of limitations period or provide for the suspension of the statute of limitations where the alleged offender has evaded the administration of justice.

Article 30: *Prosecution, Adjudication and Sanctions*

1. Each State Party shall make the commission of an offence established in accordance with this Convention liable to sanctions that take into account the gravity of that offence.
2. Each State Party shall take such measures as may be necessary to establish or maintain, in accordance with its legal system and constitutional principles, an appropriate balance between any immunities or jurisdictional privileges accorded to its public officials for the performance of their functions and the possibility, when necessary, of effectively investigating, prosecuting and adjudicating offences established in accordance with this Convention.
3. Each State Party shall endeavour to ensure that any discretionary legal powers under its domestic law relating to the prosecution of persons for offences established in accordance with this Convention are exercised to maximize the effectiveness of law enforcement measures in respect of those offences and with due regard to the need to deter the commission of such offences.
4. In the case of offences established in accordance with this Convention, each State Party shall take appropriate measures, in accordance with its domestic law and with due regard to the rights of the defence, to seek to ensure that conditions imposed in connection with decisions on release pending trial or appeal take into consideration the need to ensure the presence of the defendant at subsequent criminal proceedings.
5. Each State Party shall take into account the gravity of the offences concerned when considering the eventuality of early release or parole of persons convicted of such offences.
6. Each State Party, to the extent consistent with the fundamental principles of its legal system, shall consider establishing procedures through which a public official accused of an offence established in accordance with this

Convention may, where appropriate, be removed, suspended or reassigned by the appropriate authority, bearing in mind respect for the principle of the presumption of innocence.

7. Where warranted by the gravity of the offence, each State Party, to the extent consistent with the fundamental principles of its legal system, shall consider establishing procedures for the disqualification, by court order or any other appropriate means, for a period of time determined by its domestic law, of persons convicted of offences established in accordance with this Convention from:
   (*a*) holding public office; and
   (*b*) holding office in an enterprise owned in whole or in part by the State.
8. Paragraph 1 of this article shall be without prejudice to the exercise of disciplinary powers by the competent authorities against civil servants.
9. Nothing contained in this Convention shall affect the principle that the description of the offences established in accordance with this Convention and of the applicable legal defences or other legal principles controlling the lawfulness of conduct is reserved to the domestic law of a State Party and that such offences shall be prosecuted and punished in accordance with that law.
10. States Parties shall endeavour to promote the reintegration into society of persons convicted of offences established in accordance with this Convention.

Article 31: *Freezing, Seizure and Confiscation*

1. Each State Party shall take, to the greatest extent possible within its domestic legal system, such measures as may be necessary to enable confiscation of
   (*a*) proceeds of crime derived from offences established in accordance with this Convention or property the value of which corresponds to that of such proceeds; and
   (*b*) property, equipment or other instrumentalities used in or destined for use in offences established in accordance with this Convention.
2. Each State Party shall take such measures as may be necessary to enable the identification, tracing, freezing or

seizure of any item referred to in paragraph 1 of this article for the purpose of eventual confiscation.

3. Each State Party shall adopt, in accordance with its domestic law, such legislative and other measures as may be necessary to regulate the administration by the competent authorities of frozen, seized or confiscated property covered in paragraphs 1 and 2 of this article.
4. If such proceeds of crime have been transformed or converted, in part or in full, into other property, such property shall be liable to the measures referred to in this article instead of the proceeds.
5. If such proceeds of crime have been intermingled with property acquired from legitimate sources, such property shall, without prejudice to any powers relating to freezing or seizure, be liable to confiscation upto the assessed value of the intermingled proceeds.
6. Income or other benefits derived from such proceeds of crime, from property into which such proceeds of crime have been transformed or converted or from property with which such proceeds of crime have been intermingled shall also be liable to the measures referred to in this article, in the same manner and to the same extent as proceeds of crime.
7. For the purpose of this article and Article 55 of this Convention, each State Party shall empower its courts or other competent authorities to order that bank, financial or commercial records be made available or seized. A State Party shall not decline to act under the provisions of this paragraph on the ground of bank secrecy.
8. States Parties may consider the possibility of requiring that an offender demonstrate the lawful origin of such alleged proceeds of crime or other property liable to confiscation, to the extent that such a requirement is consistent with the fundamental principles of their domestic law and with the nature of judicial and other proceedings.
9. The provisions of this article shall not be so construed as to prejudice the rights of *bona fide* third parties.
10. Nothing contained in this article shall affect the principle that the measures to which it refers shall be defined and implemented in accordance with and subject to the provisions of the domestic law of a State Party.

Article 32: *Protection of Witnesses, Experts and Victims*

1. Each State Party shall take appropriate measures in accordance with its domestic legal system and within its means to provide effective protection from potential retaliation or intimidation for witnesses and experts who give testimony concerning offences established in accordance with this Convention and, as appropriate, for their relatives and other persons close to them.
2. The measures envisaged in paragraph 1 of this article may include, *inter alia*, without prejudice to the rights of the defendant, including the right to due process:
   (*a*) Establishing procedures for the physical protection of such persons, such as, to the extent necessary and feasible, relocating them and permitting, where appropriate, non-disclosure or limitations on the disclosure of information concerning the identity and whereabouts of such persons; and
   (*b*) Providing evidentiary rules to permit witnesses and experts to give testimony in a manner that ensures the safety of such persons, such as permitting testimony to be given through the use of communications technology such as video or other adequate means.
3. States Parties shall consider entering into agreements or arrangements with other States for the relocation of persons referred to in paragraph 1 of this article.
4. The provisions of this article shall also apply to victims insofar as they are witnesses.
5. Each State Party shall, subject to its domestic law, enable the views and concerns of victims to be presented and considered at appropriate stages of criminal proceedings against offenders in a manner not prejudicial to the rights of the defence.

Article 33: *Protection of Reporting Persons*

Each State Party shall consider incorporating into its domestic legal system appropriate measures to provide protection against any unjustified treatment for any person who reports in good faith and on reasonable grounds to the competent authorities any facts concerning offences established in accordance with this Convention.

Article 34: *Consequences of Acts of Corruption*

With due regard to the rights of third parties acquired in good faith, each State Party shall take measures, in accordance with the fundamental principles of its domestic law, to address consequences of corruption. In this context, States Parties may consider corruption a relevant factor in legal proceedings to annul or rescind a contract, withdraw a concession or other similar instrument or take any other remedial action.

Article 35: *Compensation for Damage*

Each State Party shall take such measures as may be necessary, in accordance with principles of its domestic law, to ensure that entities or persons who have suffered damage as a result of an act of corruption have the right to initiate legal proceedings against those responsible for that damage in order to obtain compensation.

Article 36: *Specialized Authorities*

Each State Party shall, in accordance with the fundamental principles of its legal system, ensure the existence of a body or bodies or persons specialized in combating corruption through law enforcement. Such body or bodies or persons shall be granted the necessary independence, in accordance with the fundamental principles of the legal system of the State Party, to be able to carry out their functions effectively and without any undue influence. Such persons or staff of such body or bodies should have the appropriate training and resources to carry out their tasks.

Article 37: *Cooperation with Law Enforcement Authorities*

1. Each State Party shall take appropriate measures to encourage persons who participate or who have participated in the commission of an offence established in accordance with this Convention to supply information useful to competent authorities for investigative and evidentiary purposes and to provide factual, specific help to competent authorities that may contribute to depriving offenders of the proceeds of crime and to recovering such proceeds.
2. Each State Party shall consider providing for the possibility,

in appropriate cases, of mitigating punishment of an accused person who provides substantial cooperation in the investigation or prosecution of an offence established in accordance with this Convention.

3. Each State Party shall consider providing for the possibility, in accordance with fundamental principles of its domestic law, of granting immunity from prosecution to a person who provides substantial cooperation in the investigation or prosecution of an offence established in accordance with this Convention.
4. Protection of such persons shall be, *mutatis mutandis*, as provided for in Article 32 of this Convention.
5. Where a person referred to in paragraph 1 of this article located in one State Party can provide substantial cooperation to the competent authorities of another State Party, the States Parties concerned may consider entering into agreements or arrangements, in accordance with their domestic law, concerning the potential provision by the other State Party of the treatment set forth in paragraphs 2 and 3 of this article.

Article 38: Cooperation between National Authorities

Each State Party shall take such measures as may be necessary to encourage, in accordance with its domestic law, cooperation between, on the one hand, its public authorities, as well as its public officials, and, on the other hand, its authorities responsible for investigating and prosecuting criminal offences. Such cooperation may include:

(*a*) Informing the latter authorities, on their own initiative, where there are reasonable grounds to believe that any of the offences established in accordance with Articles 15, 21 and 23 of this Convention has been committed; or

(*b*) Providing, upon request, to the latter authorities all necessary information.

Article 39: Cooperation between National Authorities and the Private Sector

1. Each State Party shall take such measures as may be necessary to encourage, in accordance with its domestic

law, cooperation between national investigating and prosecuting authorities and entities of the private sector, in particular financial institutions, relating to matters involving the commission of offences established in accordance with this Convention.

2. Each State Party shall consider encouraging its nationals and other persons with a habitual residence in its territory to report to the national investigating and prosecuting authorities the commission of an offence established in accordance with this Convention.

Article 40: *Bank Secrecy*

Each State Party shall ensure that, in the case of domestic criminal investigations of offences established in accordance with this Convention, there are appropriate mechanisms available within its domestic legal system to overcome obstacles that may arise out of the application of bank secrecy laws.

Article 41: *Criminal Record*

Each State Party may adopt such legislative or other measures as may be necessary to take into consideration, under such terms as and for the purpose that it deems appropriate, any previous conviction in another State of an alleged offender for the purpose of using such information in criminal proceedings relating to an offence established in accordance with this Convention.

Article 42: *Jurisdiction*

1. Each State Party shall adopt such measures as may be necessary to establish its jurisdiction over the offences established in accordance with this Convention when:
   (*a*) the offence is committed in the territory of that State Party; or
   (*b*) the offence is committed on board a vessel that is flying the flag of that State Party or an aircraft that is registered under the laws of that State Party at the time that the offence is committed.
2. Subject to Article 4 of this Convention, a State Party may also establish its jurisdiction over any such offence when:

(*a*) the offence is committed against a national of that State Party; or

(*b*) the offence is committed by a national of that State Party or a stateless person who has his or her habitual residence in its territory; or

(*c*) the offence is one of those established in accordance with Article 23, paragraph 1 (*b*) (*ii*), of this Convention and is committed outside its territory with a view to the commission of an offence established in accordance with Article 23, paragraph 1 (*a*) (*i*) or (*ii*) or (*b*) (*i*), of this Convention within its territory; or

(*d*) the offence is committed against the State Party.

3. For the purposes of Article 44 of this Convention, each State Party shall take such measures as may be necessary to establish its jurisdiction over the offences established in accordance with this Convention when the alleged offender is present in its territory and it does not extradite such person solely on the ground that he or she is one of its nationals.
4. Each State Party may also take such measures as may be necessary to establish its jurisdiction over the offences established in accordance with this Convention when the alleged offender is present in its territory and it does not extradite him or her.
5. If a State Party exercising its jurisdiction under paragraph 1 or 2 of this article has been notified, or has otherwise learned, that any other States Parties are conducting an investigation, prosecution or judicial proceeding in respect of the same conduct, the competent authorities of those States Parties shall, as appropriate, consult one another with a view to coordinating their actions.
6. Without prejudice to norms of general international law, this Convention shall not exclude the exercise of any criminal jurisdiction established by a State Party in accordance with its domestic law.

Chapter IV: *International Cooperation*

Article 43: *International Cooperation*

1. States Parties shall cooperate in criminal matters in

accordance with Articles 44 to 50 of this Convention. Where appropriate and consistent with their domestic legal system. States Parties shall consider assisting each other in investigations of and proceedings in civil and administrative matters relating to corruption.

2. In matters of international cooperation, whenever dual criminality is considered a requirement, it shall be deemed fulfilled irrespective of whether the laws of the requested State Party place the offence within the same category of offence or denominate the offence by the same terminology as the requesting State Party, if the conduct underlying the offence for which assistance is sought is a criminal offence under the laws of both States Parties.

Article 44: *Extradition*

1. This article shall apply to the offences established in accordance with this Convention where the person who is the subject of the request for extradition is present in the territory of the requested State Party, provided that the offence for which extradition is sought is punishable under the domestic law of both the requesting State Party and the requested State Party.
2. Notwithstanding the provisions of paragraph 1 of this article, a State Party whose law so permits may grant the extradition of a person for any of the offences covered by this Convention that are not punishable under its own domestic law.
3. If the request for extradition includes several separate offences, at least one of which is extraditable under this article and some of which are not extraditable by reason of their period of imprisonment but are related to offences established in accordance with this Convention, the requested State Party may apply this article also in respect of those offences.
4. Each of the offences to which this article applies shall be deemed to be included as an extraditable offence in any extradition treaty existing between States Parties. States Parties undertake to include such offences as extraditable offences in every extradition treaty to be concluded between them. A State Party whose law so permits, in case

it uses this Convention as the basis for extradition, shall not consider any of the offences established in accordance with this Convention to be a political offence.

5. If a State Party that makes extradition conditional on the existence of a treaty receives a request for extradition from another State Party with which it has no extradition treaty, it may consider this Convention the legal basis for extradition in respect of any offence to which this article applies.
6. A State Party that makes extradition conditional on the existence of a treaty shall:
   (*a*) at the time of deposit of its instrument of ratification, acceptance or approval of or accession to this Convention, inform the Secretary-General of the United Nations whether it will take this Convention as the legal basis for cooperation on extradition with other States Parties to this Convention; and
   (*b*) if it does not take this Convention as the legal basis for cooperation on extradition, seek, where appropriate, to conclude treaties on extradition with other States Parties to this Convention in order to implement this article.
7. States Parties that do not make extradition conditional on the existence of a treaty shall recognize offences to which this article applies as extraditable offences between themselves.
8. Extradition shall be subject to the conditions provided for by the domestic law of the requested State Party or by applicable extradition treaties, including, *inter alia*, conditions in relation to the minimum penalty requirement for extradition and the grounds upon which the requested State Party may refuse extradition.
9. States Parties shall, subject to their domestic law, endeavour to expedite extradition procedures and to simplify evidentiary requirements relating thereto in respect of any offence to which this article applies.
10. Subject to the provisions of its domestic law and its extradition treaties, the requested State Party may, upon being satisfied that the circumstances so warrant and are urgent and at the request of the requesting State Party, take

a person whose extradition is sought and who is present in its territory into custody or take other appropriate measures to ensure his or her presence at extradition proceedings.

11. A State Party in whose territory an alleged offender is found, if it does not extradite such person in respect of an offence to which this article applies solely on the ground that he or she is one of its nationals, shall, at the request of the State Party seeking extradition, be obliged to submit the case without undue delay to its competent authorities for the purpose of prosecution. Those authorities shall take their decision and conduct their proceedings in the same manner as in the case of any other offence of a grave nature under the domestic law of that State Party. The States Parties concerned shall cooperate with each other, in particular on procedural and evidentiary aspects, to ensure the efficiency of such prosecution.
12. Whenever a State Party is permitted under its domestic law to extradite or otherwise surrender one of its nationals only upon the condition that the person will be returned to that State Party to serve the sentence imposed as a result of the trial or proceedings for which the extradition or surrender of the person was sought and that State Party and the State Party seeking the extradition of the person agree with this option and other terms that they may deem appropriate, such conditional extradition or surrender shall be sufficient to discharge the obligation set forth in paragraph 11 of this article.
13. If extradition, sought for purposes of enforcing a sentence, is refused because the person sought is a national of the requested State Party, the requested State Party shall, if its domestic law so permits and in conformity with the requirements of such law, upon application of the requesting State Party, consider the enforcement of the sentence imposed under the domestic law of the requesting State Party or the remainder thereof.
14. Any person regarding whom proceedings are being carried out in connection with any of the offences to which this article applies shall be guaranteed fair treatment at all stages of the proceedings, including enjoyment of all

the rights and guarantees provided by the domestic law of the State Party in the territory of which that person is present.

15. Nothing in this Convention shall be interpreted as imposing an obligation to extradite if the requested State Party has substantial grounds for believing that the request has been made for the purpose of prosecuting or punishing a person on account of that person's sex, race, religion, nationality, ethnic origin or political opinions or that compliance with the request would cause prejudice to that person's position for any one of these reasons.
16. States Parties may not refuse a request for extradition on the sole ground that the offence is also considered to involve fiscal matters.
17. Before refusing extradition, the requested State Party shall, where appropriate, consult with the requesting State Party to provide it with ample opportunity to present its opinions and to provide information relevant to its allegation.
18. States Parties shall seek to conclude bilateral and multilateral agreements or arrangements to carry out or to enhance the effectiveness of extradition.

Article 45: *Transfer of Sentenced Persons*

States Parties may consider entering into bilateral or multilateral agreements or arrangements on the transfer to their territory of persons sentenced to imprisonment or other forms of deprivation of liberty for offences established in accordance with this Convention in order that they may complete their sentences there.

Article 46: *Mutual Legal Assistance*

1. States Parties shall afford one another the widest measure of mutual legal assistance in investigations, prosecutions and judicial proceedings in relation to the offences covered by this Convention.
2. Mutual legal assistance shall be afforded to the fullest extent possible under relevant laws, treaties, agreements and arrangements of the requested State Party with respect to investigations, prosecutions and judicial proceedings in

relation to the offences for which a legal person may be held liable in accordance with Article 26 of this Convention in the requesting State Party.

3. Mutual legal assistance to be afforded in accordance with this article may be requested for any of the following purposes:
   (*a*) Taking evidence or statements from persons;
   (*b*) Effecting service of judicial documents;
   (*c*) Executing searches and seizures, and freezing;
   (*d*) Examining objects and sites;
   (*e*) Providing information, evidentiary items and expert evaluations;
   (*f*) Providing originals or certified copies of relevant documents and records, including government, bank, financial, corporate or business records;
   (*g*) Identifying or tracing proceeds of crime, property, instrumentalities or other things for evidentiary purposes;
   (*h*) Facilitating the voluntary appearance of persons in the requesting State Party;
   (*i*) Any other type of assistance that is not contrary to the domestic law of the requested State Party;
   (*j*) Identifying, freezing and tracing proceeds of crime in accordance with the provisions of Chapter V of this Convention;
   (*k*) The recovery of assets, in accordance with the provisions of Chapter V of this Convention.
4. Without prejudice to domestic law, the competent authorities of a State Party may, without prior request, transmit information relating to criminal matters to a competent authority in another State Party where they believe that such information could assist the authority in undertaking or successfully concluding inquiries and criminal proceedings or could result in a request formulated by the latter State Party pursuant to this Convention.
5. The transmission of information pursuant to paragraph 4 of this article shall be without prejudice to inquiries and criminal proceedings in the State of the competent authorities providing the information. The competent

authorities receiving the information shall comply with a request that said information remain confidential, even temporarily, or with restrictions on its use. However, this shall not prevent the receiving State Party from disclosing in its proceedings information that is exculpatory to an accused person. In such a case, the receiving State Party shall notify the transmitting State Party prior to the disclosure and, if so requested, consult with the transmitting State Party. If, in an exceptional case, advance notice is not possible, the receiving State Party shall inform the transmitting State Party of the disclosure without delay.

6. The provisions of this article shall not affect the obligations under any other treaty, bilateral or multi-lateral, that governs or will govern, in whole or in part, mutual legal assistance.
7. Paragraphs 9 to 29 of this article shall apply to requests made pursuant to this article if the States Parties in question are not bound by a treaty of mutual legal assistance. If those States Parties are bound by such a treaty, the corresponding provisions of that treaty shall apply unless the States Parties agree to apply paragraphs 9 to 29 of this article in lieu thereof. States Parties are strongly encouraged to apply those paragraphs if they facilitate cooperation.
8. States Parties shall not decline to render mutual legal assistance pursuant to this article on the ground of bank secrecy.
9. *(a)* A requested State Party, in responding to a request for assistance pursuant to this article in the absence of dual criminality, shall take into account the purposes of this Convention, as set forth in Article 1;

   (b) States Parties may decline to render assistance pursuant to this article on the ground of absence of dual criminality. However, a requested State Party shall, where consistent with the basic concepts of its legal system, render assistance that does not involve coercive action. Such assistance may be refused when requests involve matters of a *demonisms* nature or matters for which the cooperation or assistance sought is available under other provisions of this Convention; and

(*c*) Each State Party may consider adopting such measures as may be necessary to enable it to provide a wider scope of assistance pursuant to this article in the absence of dual criminality.

10. A person who is being detained or is serving a sentence in the territory of one State Party whose presence in another State Party is requested for purposes of identification, testimony or otherwise providing assistance in obtaining evidence for investigations, prosecutions or judicial proceedings in relation to offences covered by this Convention may be transferred if the following conditions are met:
    (*a*) The person freely gives his or her informed consent; and
    (*b*) The competent authorities of both States Parties agree, subject to such conditions as those States Parties may deem appropriate.
11. For the purposes of paragraph 10 of this article:
    (*a*) The State Party to which the person is transferred shall have the authority and obligation to keep the person transferred in custody, unless otherwise requested or authorized by the State Party from which the person was transferred;
    (*b*) The State Party to which the person is transferred shall without delay implement its obligation to return the person to the custody of the State Party from which the person was transferred as agreed beforehand, or as otherwise agreed, by the competent authorities of both States Parties;
    (*c*) The State Party to which the person is transferred shall not require the State Party from which the person was transferred to initiate extradition proceedings for the return of the person; and
    (*d*) The person transferred shall receive credit for service of the sentence being served in the State from which he or she was transferred for time spent in the custody of the State Party to which he or she was transferred.
12. Unless the State Party from which a person is to be transferred in accordance with paragraphs 10 and 11 of this article so agrees, that person, whatever his or her

nationality, shall not be prosecuted, detained, punished or subjected to any other restriction of his or her personal liberty in the territory of the State to which that person is transferred in respect of acts, omissions or convictions prior to his or her departure from the territory of the State from which he or she was transferred.

13. Each State Party shall designate a central authority that shall have the responsibility and power to receive requests for mutual legal assistance and either to execute them or to transmit them to the competent authorities for execution. Where a State Party has a special region or territory with a separate system of mutual legal assistance, it may designate a distinct central authority that shall have the same function for that region or territory. Central authorities shall ensure the speedy and proper execution or transmission of the requests received. Where the central authority transmits the request to a competent authority for execution, it shall encourage the speedy and proper execution of the request by the competent authority. The Secretary-General of the United Nations shall be notified of the central authority designated for this purpose at the time each State Party deposits its instrument of ratification, acceptance or approval of or accession to this Convention. Requests for mutual legal assistance and any communication related thereto shall be transmitted to the central authorities designated by the States Parties. This requirement shall be without prejudice to the right of a State Party to require that such requests and communications be addressed to it through diplomatic channels and, in urgent circumstances, where the States Parties agree, through the International Criminal Police Organisation, if possible.

14. Requests shall be made in writing or, where possible, by any means capable of producing a written record, in a language acceptable to the requested State Party, under conditions allowing that State Party to establish authenticity. The Secretary-General of the United Nations shall be notified of the language or languages acceptable to each State Party at the time it deposits its instrument of ratification, acceptance or approval of or accession to this Convention. In urgent circumstances and where agreed by

the States Parties, requests may be made orally but shall be confirmed in writing forthwith.

15. A request for mutual legal assistance shall contain:
    (*a*) the identity of the authority making the request;
    (*b*) the subject matter and nature of the investigation, prosecution or judicial proceeding to which the request relates and the name and functions of the authority conducting the investigation, prosecution or judicial proceeding;
    (*c*) a summary of the relevant facts, except in relation to requests for the purpose of service of judicial documents;
    (*d*) a description of the assistance sought and details of any particular procedure that the requesting State Party wishes to be followed;
    (*e*) where possible, the identity, location and nationality of any person concerned; and
    (*f*) the purpose for which the evidence, information or action is sought.
16. The requested State Party may request additional information when it appears necessary for the execution of the request in accordance with its domestic law or when it can facilitate such execution.
17. A request shall be executed in accordance with the domestic law of the requested State Party and, to the extent not contrary to the domestic law of the requested State Party and where possible, in accordance with the procedures specified in the request.
18. Wherever possible and consistent with fundamental principles of domestic law, when an individual is in the territory of a State Party and has to be heard as a witness or expert by the judicial authorities of another State Party, the first State Party may, at the request of the other, permit the hearing to take place by video conference if it is not possible or desirable for the individual in question to appear in person in the territory of the requesting State Party. States Parties may agree that the hearing shall be conducted by a judicial authority of the requesting State Party and attended by a judicial authority of the requested State Party.

19. The requesting State Party shall not transmit or use information or evidence furnished by the requested State Party for investigations, prosecutions or judicial proceedings other than those stated in the request without the prior consent of the requested State Party. Nothing in this paragraph shall prevent the requesting State Party from disclosing in its proceedings information or evidence that is exculpatory to an accused person. In the latter case, the requesting State Party shall notify the requested State Party prior to the disclosure and, if so requested, consult with the requested State Party. If, in an exceptional case, advance notice is not possible, the requesting State Party shall inform the requested State Party of the disclosure without delay.
20. The requesting State Party may require that the requested State Party keep confidential the fact and substance of the request, except to the extent necessary to execute the request. If the requested State Party cannot comply with the requirement of confidentiality, it shall promptly inform the requesting State Party.
21. Mutual legal assistance may be refused:
    (*a*) if the request is not made in conformity with the provisions of this article;
    (*b*) if the requested State Party considers that execution of the request is likely to prejudice its sovereignty, security, *ordre public* or other essential interests;
    (*c*) if the authorities of the requested State Party would be prohibited by its domestic law from carrying out the action requested with regard to any similar offence, had it been subject to investigation, prosecution or judicial proceedings under their own jurisdiction; and
    (*d*) if it would be contrary to the legal system of the requested State Party relating to mutual legal assistance for the request to be granted.
22. States Parties may not refuse a request for mutual legal assistance on the sole ground that the offence is also considered to involve fiscal matters.
23. Reasons shall be given for any refusal of mutual legal assistance.
24. The requested State Party shall execute the request for mutual legal assistance as soon as possible and shall take

as full account as possible of any deadlines suggested by the requesting State Party and for which reasons are given, preferably in the request. The requesting State Party may make reasonable requests for information on the status and progress of measures taken by the requested State Party to satisfy its request. The requested State Party shall respond to reasonable requests by the requesting State Party on the status, and progress in its handling, of the request. The requesting State Party shall promptly inform the requested State Party when the assistance sought is no longer required.

25. Mutual legal assistance may be postponed by the requested State Party on the ground that it interferes with an ongoing investigation, prosecution or judicial proceeding.
26. Before refusing a request pursuant to paragraph 21 of this article or postponing its execution pursuant to paragraph 25 of this article, the requested State Party shall consult with the requesting State Party to consider whether assistance may be granted subject to such terms and conditions as it deems necessary. If the requesting State Party accepts assistance subject to those conditions, it shall comply with the conditions.
27. Without prejudice to the application of paragraph 12 of this article, a witness, expert or other person who, at the request of the requesting State Party, consents to give evidence in a proceeding or to assist in an investigation, prosecution or judicial proceeding in the territory of the requesting State Party shall not be prosecuted, detained, punished or subjected to any other restriction of his or her personal liberty in that territory in respect of acts, omissions or convictions prior to his or her departure from the territory of the requested State Party. Such safe conduct shall cease when the witness, expert or other person having had, for a period of fifteen consecutive days or for any period agreed upon by the States Parties from the date on which he or she has been officially informed that his or her presence is no longer required by the judicial authorities, an opportunity of leaving, has nevertheless remained voluntarily in the territory of the requesting State Party or, having left it, has returned of his or her own free will.

28. The ordinary costs of executing a request shall be borne by the requested State Party, unless otherwise agreed by the States Parties concerned. If expenses of a substantial or extraordinary nature are or will be required to fulfil the request, the States Parties shall consult to determine the terms and conditions under which the request will be executed, as well as the manner in which the costs shall be borne.
29. The requested State Party:
    (*a*) shall provide to the requesting State Party copies of government records, documents or information in its possession that under its domestic law are available to the general public; and
    (*b*) may, at its discretion, provide to the requesting State Party in whole, in part or subject to such conditions as it deems appropriate, copies of any government records, documents or information in its possession that under its domestic law are not available to the general public.
30. States Parties shall consider, as may be necessary, the possibility of concluding bilateral or multi-lateral agreements or arrangements that would serve the purposes of, give practical effect to or enhance the provisions of this article.

Article 47: Transfer of Criminal Proceedings

States Parties shall consider the possibility of transferring to one another proceedings for the prosecution of an offence established in accordance with this Convention in cases where such transfer is considered to be in the interests of the proper administration of justice, in particular in cases where several jurisdictions are involved, with a view to concentrating the prosecution.

Article 48: Law Enforcement Cooperation

1. States Parties shall cooperate closely with one another, consistent with their respective domestic legal and administrative systems, to enhance the effectiveness of law enforcement action to combat the offences covered by this Convention. States Parties shall, in particular, take effective measures:

(*a*) To enhance and, where necessary, to establish channels of communication between their competent authorities, agencies and services in order to facilitate the secure and rapid exchange of information concerning all aspects of the offences covered by this Convention, including, if the States Parties concerned deem it appropriate, links with other criminal activities;

(*b*) To cooperate with other States Parties in conducting inquiries with respect to offences covered by this Convention concerning:

(*i*) The identity, whereabouts and activities of persons suspected of involvement in such offences or the location of other persons concerned,

(*ii*) The movement of proceeds of crime or property derived from the commission of such offences,

(*iii*) The movement of property, equipment or other instrumentalities used or intended for use in the commission of such offences,

(*c*) To provide, where appropriate, necessary items or quantities of substances for analytical or investigative purposes,

(*d*) To exchange, where appropriate, information with other States Parties concerning specific means and methods used to commit offences covered by this Convention, including the use of false identities, forged, altered or false documents and other means of concealing activities,

(*e*) To facilitate effective coordination between their competent authorities, agencies and services and to promote the exchange of personnel and other experts, including, subject to bilateral agreements or arrangements between the States Parties concerned, the posting of liaison officers, and

(*f*) To exchange information and coordinate administrative and other measures taken as appropriate for the purpose of early identification of the offences covered by this Convention.

2. With a view to giving effect to this Convention, States Parties shall consider entering into bilateral or multi-lateral

agreements or arrangements on direct cooperation between their law enforcement agencies and, where such agreements or arrangements already exist, amending them. In the absence of such agreements or arrangements between the States Parties concerned, the States Parties may consider this Convention to be the basis for mutual law enforcement cooperation in respect of the offences covered by this Convention. Whenever appropriate, States Parties shall make full use of agreements or arrangements, including international or regional organisations, to enhance the cooperation between their law enforcement agencies.

3. States Parties shall endeavour to cooperate within their means to respond to offences covered by this Convention committed through the use of modem technology.

Article 49: *Joint Investigations*

States Parties shall consider concluding bilateral or multi-lateral agreements or arrangements whereby, in relation to matters that are the subject of investigations, prosecutions or judicial proceedings in one or more States, the competent authorities concerned may establish joint investigative bodies. In the absence of such agreements or arrangements, joint investigations may be undertaken by agreement on a case-by-case basis. The States Parties involved shall ensure that the sovereignty of the State Party in whose territory such investigation is to take place is fully respected.

Article 50: *Special Investigative Techniques*

1. In order to combat corruption effectively, each State Party shall, to the extent permitted by the basic principles of its domestic legal system and in accordance with the conditions prescribed by its domestic law, take such measures as may be necessary, within its means, to allow for the appropriate use by its competent authorities of controlled delivery and, where it deems appropriate, other special investigative techniques, such as electronic or other forms of surveillance and undercover operations, within its territory, and to allow for the admissibility in court of evidence derived there from.

2. For the purpose of investigating the offences covered by this Convention, States Parties are encouraged to conclude, when necessary, appropriate bilateral or multi-lateral agreements or arrangements for using such special investigative techniques in the context of cooperation at the international level. Such agreements or arrangements shall be concluded and implemented in full compliance with the principle of sovereign equality of States and shall be carried out strictly in accordance with the terms of those agreements or arrangements.
3. In the absence of an agreement or arrangement as set forth in paragraph 2 of this article, decisions to use such special investigative techniques at the international level shall be made on a case-by-case basis and may, when necessary, take into consideration financial arrangements and understandings with respect to the exercise of jurisdiction by the States Parties concerned.
4. Decisions to use controlled delivery at the international level may, with the consent of the States Parties concerned, include methods such as intercepting and allowing the goods or funds to continue intact or be removed or replaced in whole or in part.

Chapter V: *Asset Recovery*

Article 51: *General Provision*

The return of assets pursuant to this chapter is a fundamental principle of this Convention, and States Parties shall afford one another the widest measure of cooperation and assistance in this regard.

Article 52: *Prevention and Detection of Transfers of Proceeds of Crime*

1. Without prejudice to Article 14 of this Convention, each State Party shall take such measures as may be necessary, in accordance with its domestic law, to require financial institutions within its jurisdiction to verify the identity of customers, to take reasonable steps to determine the identity of beneficial owners of funds deposited into high-value accounts and to conduct enhanced scrutiny of accounts sought or maintained by or on behalf of individuals who

are, or have been, entrusted with prominent public functions and their family members and close associates. Such enhanced scrutiny shall be reasonably designed to detect suspicious transactions for the purpose of reporting to competent authorities and should not be so construed as to discourage or prohibit financial institutions from doing business with any legitimate customer.

2. In order to facilitate implementation of the measures provided for in paragraph 1 of this article, each State Party, in accordance with its domestic law and inspired by relevant initiatives of regional, interregional and multilateral organisations against money laundering, shall:
   (*a*) issue advisories regarding the types of natural or legal person to whose accounts financial institutions within its jurisdiction will be expected to apply enhanced scrutiny, the types of accounts and transactions to which to pay particular attention and appropriate account-opening, maintenance and record-keeping measures to take concerning such accounts; and
   (*b*) where appropriate, notify financial institutions within its jurisdiction, at the request of another State Party or on its own initiative, of the identity of particular natural or legal persons to whose accounts such institutions will be expected to apply enhanced scrutiny, in addition to those whom the financial institutions may otherwise identify.
3. In the context of paragraph 2 (*a*) of this article, each State Party shall implement measures to ensure that its financial institutions maintain adequate records, over an appropriate period of time, of accounts and transactions involving the persons mentioned in paragraph 1 of this article, which should, as a minimum, contain information relating to the identity of the customer as well as, as far as possible, of the beneficial owner.
4. With the aim of preventing and detecting transfers of proceeds of offences established in accordance with this Convention, each State Party shall implement appropriate and effective measures to prevent, with the help of its regulatory and oversight bodies, the establishment of banks that have no physical presence and that are not affiliated

with a regulated financial group. Moreover, States Parties may consider requiring their financial institutions to refuse to enter into or continue a correspondent banking relationship with such institutions and to guard against establishing relations with foreign financial institutions that permit their accounts to be used by banks that have no physical presence and that are not affiliated with a regulated financial group.

5. Each State Party shall consider establishing, in accordance with its domestic law, effective financial disclosure systems for appropriate public officials and shall provide for appropriate sanctions for non-compliance. Each State Party shall also consider taking such measures as may be necessary to permit its competent authorities to share that information with the competent authorities in other States Parties when necessary to investigate, claim and recovery proceeds of offences established in accordance with this Convention.
6. Each State Party shall consider taking such measures as may be necessary, in accordance with its domestic law, to require appropriate public officials having an interest in or signature or other authority over a financial account in a foreign country to report that relationship to appropriate authorities and to maintain appropriate records related to such accounts. Such measures shall also provide for appropriate sanctions for non-compliance.

Article 53: *Measures for Direct Recovery of Property*

Each State Party shall, in accordance with its domestic law:

(*a*) Take such measures as may be necessary to permit another State Party to initiate civil action in its courts to establish title to or ownership of property acquired through the commission of an offence established in accordance with this Convention;

(*b*) Take such measures as may be necessary to permit its courts to order those who have committed offences established in accordance with this Convention to pay compensation or damages to another State Party that has been harmed by such offences; and (*c*) Take such measures as may be necessary to permit its courts or competent authorities, when having to decide on confiscation, to recognize another State Party's claim as a legitimate owner of property acquired through the commission of an offence established in accordance with this Convention.

Article 54: *Mechanisms for Recovery of Property through International Cooperation in Confiscation*

1. Each State Party, in order to provide mutual legal assistance pursuant to Article 55 of this Convention with respect to property acquired through or involved in the commission of an offence established in accordance with this Convention, shall, in accordance with its domestic law:
   (*a*) Take such measures as may be necessary to permit its competent authorities to give effect to an order of confiscation issued by a court of another State Party;
   (*b*) Take such measures as may be necessary to permit its competent authorities, where they have jurisdiction, to order the confiscation of such property of foreign origin by adjudication of an offence of money-laundering or such other offence as may be within its jurisdiction or by other procedures authorized under its domestic law; and
   (*c*) Consider taking such measures as may be necessary to allow confiscation of such property without a criminal conviction in cases in which the offender cannot be prosecuted by reason of death, flight or absence or in other appropriate cases.
2. Each State Party, in order to provide mutual legal assistance upon a request made pursuant to paragraph 2 of Article 55 of this Convention, shall, in accordance with its domestic law:
   (*a*) Take such measures as may be necessary to permit its competent authorities to freeze or seize property upon a freezing or seizure order issued by a court or competent authority of a requesting State Party that provides a reasonable basis for the requested State Party to believe that there are sufficient grounds for taking such actions and that the property would

eventually be subject to an order of confiscation for purposes of paragraph 1 (*a*) of this article;

(*b*) Take such measures as may be necessary to permit its competent authorities to freeze or seize property upon a request that provides a reasonable basis for the requested State Party to believe that there are sufficient grounds for taking such actions and that the property would eventually be subject to an order of confiscation for purposes of paragraph 1 (*a*) of this article; and

(*c*) Consider taking additional measures to permit its competent authorities to preserve property for confiscation, such as on the basis of a foreign arrest or criminal charge related to the acquisition of such property.

Article 55: *International Cooperation for Purposes of Confiscation*

1. A State Party that has received a request from another State Party having jurisdiction over an offence established in accordance with this Convention for confiscation of proceeds of crime, property, equipment or other instrumentalities referred to in Article 31, paragraph 1, of this Convention situated in its territory shall, to the greatest extent possible within its domestic legal system:

   (*a*) Submit the request to its competent authorities for the purpose of obtaining an order of confiscation and, if such an order is granted, give effect to it; or

   (*b*) Submit to its competent authorities, with a view to giving effect to it to the extent requested, an order of confiscation issued by a court in the territory of the requesting State Party in accordance with Articles 31, paragraph 1, and 54, paragraph 1 (*a*), of this Convention insofar as it relates to proceeds of crime, property, equipment or other instrumentalities referred to in Article 31, paragraph 1, situated in the territory of the requested State Party.

2. Following a request made by another State Party having jurisdiction over an offence established in accordance with this Convention, the requested State Party shall take measures to identify, trace and freeze or seize proceeds of crime, property, equipment or other instrumentalities

referred to in Article 31, paragraph 1, of this Convention for the purpose of eventual confiscation to be ordered either by the requesting State Party or, pursuant to a request under paragraph 1 of this Article, by the requested State Party.

3. The provisions of Article 46 of this Convention are applicable, *mutatis mutandis*, to this article. In addition to the information specified in Article 46, paragraph 15, requests made pursuant to this article shall contain:
   (*a*) In the case of a request pertaining to paragraph 1 (*a*) of this article, a description of the property to be confiscated, including, to the extent possible, the location and, where relevant, the estimated value of the property and a statement of the facts relied upon by the requesting State Party sufficient to enable the requested State Party to seek the order under its domestic law;
   (*b*) In the case of a request pertaining to paragraph 1 (*b*) of this article, a legally admissible copy of an order of confiscation upon which the request is based issued by the requesting State Party, a statement of the facts and information as to the extent to which execution of the order is requested, a statement specifying the measures taken by the requesting State Party to provide adequate notification to *bona fide* third parties and to ensure due process and a statement that the confiscation order is final;
   (*c*) In the case of a request pertaining to paragraph 2 of this article, a statement of the facts relied upon by the requesting State Party and a description of the actions requested and, where available, a legally admissible copy of an order on which the request is based.
4. The decisions or actions provided for in paragraphs 1 and 2 of this article shall be taken by the requested State Party in accordance with and subject to the provisions of its domestic law and its procedural rules or any bilateral or multi-lateral agreement or arrangement to which it may be bound in relation to the requesting State Party.
5. Each State Party shall furnish copies of its laws and regulations that give effect to this article and of any subsequent changes to such laws and regulations or a

description thereof to the Secretary-General of the United Nations.

6. If a State Party elects to make the taking of the measures referred to in paragraphs 1 and 2 of this article conditional on the existence of a relevant treaty, that State Party shall consider this Convention the necessary and sufficient treaty basis.
7. Cooperation under this article may also be refused or provisional measures lifted if the requested State Party does not receive sufficient and timely evidence or if the property is office *de minimis* value.
8. Before lifting any provisional measure taken pursuant to this article, the requested State Party shall, wherever possible, give the requesting State Party an opportunity to present its reasons in favour of continuing the measure.
9. The provisions of this article shall not be construed as prejudicing the rights of *bona fide* third parties.

Article 56: *Special Cooperation*

Without prejudice to its domestic law, each State Party shall endeavour to take measures to permit it to forward, without prejudice to its own investigations, prosecutions or judicial proceedings, information on proceeds of offences established in accordance with this Convention to another State Party without prior request, when it considers that the disclosure of such information might assist the receiving State Party in initiating or carrying out investigations, prosecutions or judicial proceedings or might lead to a request by that State Party under this chapter of the Convention.

Article 57: *Return and Disposal of Assets*

1. Property confiscated by a State Party pursuant to Article 31 or 55 of this Convention shall be disposed of, including by return to its prior legitimate owners, pursuant to paragraph 3 of this article, by that State Party in accordance with the provisions of this Convention and its domestic law.
2. Each State Party shall adopt such legislative and other measures, in accordance with the fundamental principles of its domestic law, as may be necessary to enable its

competent authorities to return confiscated property, when acting on the request made by another State Party, in accordance with this Convention, taking into account the rights of *bona fide* third parties.

3. In accordance with Articles 46 and 55 of this Convention and paragraphs 1 and 2 of this article, the requested State Party shall:
   (*a*) In the case of embezzlement of public funds or of laundering of embezzled public funds as referred to in Articles 17 and 23 of this Convention, when confiscation was executed in accordance with Article 55 and on the basis of a final judgement in the requesting State Party, a requirement that can be waived by the requested State Party, return the confiscated property to the requesting State Party;
   (*b*) In the case of proceeds of any other offence covered by this Convention, when the confiscation was executed in accordance with Article 55 of this Convention and on the basis of a final judgement in the requesting State Party, a requirement that can be waived by the requested State Party, return the confiscated property to the requesting State Party, when the requesting State Party reasonably establishes its prior ownership of such confiscated property to the requested State Party or when the requested State Party recognizes damage to the requesting State Party as a basis for returning the confiscated property;
   (*c*) In all other cases, give priority consideration to returning confiscated property to the requesting State Party, returning such property to its prior legitimate owners or compensating the victims of the crime.
4. Where appropriate, unless States Parties decide otherwise, the requested State Party may deduct reasonable expenses incurred in investigations, prosecutions or judicial proceedings leading to the return or disposition of confiscated property pursuant to this article.
5. Where appropriate, States Parties may also give special consideration to concluding agreements or mutually acceptable arrangements, on a case-by-case basis, for the final disposal of confiscated property.

Article 58: *Financial Intelligence Unit*

States Parties shall cooperate with one another for the purpose of preventing and combating the transfer of proceeds of offences established in accordance with this Convention and of promoting ways and means of recovering such proceeds and, to that end, shall consider establishing a financial intelligence unit to be responsible for receiving, analysing and disseminating to the competent authorities reports of suspicious financial transactions.

Article 59: *Bilateral and Multi-lateral Agreements and Arrangements*

States Parties shall consider concluding bilateral or multi-lateral agreements or arrangements to enhance the effectiveness of international cooperation undertaken pursuant to this chapter of the Convention.

Chapter* VI: *Technical Assistance and Information Exchange

Article 60: *Training and Technical Assistance*

1. Each State Party shall, to the extent necessary, initiate, develop or improve specific training programmes for its personnel responsible for preventing and combating corruption. Such training programmes could deal, *inter alia*, with the following areas:
   (*a*) Effective measures to prevent, detect, investigate, punish and control corruption, including the use of evidence-gathering and investigative methods;
   (*b*) Building capacity in the development and planning of strategic anti-corruption policy;
   (*c*) Training competent authorities in the preparation of requests for mutual legal assistance that meet the requirements of this Convention;
   (*d*) Evaluation and strengthening of institutions, public service management and the management of public finances, including public procurement, and the private sector;
   (*e*) Preventing and combating the transfer of proceeds of offences established in accordance with this Convention and recovering such proceeds;
   (*f*) Detecting and freezing of the transfer of proceeds of

offences established in accordance with this Convention;

(*g*) Surveillance of the movement of proceeds of offences established in accordance with this Convention and of the methods used to transfer, conceal or disguise such proceeds;

(*h*) Appropriate and efficient legal and administrative mechanisms and methods for facilitating the return of proceeds of offences established in accordance with this Convention;

(*i*) Methods used in protecting victims and witnesses who cooperate with judicial authorities; and

(*j*) Training in national and international regulations and in languages.

2. States Parties shall, according to their capacity, consider affording one another the widest measure of technical assistance, especially for the benefit of developing countries, in their respective plans and programmes to combat corruption, including material support and training in the areas referred to in paragraph 1 of this article, and training and assistance and the mutual exchange of relevant experience and specialized knowledge, which will facilitate international cooperation between States Parties in the areas of extradition and mutual legal assistance.
3. States Parties shall strengthen, to the extent necessary, efforts to maximize operational and training activities in international and regional organisations and in the framework of relevant bilateral and multi-lateral agreements or arrangements.
4. States Parties shall consider assisting one another, upon request, in conducting evaluations, studies and research relating to the types, causes, effects and costs of corruption in their respective countries, with a view to developing, with the participation of competent authorities and society, strategies and action plans to combat corruption.
5. In order to facilitate the recovery of proceeds of offences established in accordance with this Convention, States Parties may cooperate in providing each other with the names of experts who could assist in achieving that objective.

6. States Parties shall consider using sub-regional, regional and international conferences and seminars to promote cooperation and technical assistance and to stimulate discussion on problems of mutual concern, including the special problems and needs of developing countries and countries with economies in transition.
7. States Parties shall consider establishing voluntary mechanisms with a view to contributing financially to the efforts of developing countries and countries with economies in transition to apply this Convention through technical assistance programmes and projects.
8. Each State Party shall consider making voluntary contributions to the United Nations Office on Drugs and Crime for the purpose of fostering, through the Office, programmes and projects in developing countries with a view to implementing this Convention.

Article 61: Collection, Exchange and Analysis of Information on Corruption

1. Each State Party shall consider analysing, in consultation with experts, trends in corruption in its territory, as well as the circumstances in which corruption offences are committed.
2. States Parties shall consider developing and sharing with each other and through international and regional organisations statistics, analytical expertise concerning corruption and information with a view to developing, insofar as possible, common definitions, standards and methodologies, as well as information on best practices to prevent and combat corruption.
3. Each State Party shall consider monitoring its policies and actual measures to combat corruption and making assessments of their effectiveness and efficiency.

Article 62: Other Measures—Implementation of the Convention through Economic Development and Technical Assistance

1. States Parties shall take measures conducive to the optimal implementation of this Convention to the extent possible, through international cooperation, taking into account the

negative effects of corruption on society in general, in particular on sustainable development.

2. States Parties shall make concrete efforts to the extent possible and in coordination with each other, as well as with international and regional organisations:
   (*a*) To enhance their cooperation at various levels with developing countries, with a view to strengthening the capacity of the latter to prevent and combat corruption;
   (*b*) To enhance financial and material assistance to support the efforts of developing countries to prevent and fight corruption effectively and to help them implement this Convention successfully;
   (*c*) To provide technical assistance to developing countries and countries with economies in transition to assist them in meeting their needs for the implementation of this Convention. To that end, States Parties shall endeavour to make adequate and regular voluntary contributions to an account specifically designated for that purpose in a United Nations funding mechanism. States Parties may also give special consideration, in accordance with their domestic law and the provisions of this Convention, to contributing to that account a percentage of the money or of the corresponding value of proceeds of crime or property confiscated in accordance with the provisions of this Convention;
   (*d*) To encourage and persuade other States and financial institutions as appropriate to join them in efforts in accordance with this article, in particular by providing more training programmes and modern equipment to developing countries in order to assist them in achieving the objectives of this Convention.
3. To the extent possible, these measures shall be without prejudice to existing foreign assistance commitments or to other financial cooperation arrangements at the bilateral, regional or international level.
4. States Parties may conclude bilateral or multi-lateral agreements or arrangements on material and logistical assistance, taking into consideration the financial

arrangements necessary for the means of international cooperation provided for by this Convention to be effective and for the prevention, detection and control of corruption.

Chapter VII: *Mechanisms for Implementation*

Article 63: *Conference of the States Parties to the Convention*

1. A Conference of the States Parties to the Convention is hereby established to improve the capacity of and cooperation between States Parties to achieve the objectives set forth in this Convention and to promote and review its implementation.
2. The Secretary-General of the United Nations shall convene the Conference of the States Parties not later than one year following the entry into force of this Convention. Thereafter, regular meetings of the Conference of the States Parties shall be held in accordance with the rules of procedure adopted by the Conference.
3. The Conference of the States Parties shall adopt rules of procedure and rules governing the functioning of the activities set forth in this article, including rules concerning the admission and participation of observers, and the payment of expenses incurred in carrying out those activities.
4. The Conference of the States Parties shall agree upon activities, procedures and methods of work to achieve the objectives set forth in paragraph 1 of this article, including:
   (*a*) Facilitating activities by States Parties under Articles 60 and 62 and Chapters II to V of this Convention, including by encouraging the mobilization of voluntary contributions;
   (*b*) Facilitating the exchange of information among States Parties on patterns and trends in corruption and on successful practices for preventing and combating it and for the return of proceeds of crime, through, *inter alia*, the publication of relevant information as mentioned in this article;
   (*c*) Cooperating with relevant international and regional organisations and mechanisms and non-governmental organisations;

(*d*) Making appropriate use of relevant information produced by other international and regional mechanisms for combating and preventing corruption in order to avoid unnecessary duplication of work;

(*e*) Reviewing periodically the implementation of this Convention by its States Parties;

(*f*) Making recommendations to improve this Convention and its implementation; and

(*g*) Taking note of the technical assistance requirements of States Parties with regard to the implementation of this Convention and recommending any action it may deem necessary in that respect.

5. For the purpose of paragraph 4 of this article, the Conference of the States Parties shall acquire the necessary knowledge of the measures taken by States Parties in implementing this Convention and the difficulties encountered by them in doing so through information provided by them and through such supplemental review mechanisms as may be established by the Conference of the States Parties.

6. Each State Party shall provide the Conference of the States Parties with information on its programmes, plans and practices, as well as on legislative and administrative measures to implement this Convention, as required by the Conference of the States Parties. The Conference of the States Parties shall examine the most effective way of receiving and acting upon information, including, *inter alia*, information received from States Parties and from competent international organisations. Inputs received from relevant non-governmental organisations duly accredited in accordance with procedures to be decided upon by the Conference of the States Parties may also be considered.

7. Pursuant to paragraphs 4 to 6 of this article, the Conference of the States Parties shall establish, if it deems it necessary, any appropriate mechanism or body to assist in the effective implementation of the Convention.

Article 64: Secretariat

1. The Secretary-General of the United Nations shall provide

the necessary secretariat services to the Conference of the States Parties to the Convention.

2. The secretariat shall:
   (*a*) assist the Conference of the States Parties in carrying out the activities set forth in Article 63 of this Convention and make arrangements and provide the necessary services for the sessions of the Conference of the States Parties;
   (*b*) upon request, assist States Parties in providing information to the Conference of the States Parties as envisaged in Article 63, paragraphs 5 and 6, of this Convention; and
   (*c*) ensure the necessary coordination with the secretariats of relevant international and regional organisations.

Chapter VIII: *Final Provisions*

Article 65: *Implementation of the Convention*

1. Each State Party shall take the necessary measures, including legislative and administrative measures, in accordance with fundamental principles of its domestic law, to ensure the implementation of its obligations under this Convention.
2. Each State Party may adopt more strict or severe measures than those provided for by this Convention for preventing and combating corruption.

Article 66: *Settlement of Disputes*

1. States Parties shall endeavour to settle disputes concerning the interpretation or application of this Convention through negotiation.
2. Any dispute between two or more States Parties concerning the interpretation or application of this Convention that cannot be settled through negotiation within a reasonable time shall, at the request of one of those States Parties, be submitted to arbitration. If, six months after the date of the request for arbitration, those States Parties are unable to agree on the organisation of the arbitration, any one of those States Parties may refer the dispute to the International

Court of Justice by request in accordance with the Statute of the Court.

3. Each State Party may, at the time of signature, ratification, acceptance or approval of or accession to this Convention, declare that it does not consider itself bound by paragraph 2 of this article. The other States Parties shall not be bound by paragraph 2 of this article with respect to any State Party that has made such a reservation.
4. Any State Party that has made a reservation in accordance with paragraph 3 of this article may at any time withdraw that reservation by notification to the Secretary-General of the United Nations.

Article 67: *Signature, Ratification, Acceptance, Approval and Accession*

1. This Convention shall be open to all States for signature from 9 to 11 December, 2003 in Merida, Mexico, and thereafter at United Nations Headquarters in New York until 9 December, 2005.
2. This Convention shall also be open for signature by regional economic integration organisations provided that at least one member State of such organization has signed this Convention in accordance with paragraph 1 of this article.
3. This Convention is subject to ratification, acceptance or approval. Instruments of ratification, acceptance or approval shall be deposited with the Secretary-General of the United Nations. A regional economic integration organisation may deposit its instrument of ratification, acceptance or approval if at least one of its member States has done likewise. In that instrument of ratification, acceptance or approval, such organisation shall declare the extent of its competence with respect to the matters governed by this Convention. Such organisation shall also inform the depositary of any relevant modification in the extent of its competence.
4. This Convention is open for accession by any State or any regional economic integration organisation of which at least one member State is a Party to this Convention. Instruments of accession shall be deposited with the Secretary-General of the United Nations. At the time of its accession, a regional economic integration organisation shall declare the extent of its competence with respect to matters governed by this

Convention. Such organisation shall also inform the depositary of any relevant modification in the extent of its competence.

Article 68: *Entry into Force*

1. This Convention shall enter into force on the ninetieth day after the date of deposit of the thirtieth instrument of ratification, acceptance, approval or accession. For the purpose of this paragraph, any instrument deposited by a regional economic integration organisation shall not be counted as additional to those deposited by member States of such organisation.
2. For each State or regional economic integration organisation ratifying, accepting, approving or acceding to this Convention after the deposit of the thirtieth instrument of such action, this Convention shall enter into force on the thirtieth-day after the date of deposit by such State or organisation of the relevant instrument or on the date this Convention enters into force pursuant to paragraph 1 of this article, whichever is later.

Article 69: *Amendment*

1. After the expiry of five years from the entry into force of this Convention, a State Party may propose an amendment and transmit it to the Secretary-General of the United Nations, who shall thereupon communicate the proposed amendment to the States Parties and to the Conference of the States Parties to the Convention for the purpose of considering and deciding on the proposal. The Conference of the States Parties shall make every effort to achieve consensus on each amendment. If all efforts at consensus have been exhausted and no agreement has been reached, the amendment shall, as a last resort, require for its adoption a two-thirds majority vote of the States Parties present and voting at the meeting of the Conference of the States Parties.
2. Regional economic integration organisations, in matters within their competence, shall exercise their right to vote under this article with a number of votes equal to the

number of their member States that are Parties to this Convention. Such organisations shall not exercise their right to vote if their member States exercise theirs and *vice versa*.

3. An amendment adopted in accordance with paragraph 1 of this article is subject to ratification, acceptance or approval by States Parties.
4. An amendment adopted in accordance with paragraph 1 of this article shall enter into force in respect of a State Party ninety days after the date of the deposit with the Secretary-General of the United Nations of an instrument of ratification, acceptance or approval of such amendment.
5. When an amendment enters into force, it shall be binding on those States Parties which have expressed their consent to be bound by it. Other States Parties shall still be bound by the provisions of this Convention and any earlier amendments that they have ratified, accepted or approved.

Article 70: *Denunciation*

1. A State Party may denounce this Convention by written notification to the Secretary-General of the United Nations. Such denunciation shall become effective one year after the date of receipt of the notification by the Secretary-General.
2. A regional economic integration organisation shall cease to be a Party to this Convention when all of its member States have denounced it.

Article 71: *Depositary and Languages*

1. The Secretary-General of the United Nations is designated depositary of this Convention.
2. The original of this Convention, of which the Arabic, Chinese, English, French, Russian and Spanish texts are equally authentic, shall be deposited with the Secretary-General of the United Nations.

In *Witness Whereof*, the undersigned plenipotentiaries, being duly authorized thereto by their respective Governments, have signed this Convention.

Report of TI on UNCAC Follow-up

Background

The UN Convention Against Corruption (UNCAC) represents a crucial step in building an international framework to combat corruption. In today's global economy, corruption has become a worldwide phenomenon making it essential to have an international convention that binds all countries. Because of its universal reach, UNCAC makes it possible to tackle problems that cannot be addressed through existing regional conventions.

Experience with other anti-corruption conventions has demonstrated the importance of a systematic monitoring process to ensure timely and effective implementation by national governments. UNCAC provides for a Conference of the States Parties (CSP) to the Convention which has broad responsibilities to promote and review its implementation, including establishing "any appropriate mechanism or body to assist in the effective implementation of the Convention." The first meeting of the CSP will be held in December of 2006.

Transparency International (TI) organised a Study Group on a Follow-up Process for UNCAC to develop ideas for consideration by the CSP. The Study Group consists of individuals with extensive experience with monitoring of other anti-corruption conventions. They participated as individuals, not as representatives of the organisations with which they are affiliated. The Study Group held four meetings: in Paris on 19 December, 2004 and 18 March, 2005 and in Berlin on 22-23 June and 23-24 September, 2005. On 24 January, 2006, a meeting was held in Vienna at which representatives of nineteen governments commented on the work of the Study Group.

Representatives of the following countries including most of the members of the friends of the Convention group attended the 24 January meeting: Argentina, Austria, Canada, Egypt, Finland, France, Japan, Jordan, Mexico, Netherlands, Nigeria, Norway, Pakistan, Peru, Poland, Russia, South Africa, UK and the US.

The Study Group spent substantial time reviewing the monitoring processes of other anti-corruption conventions. These provide important background for the consideration of UNCAC monitoring and information on these processes is contained in the Appendix and in the Attachment to this report. The Study Group also analysed the concerns about monitoring that were raised during the Vienna negotiations that led to the adoption of UNCAC and considered how these should be addressed. This report presents TI's synthesis of the Study Group's work. TI takes sole responsibility for its contents.

During the work of the Study Group it became clear that the issues of implementation, monitoring, and technical assistance were closely inter-connected. Therefore, this Report deals not just with monitoring, but more broadly, with the need for a "Follow-up Process for UNCAC."

TI gratefully acknowledges the support of the United Nations Foundation for the work of the Study Group and the support TI is receiving from the Foreign Ministry of Finland. TI also wishes to express its appreciation to the experts who contributed the eleven reviews of monitoring systems attached to the Report.

Relevant UNCAC Provisions

UNCAC contains detailed provisions dealing with steps to promote effective implementation. These provisions establish a solid framework for action by the Conference of States Parties on a process to promote implementation, encourage technical assistance, and conduct follow-up monitoring. The proposals made in this Report are consistent with these provisions.

Chapter VI of UNCAC covers "Technical Assistance and Information Exchange," including:

- Training and technical assistance.
- Collection, exchange and analysis of information on corruption.
- Implementation of the Convention through technical assistance to developing countries and countries in transition.

Chapter VII covers "Mechanisms for Implementation", and outlines the responsibilities of the Conference of the States Parties to promote and review implementation. These include:

- Reviewing periodically the implementation of the Convention by the States Parties.
- Making recommendations to improve the Convention and its implementation.

- Receiving reports by governments on measures taken to implement the Convention and the difficulties encountered by them, including information on programme plans and practices as well as legislative and administrative measures to implement the Convention.
- Obtaining information on programmes, plans and practices to implement the Convention from international organisations, and from relevant non-governmental organisations.
- Cooperating with other international and regional organisations and Non-Governmental Organisations (NGOs).
- Making appropriate use of information produced by other mechanisms for combating corruption in order to avoid unnecessary duplication of work.
- Making recommendations regarding technical assistance requirements.
- Establishing, if deemed necessary by the Conference of States Parties, any appropriate mechanism or body to assist in the effective implementation of the Convention.
- Providing Secretariat services to the Conference of States Parties.

Follow-up Process: Importance and Significance

A. *Basic Rationale*

UNCAC represents the collective commitment by more than 140 countries to create an international framework for combating corruption. The parties recognise that, in a global economy, corruption has taken on global dimensions. Governments acting alone, or even in the framework of regional conventions cannot address global corruption effectively. Adoption and ratification of UNCAC are initial steps. To make UNCAC work will require a follow-up process of many years duration.

A follow-up process is necessary because much of UNCAC is not self-executing and numerous actions by national governments are needed to implement the Convention. Legislatures must pass laws implementing provisions of UNCAC. Governments must also provide funding and staffing for agencies administering anti-corruption programmes. Most importantly, government leaders must maintain the political will to overcome opposition to enforcement and other controversial anti-corruption actions. UNCAC monitoring faces unique challenges:

- UNCAC has the largest and most diverse number of parties of any anti-corruption convention. More than 140 countries have signed UNCAC and are expected to ratify and become parties. This compares with 36 OECD parties, 33 OAS parties, and 39 GRECO parties. UNCAC parties also have a greater diversity in political, legal, and economic systems than the other conventions.
- UNCAC has the broadest scope of any convention. However, governments have varying interests in particular provisions of UNCAC.

These challenges make monitoring UNCAC even more important than under other conventions. They also make it more difficult to conduct an effective and politically acceptable monitoring process.

UNCAC's worldwide membership is its greatest strength. However, the large number of parties, and their wide diversity, present a complex challenge for achieving successful collective action. Many developing countries are likely to need technical assistance. In both developed and developing countries, there may be political resistance to the reforms called for by UNCAC. Delays in some countries will be exploited by advocates of delay in other countries. There will also be changes in governments.

For all of these reasons, a well-organised follow-up process is essential to make sure that UNCAC will become a functioning international framework for combating corruption.

B. *Benefits of Follow-up Process*

The follow-up process can provide benefits to individual governments, as well as to UNCAC's collective objective.

- It permits early identification of implementation problems and needs for technical assistance.
- It facilitates timely provision of technical assistance and stimulates coordination between UNDP, the World Bank, other international financial institutions and bilateral.

- It provides opportunities for exchanging best practices and other forms of cooperation.
- In view of UNCAC's very broad scope, the follow-up process can provide guidance to governments on priorities for implementation.
- It maintains momentum for implementation by assuring governments willing to move promptly that other governments will be encouraged to meet their commitments.
- It facilitates the establishment of expert groups on issues where collective action is most essential, for example, recovery of proceeds of corruption deposited in foreign banks, mutual legal assistance and anti-money-laundering.
- It provides information on the status of implementation, including public recognition of progress made.

C. *Experience with Other Conventions Shows Monitoring is Key to Progress*

- There was no monitoring of the OAS Convention for four years after it became effective and there was little government action against corruption. Monitoring started in 2001 and this has stimulated government action.
- OECD monitoring sailed through its first phase, reviewing implementing laws. But review of national enforcement programmes was slowed down for two years because of inadequate funding for monitoring of enforcement. Action on enforcement lagged until monitoring was fully resumed.
- The GRECO process provides a follow-up procedure which assesses measures taken by governments to implement recommendations emanating from GRECO country reviews. As a result, there has been substantial progress in implementing the Council of Europe's anti-corruption conventions.

D. *Why Follow-up Process Works*

Follow-up reviews have an impact by bringing a variety of influences into play:

- Reporting schedules or review team visits stimulate government action.

- Progress reviews, such as OECD's regular "tours de table," provide a forum for peer group pressure by other governments.
- Country visits enable private sector and civil society groups to provide non-governmental assessment of progress on implementation.
- Reports from follow-up reviews build public pressure for action by lagging governments.
- Reviews call attention to technical assistance needs.

E. *Follow-up is Crucial for Success of UNCAC*

If UNCAC is properly implemented it will result in major reductions in corruption, producing great benefits in terms of better democratic governance, accelerated international development, more efficient government procurement, stronger competition, and alleviation of poverty around the world. An effective follow-up process ensures that such implementation will take place and that the goals of UNCAC can be achieved. Without follow-up there is a high risk that UNCAC will become another example of the futility of high aspirations.

Monitoring Organisation

A. *Conference of States Parties*

- Under the Convention, the Conference of States Parties (CSP) has responsibility for follow-up monitoring and the UNCAC Secretariat operates under the supervision of the CSP.
- Because the CSP is likely to consist of delegates from more than a hundred countries, and will meet annually in the first three years and then every two years, consideration should be given to establishing a CSP sub-group of a reasonable size that can work with UNODC between CSP meetings. There is substantial experience from other UN review processes for the creation of such sub-groups.

B. *UNCAC Secretariat*

- A strong secretariat will be needed to manage UNCAC's follow-up monitoring programme. UNODC has been designated by the UN Secretary-General as the secretariat for the Conference of States Parties. The benefits of using the staff familiar with the negotiation of the convention for follow-up monitoring are confirmed by OECD and GRECO experience.

- The key to effective monitoring is strong leadership and a competent professional staff. The experience of OECD and GRECO indicates that the staff required is quite small. The OECD reviews are currently being managed by a staff of eight persons and GRECO is currently employing ten.
- The record of UNODC in managing the development of both UNCAC and UNTOC with a small professional staff provides assurance that UNODC can manage the UNCAC monitoring programme successfully and cost-effectively.
- Collaboration with the secretariats that support the other monitoring programmes would augment UNODC's capacity.
- A roster of experts should be established, including nominations from member governments and from other monitoring organisations. Persons with specialized monitoring experience are in short supply and funding for a training programme is likely to be needed.

C. *Funding*

Funding for monitoring should be provided from the regular UNODC budget. Such funding would be preferable to reliance on special contributions from wealthier countries from the perspective of public credibility. Dependable multi-year funding commitments will be needed to permit adequate planning and staffing.

- Once it is in full operation, an estimated cost in the range of € 5 million per year for UNCAC follow-up reviews would seem reasonable. The costs of OECD and GRECO monitoring programmes are in the range of € 1-2 million per year, not including the costs incurred by the country being monitored. OECD and GRECO are widely considered the most effective monitoring programmes and include country visits by review teams. The € 5 million estimate for UNCAC monitoring recognises UNCAC's larger number of parties and broader scope. The costs of monitoring are very modest when compared with the benefits, measured in terms of progress in reducing corruption.

Monitoring Programmes

This section will suggest possible follow-up monitoring programmes, recognising that such programmes will need to evolve overtime.

- The first phase should be a survey of implementation designed to identify rate of progress, potential problems and technical assistance needs. It should be authorised by the Conference of the States Parties (CSP) in December 2006 and the results from the survey should be presented at the second CSP in late 2007.
- Subsequent follow-up programmes should be defined based on the results of the survey of implementation.

A. *Phase I: Survey of Implementation*

The first phase of UNCAC follow-up monitoring should be a survey of the status of implementation by the Parties, to be conducted in 2007. The purpose would be to obtain data providing a basis for decisions on actions needed to strengthen implementation, such as providing technical assistance, preparing guidance documents and model laws, and conducting workshops. The implementation survey should involve the following stages:

1. *Self-Evaluation*: Governments should respond to a questionnaire, prepared by the Secretariat, covering the following:

Status of implementation, indicating provisions that have been implemented and those that have not

Identification of obstacles to implementation

Action plan to overcome obstacles, including technical assistance needs and priorities for future progress.

In drafting the questionnaire the Secretariat should request enough information to obtain a reliable picture, without making this an overly burdensome exercise. Civil society organisations, the private sector and trade unions should be invited to make submissions at this stage.

2. *Review of Responses*: The responses should be reviewed by the Secretariat and by experts chosen by the Secretariat. The review process should include discussion with submitting governments in case of questions.

3. *Report to Conference of States Parties*: The Secretariat should prepare a report summarising the country responses and proposed priorities for consideration at the 2007 Conference of States Parties. This report should be published.

4. *Proposals on Technical Assistance*: The Secretariat should also conduct a survey of technical assistance needs and proposals for addressing such needs for consideration at the 2007 Conference of States Parties.

5. *Follow-up Surveys*: Additional surveys of implementation should be conducted periodically, including reports by new parties and updates by other parties. The frequency of follow-up surveys will depend on how rapidly progress is made.

B. *Subsequent Phases: Monitoring of Specific Provisions*

In subsequent years the follow-up programme should focus on monitoring of progress on specific UNCAC provisions. The Secretariat should manage the monitoring process and identify provisions to be monitored each year, taking into account the results of the survey of implementation, availability of technical assistance, as well as ability to achieve timely results.

- Early priority should be given to UNCAC monitoring of cross-border issues, particularly those requiring North-South participation, where UNCAC has the greatest comparative advantage over other conventions. These should include asset recovery mutual legal assistance and cross-border bribery and extortion.
- The monitoring process for each of the issues should be tailored to the nature of the issue. For example, with respect to asset recovery it might be useful to begin by forming a working group consisting of (*i*) several countries whose former leaders had deposited substantial funds in foreign banks, and (*ii*) leading banking centres, such as Switzerland, the UK and the US. This group should explore the development of uniform expedited procedures for the identification, freezing and repatriation of the proceeds of

corruption. Consideration should also be given to the investment of frozen funds in the country from which such funds were taken by the World Bank or other financial institutions, until the conclusion of litigation.

- Another priority should be the development of best practices for the implementation of UNCAC's preventive measures. This should be done in cooperation with the secretariats administering the other anti-corruption conventions, several of which have extensive experience with the implementation of preventive measures. Cooperation on the development of best practices would provide a basis for determining how monitoring of implementation of preventive measures could be allocated between the UNCAC secretariat and the secretariats of the regional conventions.
- In future years, monitoring programmes for a broader range of UNCAC provisions should be conducted.
- The timing of monitoring reviews for particular countries will require flexibility. A reasonable balance should be maintained between giving countries enough time for implementation, while ensuring collective momentum.
- It may be useful to conduct pilot projects which could serve as a basis for future monitoring work. Such projects could conduct test runs of monitoring models with a limited number of countries in order to develop suitable techniques that are effective without being overly burdensome.

C. *Monitoring Methods*

- The UNCAC follow-up process should utilise a variety of monitoring methods including questionnaires, expert reviews, peer reviews and country visits. Selection should be based on suitability of the particular method or combination of methods for the issue being reviewed.
- Use of outside experts provides an important method to supplement the professional resources of the Secretariat and thereby enables it to operate with a small staff.
- Country visits are indispensable for issues where a reliable assessment requires in puts from different sources of information, including not only government officials but also the private sector and civil society. Country visits also

enable the monitors to conduct probing exchanges to determine the reliability of differing inputs. Country visits can have another important benefit, namely promoting public interest in UNCAC and its implementation by concerned groups and media. A part of the visit should provide for public participation.

- Peer groups can be organised on a regional basis, or on other bases such as level of economic development or special interest in particular UNCAC provisions such as those on asset recovery or money-laundering. In the case of regional peer groups, cooperation should be sought from monitoring groups for the regional conventions.
- The objectivity of the reviews is essential to their credibility. Reviewers should not be citizens of the country being reviewed and should not be selected or approved by that government.

D. *Need for Independent Reports, Transparency and Diverse Sources of Information*

- One of the key outputs of the monitoring programme in subsequent phases should be independent country reports on the status of implementation and technical assistance needs. These reports should contain conclusions and recommendations. They should be prepared by the Secretariat or by independent experts selected by the Secretariat.
- Participation by NGOs, the private sector and labour unions is important to ensure that the monitoring programme obtains a balanced picture.
- Questionnaires should be made public and governments should be encouraged to make their responses public.
- Monitoring reports, identifying deficiencies in implementing UNCAC provisions, should also be made public. Publication provides the best assurance that the deficiencies will be corrected.
- Country visits should include a press conference or other public event to encourage public interest and support for UNCAC implementation.
- NGOs can strengthen UNCAC monitoring by taking actions in addition to participating in UNODC monitoring

reviews. Such actions include promoting government support for monitoring, filling gaps in official monitoring programmes, developing innovative approaches, and evaluating and reporting on the effectiveness of official monitoring programme. NGOs have taken such actions in support of OECD, OAS and other anti-corruption conventions. Such an NGO role is likely to be even more important for UNCAC.

E. *Promoting Consistent Interpretation of UNCAC Provisions*

- The monitoring process can play an important role in promoting consistent implementation and interpretation of UNCAC provisions. Consistency is important to the success of UNCAC in the global economy because

  It assists prosecutors in the application of UNCACs mutual legal assistance provisions.

  It benefits the many companies doing business in multiple jurisdictions.

  It makes it easier for citizens to hold governments and private actors accountable.

  Consistency could be promoted by publishing official commentaries on potentially ambiguous provisions, as has been done by the OECD Working Group on Bribery.

- The Secretariat could also provide a forum where governments, companies or others could raise concerns or bring complaints about government actions that appear seriously inconsistent with the letter or spirit of UNCAC. The Secretariat could evaluate such concerns, and where appropriate meet with the government whose actions are being questioned in order to promote consistent implementation and might make arrangements for mediation.

Major Concerns about UNCAC Monitoring

Concerns about UNCAC monitoring were raised during the Vienna negotiations. It is essential that these concerns are addressed to ensure support for monitoring at the Conference of States Parties.

A. *Cost and Effectiveness*

Concerns:

- Can UNCAC monitoring operate at a reasonable cost and without building a large staff?
- Will UNCAC monitoring be effective?

Response: The record of UNODC in managing the development of UNCAC with a small staff provides assurance that UNODC can manage the follow-up process effectively and efficiently.

B. *Impact on Technical Assistance Funding*

Concern: Would funds for monitoring reduce funds available for technical assistance?

Response: The following points should help to place this concern in perspective:

- The cost of follow-up and monitoring is likely to be only a small fraction of the cost of technical assistance.
- The cost of follow-up and monitoring should come from the UNODC budget, while technical assistance should be funded by UNDP, the World Bank, regional multilateral development banks and bilateral donors.
- Funding available for technical assistance could well be increased by providing for close cooperation between monitoring reviews and technical assistance. Monitoring should provide information about the need for technical assistance.

C. *Duplicative Reviews*

Concerns

- Would UNCAC monitoring duplicate reviews conducted under other anti-corruption conventions?
- Would UNCAC monitoring undermine support for existing regional monitoring programmes and hinder efforts to develop a monitoring programme for the African Union Convention?

Response: Duplicative monitoring became a problem prior to UNCAC because pre-existing anti-corruption conventions developed without consideration of the effect on other conventions with similar provisions and overlapping membership. Because UNCAC is the only convention with global membership, it provides the opportunity to address the duplication problem. This can be done by coordinating UNCAC monitoring with other anti-corruption monitoring programmes.

D. *Fairness of Reviews*

Concerns

- Would developing countries be unfairly criticised for deficiencies they do not have the capability to correct?
- Would weaker countries be treated more harshly than powerful countries?

Response: Providing technical assistance to developing countries to enable them to implement UNCAC should alleviate concerns about unfair criticism and lack of capacity. Experience under existing monitoring programmes demonstrates that both weak and powerful countries can be treated fairly and equally. The use of peer groups with regional participation to conduct reviews can provide assurance of fair treatment.

E. *Timing of Reviews*

Concern: Would countries be reviewed before they have had adequate time to implement UNCAC provisions?

Response: The timing of reviews should take into account that not all provisions of UNCAC can be implemented at the same time and that some countries need more time than others.

F. *Infringement of Sovereignty and Intrusiveness*

Concern: Would UNCAC monitoring be an infringement of sovereignty and an intrusion in national affairs?

Response: Experience with other anti-corruption conventions demonstrates that monitoring programmes can be conducted using methods that the many countries which have participated in such programmes have not considered to be infringements of sovereignty or intrusions in their national affairs. The objective should be to use methods that are effective but not unduly burdensome. UNCAC provisions on implementation and on the mandate of the Conference of States Parties accentuate a positive, constructive and supportive approach. Monitoring reviews should be regarded as a process of mutual support and encouragement.

Technical Assistance Needs

The importance for the success of UNCAC of providing capacity-building assistance is widely recognised. However, the development of a successful technical assistance programme for UNCAC will require cooperation among international, regional and bilateral donor agencies. It will also require agreement on priorities for the implementation of different UNCAC provisions and reconciliation of competing interests among recipient countries, since demand for technical assistance is likely to exceed available funding. It is essential that UNODC work with UNDP, the World Bank and other donor agencies and governments to develop an effective process for resolving these issues.

UNCAC-related technical assistance will need to take into account existing donor funding for governance and anti-corruption activities. Donors already consider anti-corruption strategies in formulating their development assistance programmes. Furthermore, there already exist donor coordination arrangements at country level in many countries. It is also necessary to take into account the different ways that donors operate. Some donors operate decentralised country programmes and may prefer to provide technical assistance for UNCAC implementation through such programmes. Others may prefer to contribute to a central fund.

In view of the broad scope of UNCAC and the diversity in the administrative and legal capabilities of the parties, it is essential that technical assistance be broadly conceived. It should encompass all forms of capacity-building assistance that will enable governments to implement UNCAC.

Technical assistance programmes must be carefully selected and administered to ensure that tangible results are achieved. This is essential to maintain public support for the long period for which technical support will be needed.

The following recommendations should be considered.

A. *Donor Commitment to Provide Technical Assistance*

In preparation for the first Conference of States Parties, discussions should be held with leading donor agencies, particularly UNDP and the World Bank, as well as other multi-lateral development banks and bilateral agencies. The objective should be to have these agencies make a public statement at the Conference of States Parties that they will assign high priority to providing funding for developing countries for UNCAC implementation.

B. *Survey of Technical Assistance Needs*

An important objective of the survey of implementation called for under Section VIII-A of this Report is to obtain information on technical assistance needs and on what technical assistance is already being provided. The responses to the survey should enable the Secretariat to assess technical assistance needs for particular UNCAC provisions as well as the countries in need of such assistance.

Alongside the survey of technical assistance needs, UNCAC's Secretariat should work with UNDP, the World Bank and other donors to assess existing and planned technical assistance activities relevant for UNCAC implementation.

Based on the information collected, the Secretariat should make a report to the Conference of States Parties and to donor agencies on the technical assistance needs and available funds and make recommendations on technical assistance priorities.

C. *Longer-Term Cooperation*

The benefits of close cooperation between UNODC, UNDP, the World Bank and other donor agencies are clear. It is beyond the scope of this Report to make specific suggestions regarding the modalities for achieving effective cooperation. One possibility would be to organise a technical assistance working group, including the leading donor agencies, that would meet with UNODC on a regular basis to review the status of UNCAC implementation and make recommendations to donor agencies regarding priorities for technical assistance. Such a working group should also consider which technical assistance needs could be best served through creation of special funds.

We urge the leaders of UNODC, UNDP and the World Bank to meet before the Conference of States Parties to develop suitable modalities for cooperation. OECD-DAC should play an important role in making inputs to such a meeting.

D. *Annual Public Report on Funding Status*

In order to ensure that UNCAC-related technical assistance remains a priority and to facilitate informed decision-making by all donors, UNODC should work with UNDP and the World Bank to publish an annual report on UNCAC-related technical assistance.

UNCAC and Other Monitoring Programmes

Concern about duplicative monitoring for different anti-corruption conventions is an obstacle to the establishment of an UNCAC monitoring programme. For that reason, UNODC should take the initiative to organise a coordinating group with representatives from the monitoring organisations of the other anti-corruption conventions.

A. *Avoiding Duplicative Monitoring Programmes*

- Anti-corruption conventions adopted before UNCAC did not take into consideration the existence of other conventions. The adoption of UNCAC provides an opportunity to think through and rationalise the relationship among the different anti-corruption conventions and their monitoring programmes. Regional conventions and the OECD Convention should be regarded as important building blocks of the system for combating corruption for which UNCAC can provide the unifying worldwide framework.
- Concern that UNCAC monitoring would duplicate monitoring under other anti-corruption conventions can be addressed through cooperation and collaboration among the different monitoring organisations. Paragraphs 4 (*c*) and (*d*) of Article 63 of UNCAC refer to cooperation with relevant international and regional organisations and to making use of information produced by other mechanisms for combating and preventing corruption "in order to avoid unnecessary duplication of work." These

provisions provide the basis for cooperation in the conduct of UNCAC's monitoring programme.

- There is a practical incentive for cooperation among the organisations administering anti-corruption conventions because they all have serious resource constraints. Collaboration should enable each programme to accomplish more with its available resources. Moreover, it is important for UNCAC to build on rather than undermine existing regional mechanisms.
- Because each convention has a different political constituency, there may be some resistance to cooperation. It may be argued that monitoring reviews conducted by another organisation would lack legitimacy. The interests of legitimacy and avoiding duplication need to be reconciled.

  The principal criterion should be pragmatic, not legalistic, i.e., focusing primarily on the adequacy of the review process, not on which organisation has legal authority to conduct the review.

  Focus on legal authority would lead to irresolvable differences, with each monitoring organisation claiming authority to monitor all issues within the scope of its convention. The issue should not be whether the UNCAC review process has the authority to monitor how an OECD country enforces the prohibition on foreign bribery, but rather whether it would be useful for the UNCAC process to do so after OECD has already done so.
- Cooperation between UNCAC and other monitoring programmes should be considered in two stages, which are outlined below. The first stage, primarily involving exchanges of information, should be non-controversial. The second stage, which would promote coordination and collaboration, including understandings regarding priorities for monitoring particular issues, may be more controversial.

B. *Stage* 1: *Cooperation among Monitoring Programmes*

A procedure for cooperation should be established promptly. This should include such steps as:

- Hold regular meetings of representatives of monitoring organisations to discuss their plans for reviews, including countries and issues to be reviewed, and how to share experience and avoid duplication.
- Designate liaison representatives to maintain regular contacts between annual meetings.
- Exchange information from prior reviews, including access to reports and other relevant data.
- Develop roster of experts on subjects of common interest.

C. *Stage 2: Coordination and Collaboration*

As soon as possible the procedure for cooperation established in Stage 1 should be expanded to consider steps to promote coordination and collaboration, including understandings on priorities for monitoring different issues. All conventions, other than OECD, have broad scopes, with UNCAC having the broadest scope. Given the limited resources for monitoring, only a few provisions can be monitored in any year. Thus, monitoring organisations need to establish priorities, and it would be useful to take into account the priorities of the other programmes.

The exchange of information contemplated in Stage 1 should provide the basis for developing understandings about which issues should be given priority by each monitoring programme. It is recognised that each convention is a separate legal instrument, and each organisation has its own procedure for deciding on priorities for monitoring. However, there should be room for coordination and collaboration, taking into account the comparative advantages of different organisations.

The following points illustrate how prioritization might work; they are intended only as a starting point for consideration:

- *UNCAC Review Process*: A global process is best for monitoring issues where worldwide cooperation, particularly North-South cooperation, is needed. Examples include mutual legal assistance, asset recovery, cross-border bribery and extortion.
- *Regional Monitoring Bodies*: These provide useful fora for cooperation and mutual support among countries with similar legal and economic systems. Regional monitoring organisations should wherever possible take responsibility

for monitoring issues of particular concern to specific regional monitoring mechanisms, such as those of GRECO, the OAS etc. Support for implementation of preventive measures might also be conducted at the regional level because examples of best practices from within the region are likely to be considered more relevant; implementation should be monitored by experts from the region.

- *OECD*: The UNCAC Secretariat should work with OECD Working Group on techniques for UNCAC monitoring of foreign bribery prohibitions in non-OECD countries, taking advantage of OECD's extensive experience with foreign bribery issues and its well-developed follow-up monitoring programme.
- *FATF*: UNODC should work with FATE, as well as with regional anti-money laundering organisations, on UNCAC monitoring of anti-money-laundering provisions in countries that are not FATF members.

Prioritisation should be regarded as a practical way to allocate limited monitoring resources in a cooperative and cost-effective way. UNCAC should retain legal authority to monitor any issue covered by its provisions. There should be flexibility in working out arrangements for different issues and for different regions taking into account capabilities and level of interest of regional monitoring organisations.

Decisions regarding prioritisation should be regarded as practical steps to allocate limited monitoring resources in a cooperative and cost effective way Prioritisation should not mean exclusive responsibility; cooperation between UNCAC and regional organisations will be necessary on many issues. Understandings regarding priorities will need to be reviewed periodically in the light of developing experience with UNCAC and with the regional conventions.

In principle, it seems appealing to make an allocation of follow-up programmes under which the UNCAC monitoring programme would have responsibility primarily for issues requiring global participation, while the programmes for regional conventions would be responsible for most other issues. However, it is premature to make firm decisions. There are substantial uncertainties about the follow-up programmes of the other anti-corruption conventions. As indicated in the review of monitoring programmes in the Appendix which follows, only the Council of Europe and OECD have strong programmes. The programme of the Inter-American Convention is still weak and it is uncertain when it will obtain more adequate support. The regional programmes for Africa and Asia are still in a formative stage. It would be useful to have a concept describing how a strong global monitoring programme should relate to strong regional monitoring programmes. However, for the near term monitoring is in an evolutionary phase, where the principal focus has to be on what can be made to work with existing organisations and available resources.

Lessons Learned

A. *Monitoring Should Start Promptly*

- Starting a monitoring programme promptly after a convention enters into force has great advantages. At that time, there will be strong support for the convention, and the monitoring process can build on that momentum. The monitoring process can be staffed by persons with first-hand experience in the drafting and negotiation of the Convention. In the case of OECD, there was a seamless transition from working on the preparation and adoption of the Convention to monitoring its implementation.
- The experience with the OAS Convention demonstrates the difficulties caused by delay. Monitoring did not begin until four years after entry into force. By that time, support for the Convention had diminished, and it has been difficult to build an effective monitoring programme.

B. *Strong Secretariat is Needed*

- Experience with existing monitoring mechanisms makes clear that a capable secretariat is needed to manage the monitoring process. Adequate staffing for the secretariat is critical to the success of the monitoring programme.
- One of the strengths of the OECD and GRECO review processes is the support from their secretariats, which have generally been adequately staffed. The OAS process has had only limited secretariat support.

C. ***Adequate Funding is Essential***

- Adequate funding is needed to support the secretariat and to conduct monitoring reviews. Because monitoring must be organised as a continuing, long-term programme, funding must be secure and dependable.
- Funding from the regular budget of the sponsoring international organisation is preferable to reliance on contributions from wealthier countries. The first phase of OECD monitoring was funded by individual contributions from several countries. However, after country visits began it became necessary to obtain funding from the OECD budget.
- The OAS experience shows that monitoring can be impaired by inadequate funding. The OECD programme was also hampered by inadequate funding during 2002-03.

D. ***Wide Range of Monitoring Methods should be Used***

Experience has been obtained with a wide variety of monitoring methods. The method used should be based on suitability for particular issues.

- *Questionnaires* directed to governments are a common starting point to determine the rate of progress on implementation of convention provisions. While questionnaires are useful, they are not sufficient when it comes to complex issues where inputs from different sources are needed. Response rates can be inadequate and shortcomings in government programmes may not be adequately disclosed.
- *Country Visits* provide the most effective method for obtaining inputs from multiple sources and for in-depth questioning by reviewers. Country visits are conducted by OECD and GRECO, as well as by FATF and NEPAD reviews. They are more expensive than questionnaires but provide better and more balanced information. Country visits can be conducted by the staff of the secretariat, peer reviewers, expert reviewers, or a combination of the foregoing.
- *Peer Reviews* can be conducted by small teams composed

of persons from other parties, working with staff from secretariat. OECD uses two lead reviewers, one from a party with legal institutions similar to the country being reviewed and one from a country with different institutions. GRECO evaluation teams consist of 3 to 4 experts from different member states.

- *Expert Reviewers*: The use of a roster of experts can help expand the resources of the secretariat, without expanding its full-time staff. It is particularly necessary when conventions cover a wide range of technical fields not all of which can be represented on the full-time staff. It is particularly necessary when the conventions cover a wide range of technical fields not all of which can be represented on the full-time staff.
- *Plenary Reviews*: Monitoring systems commonly include plenary reviews, at which reports and recommendations from monitoring reviews are presented to all member governments. This is desirable politically but can become unwieldy when the plenary group is very large and there is a strict requirement for consensus.

  The OECD Working Group on Bribery includes representatives from all 36 parties and meets five times each year. Each meeting includes reports on country reviews and also a "tour de table" at which government representatives report on the steps taken to enforce the OECD convention. This has proved very helpful in maintaining peer pressure.

- *Horizontal Reviews*: This approach is useful for conventions with broad scope such as UNCAC, and involves separate rounds of reviews covering a limited number of issues based on a method of prioritization. Parties are reviewed on selected issues before starting the next round. These are used by GRECO and OAS.
- *Vertical Reviews*: These reviews cover all provisions of a convention for each country. These are used by OECD and FATE but are impractical for conventions with broad scope such as UNCAC.

E. *Monitoring Reviews should Identify Deficiencies and Provide for Action Plans and Follow-up*

- *Country reports* should be prepared by the secretariat, by independent experts, or by a combination of the two.
- *Clear conclusions and recommendations* should be included in country reports.
- *Country action plans* to correct deficiencies should be required as part of review process.
- *Follow-up reviews* should be conducted to ensure that deficiencies identified by the reviews are corrected.

F. *Participation by NGOs, Private Sector, and Trade Unions is Essential*

- Assessing corruption and the effectiveness of anti-corruption measures is always difficult, and it is not enough to rely solely on the perspectives of government officials. Inputs from non-governmental organisations, the private sector and trade unions are essential to provide monitors with a balanced picture. There is specific provision for NGO inputs into the OECD, OAS and NEPAD review processes. Such inputs are also generally obtained under the GRECO process.
- The importance of civil society participation in anti-corruption efforts is recognised in Article 13 of the UNCAC. Article 63 refers to inputs from relevant non-governmental organisations.
- It is essential for an effective monitoring process that it provide for official channels for written and oral civil society inputs.
- NGOs have played an important role in getting monitoring programmes launched, in making sure that they don't lose steam, and in publicizing their results. The role of NGOs can become controversial, when they press for actions that governments are reluctant to take, but that only confirms that the NGO role is important. In particular, TI played a role in getting OAS monitoring launched and in pushing for adequate funding for OECD monitoring at points when government support was flagging.

- NGOs should be encouraged to conduct their own monitoring programmes, which can supplement official monitoring programmes. For example, TI, with the use of its national chapters, prepares an annual progress report on national enforcement of the OECD convention which it submits to OECD's Working Group on Bribery and also issues publicly.

G. *Monitoring Programmes should be Conducted in Transparent Manner*

- *Reports* by monitoring bodies should be made public, including website publication, promptly after conclusion of reviews. This is done under many of the monitoring systems, including OAS, OECD and GRECO. FATE started publishing reports and summaries in 2005. Publication of monitoring reports makes participating governments accountable to their own public.
- *Questionnaires* that governments are asked to fill out should be made public, including website publication. The OAS, OECD and GRECO questionnaires are published on their respective websites.
- *Government responses* are made public under the review processes for the OAS Convention and the ADB-OECD Action Plan for Asia-Pacific. Under OAS, countries can refuse but almost all countries release their responses. Under OECD, it is left to countries to decide whether to publish their responses. Requiring publication of government responses can arguably make such responses less candid. In TI's view, there is a clear public interest in making government responses public and this outweighs possible inhibition in governmental candor.

Findings and Recommendations

- *Follow-up essential*: A follow-up and monitoring process is essential to enable UNCAC to become an effective framework for combating corruption around the world. Such a process should be authorised at the December 2006 Conference of States Parties and should start in 2007. This would sustain momentum for implementation and promote public confidence in UNCAC.

- *Objective*: The objective of the follow-up process should be to ensure the evolution of UNCAC into an effective global framework for combating corruption. This will take time because UNCAC is a complicated instrument. Not all UNCAC provisions can be implemented at the same time and governments should be allowed to make progress at different rates.
- *Secretariat*: A strong secretariat with adequate and dependable funding is needed to manage the follow-up process.

  Experience with other anti-corruption conventions shows that an effective monitoring process can be conducted with a small staff at relatively modest cost. The successful role played by the UN Office on Drugs and Crime (UNODC) in the development of UNCAC provides assurance that it has the managerial and professional capability to conduct an effective follow-up programme.

- *Follow-up process*: The follow-up process should begin by asking governments to identify potential implementation problems, needs for technical assistance, and action plans for implementation.

  The Secretariat should work closely with donor agencies to facilitate the provision of technical assistance.
  After reasonable time for implementation, periodic reviews should be conducted to evaluate the adequacy of national implementation and enforcement.

- *Coordination*: UNCAC monitoring reviews should be coordinated with the monitoring programmes of other anti-corruption conventions in order to avoid duplicative monitoring and to take advantage of regional capabilities.
- *Transparency*: The follow-up process should be conducted transparently because public support for reducing corruption is the best lever for achieving UNCAC's objectives. Active involvement by the private sector, trade unions and civil society is essential.

5

Convention Against Transnational Organized Crime: Reviewing the Reports and Notes

UN CONVENTION AGAINST TRANSNATIONAL ORGANIZED CRIME

Adopted	: 15 November, 2000 by the General Assembly of the United Nations.
Signatories	: 147 (as of 7 October, 2005) Opened for signature on 12 December, 2000.
Parties	: 110 (as of 7 October, 2005).
Entry into force	: 29 September, 2003.
Open to	: All countries and regional economic organisations Website for updated information.

The UN Convention against Transnational Organized Crime (UNTOC), adopted in November 2000, recognises that corruption is an integral component of transnational organised crime and must be addressed as part of efforts to combat organised crime.

The obligations of the parties fall into the following categories:

1. *Prevention*: In general terms, the Convention calls for effective measures to promote integrity and to prevent the corruption of public officials and specifically calls for public authorities to be provided with adequate independence in order to deter the exertion of inappropriate influence on their actions.
2. *Criminalisation*: As part of the Convention's international framework for addressing transnational organised crime, requires States Parties to criminalise corruption, focusing

particularly on bribery of public officials. It also calls for effective measures to detect and punish the corruption of public officials and specifically calls for public authorities to be provided with adequate independence in order to deter the exertion of inappropriate influence on their actions.

3. *Anti-money Laundering*: UNTOC also requires criminalisation of money-laundering and the establishment of a domestic regulatory and supervisory regime for banks and other financial institutions to combat money laundering. States are also called on to fight corruption in the private sector.
4. *International Cooperation*: To fulfil its aim of addressing cross-order aspects of organised crime, UNTOC provides for a broad framework for mutual legal assistance, extradition, law-enforcement cooperation and technical assistance and training. This international cooperation has the potential to improve mutual law enforcement assistance, notably in extradition and investigations. These provisions provided the basis for the international cooperation provisions in the UN Convention against Corruption. The provisions are largely mandatory and cover specific aspects of law enforcement cooperation such as extradition, gathering and transferring evidence, assisting investigations and prosecutions. They include requirements that states parties consider joint investigations, special investigative techniques and the transfer of criminal proceedings.

General Assembly

Fifty-fifth session
Agenda item 105
Crime prevention and criminal justice

Crime Prevention and Criminal Justice

Report of the Ad Hoc Committee on the Elaboration of a Convention against Transnational Organized Crime on the work of its first to eleventh sessions.

Introduction

1. On the recommendation of the Commission on Crime Prevention and Criminal Justice and the Economic and Social Council (Council resolution 1998/14 of 28 July, 1998), the General Assembly adopted resolution 53/111 of 9 December, 1998, in which it decided to establish an open-ended inter-governmental ad hoc committee for the purpose of elaborating a comprehensive international convention against transnational organized crime and of discussing the elaboration, as appropriate of international instruments addressing trafficking in women and children, combating the illicit manufacturing of and trafficking in firearms, their parts and components and ammunition, and illegal trafficking in and transporting of migrants, including by sea. In its resolution 53/114 of 9 December, 1998, the Assembly called upon the Ad Hoc Committee on the Elaboration of a Convention against Transnational Organized Crime to devote attention to the drafting of the main text of the convention, as well as of the above-mentioned international instruments.
2. In its resolution 54/126 of 17 December, 1999, entitled "Draft United Nations Convention against Transnational Organized Crime and the draft protocols thereto", the General Assembly requested the Ad Hoc Committee to continue its work, in accordance with resolutions 53/111 and 53/114, and to intensify its work in order to complete it in 2000; decided that the Ad Hoc Committee should be convened in 2000 as required, holding no fewer than four sessions of two weeks each; requested the Ad Hoc Committee to schedule sufficient time, subject to the availability of funds from the regular budget or extra-budgetary resources, for the negotiation of the draft protocols addressing trafficking in persons, especially women and children, the illicit manufacturing of and trafficking in firearms, their parts and components and ammunition, and illegal trafficking in and transportation of migrants, including by sea, in order to enhance the possibility of their completion at the same time as the draft Convention; and decided that the Ad Hoc Committee should submit the final text of the Convention

and protocols thereto to the Assembly for early adoption prior to a high-level signing conference.

3. In its resolution 54/127 of 17 December, 1999, the General Assembly requested the Secretary-General, within existing or extra budgetary resources, to convene an expert group of no more than 20 members, with equitable geographical representation, to prepare a study on the illicit manufacturing of and trafficking in explosives by criminals and their use for criminal purposes; and directed the Ad Hoc Committee, following the completion of the study, to consider the possible elaboration of an international instrument on the illicit manufacturing of and trafficking in explosives.
4. In its resolution 54/128 of 17 December, 1999, the General Assembly directed the Ad Hoc Committee to incorporate into the Draft Convention measures against corruption linked to organized crime, including provisions regarding the sanctioning of acts of corruption involving public officials; and requested the Ad Hoc Committee, using such time as its schedule permitted and with extra-budgetary resources provided for that purpose, to explore the desirability of an international instrument against corruption, either ancillary to or independent of the Convention, to be developed after the finalization of the Convention and the three additional instruments referred to in resolution 53/111 and to present its views to the Commission on Crime Prevention and Criminal Justice.
5. In its resolution 54/129 of 17 December, 1999, the General Assembly accepted with appreciation the offer of the Government of Italy to host a high-level political signing conference in Palermo for the purpose of signing the United Nations Convention against Transnational Organized Crime (Palermo Convention) and protocols thereto; and requested the Secretary-General to schedule the Conference for a period of upto one week before the end of the Millennium Assembly in 2000.
6. The Ad Hoc Committee held eleven sessions, as follows: first session from 19-29 January, 1999; second session from 8 to 12 March, 1999; third session from 28 April to 3 May, 1999, in parallel with the eighth session of the Commission on Crime

Prevention and Criminal Justice; fourth session from 25 June to 9 July, 1999; fifth session from 4 to 15 October, 1999; sixth session from 6 to 17 December, 1999; seventh session from 17 to 28 January, 2000; eighth session from 21 February to 3 March, 2000; ninth session from 5 to 16 June, 2000; tenth session from 17 to 28 July, 2000; and eleventh session from 2 to 28 October, 2000.

7. The present report is submitted to the General Assembly at its fifty-fifth session pursuant to resolution 54/126 to apprise the Assembly of the work of the Ad Hoc Committee in implementing its mandate and to submit its recommendations to the Assembly for consideration and action.

Background

8. In its resolution 49/159 of 23 December, 1994, the General Assembly approved the Naples Political Declaration and Global Action Plan against Organized Transnational Crime (A/49/748, annex, sect. I) and urged States to implement them as a matter of urgency. In the Naples Political Declaration and Global Action Plan against Organized Transnational Crime, the World Ministerial Conference on Organized Transnational Crime requested the Commission on Crime Prevention and Criminal Justice to initiate the process of requesting the views of Governments on the impact of a convention or conventions against organized transnational crime and on the issues that could be covered therein.
9. The Regional Ministerial Workshop on Follow-up to the Naples Political Declaration and Global Action Plan against Organized Transnational Crime, held in Buenos Aires from 27 to 30 November, 1995, adopted the Buenos Aires Declaration on Prevention and Control of Organized Transnational Crime (E/CN.15/1996/2/ Add. 1). The States of the Latin American and Caribbean region expressed the interest of their Governments in the further study of the advantages of an international convention against organized transnational crime during the fifth session of the Commission, and proposed elements for inclusion in the convention.

10. In resolution 51/120 of 12 December, 1996, the General Assembly took note of the proposed draft United Nations framework convention against organized crime, introduced by Poland at the fifty-first session of the General Assembly (A/C.3/51/7, annex). The Assembly requested the Commission to consider, as a matter of priority, the question of the elaboration of an international convention against organized transnational crime, taking into account the views of all States on this matter, with a view to finalizing its work on the question as soon as possible.
11. The African Regional Ministerial Workshop on Organized Transnational Crime and Corruption, held in Dakar from 21-23 July, 1997, adopted the Dakar Declaration on the Prevention and Control of Organized Transnational Crime and Corruption (E/CN.15/1998/6/Add. l). The States of the African region expressed their strong support for the elaboration of an international convention against organized transnational crime and made specific suggestions to that end. They called upon all States to contribute to and be actively engaged in the elaboration of such an instrument, making every possible effort to resolve differences and overcome conceptual or substantive difficulties, in order to permit the process to be completed in the shortest time possible.
12. In its resolution 52/85 of 12 December, 1997, the General Assembly took note of the report of the informal meeting on the question of the elaboration of an international convention against organized transnational crime, held in Palermo, Italy, from 6-8 April, 1997 (E/CN.15/1997/7/Add. 2), organized and hosted by the Fondazione Giovanni e Francesca Falcone. The Assembly decided to establish an inter-seasonal open-ended inter-governmental group of experts for the purpose of elaborating a preliminary draft of a possible comprehensive international convention against organized transnational crime, which would submit a report thereon to the Commission at its seventh session.
13. The inter-governmental group of experts held its meeting in Warsaw, from 2-6 February, 1998, and submitted a report to the Commission at its seventh session, containing an outline of options for the contents of the international

convention against organized transnational crime (E/CN.15/1998/5).

14. The Asian Regional Ministerial Workshop on Organized Transnational Crime and Corruption, held in Manila from 23-25 March, 1998, adopted the Manila Declaration on the Prevention and Control of Transnational Crime (E/CN.15/1998/6/Add. 2). The States of the region of Asia and the Pacific welcomed the results achieved by the inter-sessional open-ended inter-governmental group of experts. They believed that the outline of options for the contents of the convention served as a solid basis for its further development. They strongly supported such an endeavour and confirmed their commitment to play an active role in the efforts to resolve differences and overcome conceptual or substantive difficulties so that the process could speedily move towards its conclusion. They urged the Commission to take advantage of the existing momentum and the consensus achieved on the desirability of such a convention, with a view to speeding up the process of its drafting and finalizing such a project as soon as possible.

15. At its seventh session, the Commission established an in-sessional working group on the implementation of the Naples Political Declaration and Global Action Plan against Organized Transnational Crime, which discussed the draft convention against organized transnational crime. The working group agreed that the development of the convention must proceed at a vigorous pace, with a view to completing the negotiation process, if possible, by the year 2000. The working group carried out a thorough discussion of the options compiled in the report of the meeting of the inter-sessional inter-governmental group of experts. In particular, it discussed the chapters on the scope of application of the convention; participation in an organized crime group; money-laundering; corporate criminal liability; sanctions; confiscation; transparency of transactions; jurisdiction; extradition; the obligation to extradite or prosecute *(aut dedere aut judicare)*; extradition of nationals; and consideration of requests for extradition.

16. The informal group of the "Friends of the Chair", which was established pursuant to the recommendation of the

Commission at its seventh session to assist the Chairman of the Ad Hoc Committee, held its first meeting in Rome from 17-18 July, 1998. At that meeting, the informal group reviewed and endorsed the provisional agenda of the informal preparatory meeting of the Ad Hoc Committee, which the Government of Argentina had generously offered to host in Buenos Aires in order to enable the continuation without interruption of the work on the development of the convention. The informal group also reviewed a provisional time-table for its work and the work of the Ad Hoc Committee, submitted by the Secretariat.

17. The informal preparatory meeting of the Ad Hoc Committee was held in Buenos Aires from 31 August to 4 September, 1998. By completing the first reading of the outline of options for the contents of the convention and discussing several outstanding issues regarding Articles 1-13, the meeting produced a new consolidated draft text of the convention, which would provide the basis for the work of the Ad Hoc Committee at its first meeting. The informal preparatory meeting was assisted by contributions submitted by Governments prior to and during the meeting.
18. The second meeting of the informal group of the Friends of the Chair was held in Buenos Aires during the above-mentioned informal preparatory meeting of the Ad Hoc Committee. The informal group approved the time-table of its meetings and those of the Ad Hoc Committee until the envisaged completion of the mandated functions of the Ad Hoc Committee in the year 2000.
19. The third meeting of the Friends of the Chair was held in Vienna on 5 and 6 November, 1998. It reviewed and endorsed the provisional agenda and organisation of work of the first session of the Ad Hoc Committee.

Proceedings of the Ad Hoc Committee

A. *First Session*

20. The Ad Hoc Committee on the Elaboration of a Convention against Transnational Organized Crime held its first session in Vienna from 19-29 January, 1999, during which it held 18 meetings.

21. In its resolution 53/111, the General Assembly had decided to accept the recommendation of the Commission on Crime Prevention and Criminal Justice to elect Luigi Lauriola (Italy) as the Chairman of the Ad Hoc Committee. Mr. Lauriola indicated that he was acting in his personal capacity and not as a representative of his country or of any regional group. Following informal consultations, the Ad Hoc Committee elected the following additional officers:

Vice-Chairmen	:	Kiyotaka Akasaka (Japan)[1]
		Nabil Ammar (Tunisia)[2]
		Demetrio Boersner (Venezuela)[3]
		Zuzana Chuda (Slovakia)
		Eric Danon (France)[4]
		Roberta Lajous (Mexico)[5]
		Patricio Palacios (Ecuador)
		Janusz Rydzkowski (Poland)
		Shaukat Umer (Pakistan)
Rapporteur	:	Peter Gastrow (South Africa)

22. The Executive Director of the Office for Drug Control and Crime Prevention of the Secretariat made a statement in which he expressed his conviction that the convention, as the first international instrument to be negotiated on action against transnational organized crime, would be a milestone in international efforts to curb the phenomenon.
23. The first session of the Ad Hoc Committee was attended by representatives of 91 States. Also attending the session were observers for entities maintaining permanent observer missions to the United Nations, organisations of the United Nations system, institutes of the United Nations Crime Prevention and Criminal Justice Programme network, inter-governmental organisations and non-governmental organisations.

---

1. Replaced subsequently by Kiyoshi Koinuma (Japan).
2. Replaced subsequently by Emna Lazougli (Tunisia).
3. For the work of the Ad Hoc Committee in 1999.
4. Replaced subsequently by Bèrengère Quincy (France).
5. For the work of the Ad Hoc Committee in 2000; replaced subsequently by Olga Pellicer Silva (Mexico).

24. The Ad Hoc Committee was of the view that the election of an expanded bureau would reduce the need for sessions of the informal working group established to assist the Chairman of the Ad Hoc Committee (the informal group of the Friends of the Chair), which had functioned during the preparatory phase. It recommended that, subject to the availability of resources, the sessions of the informal group of the Friends of the Chair that had been foreseen should be converted into sessions of the Ad Hoc Committee, with interpretation in the six official languages of the United Nations.
25. The Ad Hoc Committee based its work on a document containing the Draft United Nations Convention against Transnational Organized Crime (A/AC.254/4) and on proposals and contributions submitted by Governments (A/AC.254/5 and Add. 2). The Chairman noted that the text contained in document A/AC.254/4 had been the result of discussions and consultations held during the following: the meeting of the inter-sessional open-ended inter-governmental group of experts on the elaboration of a preliminary draft of a possible comprehensive international convention against organized transnational crime, held in Warsaw from 2-6 February, 1998; the seventh session of the Commission on Crime Prevention and Criminal Justice, held in Vienna from 21-30 April, 1998; and the informal preparatory meeting of the Ad Hoc Committee, held in Buenos Aires from 31 August - 4 September, 1998. The draft contained a number of options. On the recommendation of its Chairman, the Ad Hoc Committee decided to focus at its first session on eliminating options, in order to produce a consolidated text that would be the basis for the drafting and negotiation work that it would undertake at its subsequent sessions.
26. The Ad Hoc Committee discussed the draft protocol against illicit manufacturing of and trafficking in firearms, their parts and components and ammunition and the draft protocol against illegal trafficking in and transporting of migrants.
27. The representative of the United States of America introduced the draft protocol to combat international

trafficking in women and children, supplementary to the United Nations Convention against Transnational Organized Crime (A/AC.254/4/Add.3). The representative of Argentina introduced draft elements for an agreement on the prevention, suppression and punishment of international trafficking in women and children, supplementary to the Convention against Transnational Organized Crime (A/AC.254/8). The observers for two non-governmental organisations made statements. The delegations of Argentina and the United States undertook to produce a combined text to serve as the basis for future consideration of the draft instrument by the Ad Hoc Committee.

28. Prior to its consideration of the additional international legal instruments, the Ad Hoc Committee discussed the relationship between those instruments and the convention against transnational organized crime. Pursuant to General Assembly resolutions 53/111 and 53/114, the convention was to be a self-sufficient and free-standing instrument. The highest priority would be given to the signature, ratification and entry into force of the convention and every effort should be made to negotiate a text that would be conducive to meeting that priority. The additional international legal instruments were viewed in principle as optional protocols to the convention, covering areas that required specificity, which the convention could not meet. There was a need to ensure that the optional protocols would be consistent with the convention, not only to ensure compatibility, but also to maximize the relevance and applicability of general provisions, such as those pertaining to international cooperation, which would be covered under the convention. However, it was pointed out that each instrument was intended to meet specific concerns. Consequently, the instruments might require a broad scope. In that case, also in line with the relevant resolutions of the Economic and Social Council and the General Assembly, the possibility that the additional international legal instruments might be independent from the convention could not be excluded. There was a discussion on whether signature of or accession to the protocols would be possible without prior signature

of or accession to the convention, the general preference being towards requiring prior signature of or accession to the convention. The Ad Hoc Committee deemed that it was more appropriate to discuss that issue, together with the question of reservations, when considering the relevant articles of the draft convention.

B. *Second Session*

29. The Ad Hoc Committee held its second session in Vienna from 8-12 March, 1999, during which it held 10 meetings.
30. The second session of the Ad Hoc Committee was attended by representatives of 95 States. Also attending the session were observers for entities maintaining permanent observer missions to the United Nations, organisations of the United Nations system, institutes of the United Nations Crime Prevention and Criminal Justice Programme network, inter-governmental organisations and non-governmental organisations.
31. The Ad Hoc Committee discussed Articles 1, 2, 2 *bis,* 3 and 24-30 of the draft Convention. The Ad Hoc Committee based its work on a document containing a revised draft text of the draft United Nations Convention against Transnational Organized Crime (A/AC. 254/4/Rev. l) and on proposals and contributions submitted by Governments. The Chairman noted that the revised text contained in document A/AC.254/4/Rev. l had been the result of discussions and consultations held during the first session.
32. The representative of Argentina introduced amendments to the revised draft Protocol to Prevent, Suppress and Punish Trafficking in Women and Children, supplementary to the United Nations Convention against Transnational Organized Crime.
33. The Ad Hoc Committee based its discussion on a document containing a revised text of the draft Protocol to Prevent, Suppress and Punish Trafficking in Women and Children, supplementing the United Nations Convention against Transnational Organized Crime (A/AC. 254/4/Add.3/Rev. l). That text was a proposal submitted by Argentina and the United States pursuant to the commitment those States had made at the first session of the Ad Hoc Committee.

The Ad Hoc Committee carried out a first reading of Articles 1 and 2 of the draft Protocol.

34. During the first reading of the draft Protocol, there was discussion on whether the Protocol would address trafficking in women and children or trafficking in persons. The Secretariat was requested to clarify the question of whether, by considering trafficking in persons, the Ad Hoc Committee would be departing from the mandate given to it by the General Assembly and, if that were the case, whether it would be competent to do so. The Secretariat undertook to explore the matter and to inform the Ad Hoc Committee of its findings.

C. *Third Session*

35. The Ad Hoc Committee held its third session in Vienna from 28 April-3 May, 1999, during which it held eight meetings.
36. After the opening of the third session of the Ad Hoc Committee by its Chairman, the Secretary called the attention of the Ad Hoc Committee to outstanding matters. In connection with the additional instrument on trafficking in women and children, the Secretary recalled that at its second session the Ad Hoc Committee had made a request that the Secretariat clarify whether, by considering trafficking in persons, the Ad Hoc Committee would be departing from the mandate given to it by the General Assembly and, if that were the case, whether it would be competent to do so. The Secretariat had consulted the Senior Legal Liaison Officer of the United Nations Office at Vienna and brought to the attention of the Ad Hoc Committee his response. According to the Senior Legal Liaison Officer, in its resolutions 53/111 and 53/114, the General Assembly had clearly defined the subjects for which new instruments were required. If the Assembly had wanted any other subjects to be included, it would have said so. Moreover, the recommendations of the Economic and Social Council (e.g. Council resolutions 1998/14 and 1998/20), which formed the basis for the Assembly resolutions, referred to trafficking in women and children and not to trafficking in persons. Those resolutions had been adopted unanimously and the terms used therein

reflected the desires of the Assembly. If, however, the Ad Hoc Committee, after considering the issues before it, had come to the conclusion that, instead of developing an instrument addressing trafficking in women and children, it would be in the general interest to develop an instrument dealing with trafficking in persons, it might wish to request the Assembly to modify its mandate in that connection.

37. The third session of the Ad Hoc Committee was attended by representatives of 111 States. Also attending the session were observers for entities maintaining permanent observer missions to the United Nations, organisations of the United Nations system, institutes of the United Nations Crime Prevention and Criminal Justice Programme network, inter-governmental organisations and non-governmental organisations.

38. The Ad Hoc Committee discussed Articles 4, 4 *bis*, 7 and 8. In accordance with the request of its Chairman, the Ad Hoc Committee sought to reach agreement on a single text that would reflect, to the extent possible, the emerging consensus and would form the basis for further drafting. The Ad Hoc Committee based its work on a document containing a revised text of the draft United Nations Convention against Transnational Organized Crime (A/AC. 254/4/Rev. 2) and on proposals and contributions submitted by Governments.

39. The Ad Hoc Committee had carried out a first reading of Articles 1-8 of the draft text at its first session. Pursuant to the suggestion of its Chairman, the Ad Hoc Committee completed its first reading of the draft text, beginning with Article 9. The Ad Hoc Committee based its work on a document containing a revised text of the draft international legal instrument against illicit manufacturing of and trafficking in firearms, their parts and components and ammunition (A/AC.254/4/Add. 2/Rev. l) and on proposals and contributions submitted by Governments.

D. *Fourth Session*

40. The Ad Hoc Committee held its fourth session in Vienna from 28 June - 9 July 1999, during which it held 20 meetings.

41. The fourth session of the Ad Hoc Committee was attended by representatives of 97 States. Also attending the session were observers for entities maintaining permanent observer missions to the United Nations, organisations of the United Nations system, institutes of the United Nations Crime Prevention and Criminal Justice Programme network, intergovernmental organisations and non-governmental organisations.
42. The Ad Hoc Committee discussed Articles 4 *ter*, 5, 6, 9 and 14 (paras. 1-13). In continuing its second reading of the draft Convention and in accordance with the request of its Chairman, the Ad Hoc Committee sought to reach agreement on a single text that would reflect, to the extent possible, the points of convergence and would form the basis for further drafting. The Ad Hoc Committee based its work on a document containing a revised text of the draft United Nations Convention against Transnational Organized Crime (A/AC. 254/4/Rev. 3) and on proposals and contributions submitted by Governments.
43. The Ad Hoc Committee discussed the additional international legal instrument against illegal trafficking in and transporting of migrants, including by sea. It based its work on a document containing a revised text of the draft protocol against the smuggling of migrants by land, air and sea, supplementing the United Nations Convention against Transnational Organized Crime (A/A C. 254/4/Add. 1/ Rev. 1), and on proposals and contributions submitted by Governments.
44. The Ad Hoc Committee also discussed the additional international legal instrument against trafficking in women and children. It based its work on a document containing a revised text of the draft protocol to prevent, suppress and punish trafficking in persons, especially women and children, supplementing the United Nations Convention against Transnational Organized Crime (A/AC.254/4/ Add. 3/Rev. 2), and on proposals and contributions submitted by Governments. The Chairman explained that the title of the draft protocol reflected the relevant recommendation of the Commission on Crime Prevention and Criminal Justice at its eighth session, on which the

General Assembly was expected to take action at its fifty-fourth session.

E. *Fifth Session*

45. The Ad Hoc Committee held its fifth session in Vienna from 4-15 October, 1999, during which it held 20 meetings.
46. The fifth session of the Ad Hoc Committee was attended by representatives of 114 States. Also attending the session were observers for entities maintaining permanent observer missions to the United Nations, organisations of the United Nations system, institutes of the United Nations Crime Prevention and Criminal Justice Programme network, inter-governmental organisations and non-governmental organisations.
47. The Ad Hoc Committee discussed Articles 14 (paras. 14-22), 10, 4, 4 *bis*, 7, 7 *bis*, 7 *ter* and 15-19 of the draft Convention. In continuing its second reading of the draft Convention and in accordance with the request of its Chairman, the Ad Hoc Committee sought to reach agreement on a single text that would reflect, to the extent possible, the points of convergence and would form the basis for further drafting. The Ad Hoc Committee based its work on a document containing a revised text of the draft United Nations Convention against Transnational Organized Crime (A/AC. 254/4/Rev. 4) and on proposals and contributions submitted by Governments.
48. The Ad Hoc Committee discussed the additional international legal instrument on combating the illicit manufacturing of and trafficking in firearms, their parts and components and ammunition. It based its work on a document containing a revised text of the draft Protocol against the Illicit Manufacturing of and Trafficking in Firearms, Ammunition and Other Related Materials, supplementary to the United Nations Convention against Transnational Organized Crime (A/AC. 25 4/4/Add. 2/Rev. 2), and on proposals and contributions submitted by Governments.
49. At its fourth session, the Ad Hoc Committee had decided

that, in future, informal consultation meetings should be organized in order to facilitate the implementation of its mandate. The holding of those meetings would depend on the availability of extra-budgetary resources and would meet the following conditions: (*a*) the informal consultations would be conducted strictly in accordance with the decisions of the General Assembly; (*b*) provision would be made for interpretation in all official languages of the United Nations; (*c*) the documentation and agenda for the informal consultations would be made available well in advance of the meetings and sufficient advance notice of the time and place of the meetings would be provided; (*d*) the informal consultations would be an open-ended and transparent mechanism to assist the Ad Hoc Committee, which would remain the only decision-making body, by making recommendations; (*e*) the informal consultations would be held only as parallel in-session meetings and their subjects would not overlap those being considered by the Ad Hoc Committee in plenary; (*f*) no more than two meetings, including the plenary, would be held at the same time during the sessions of the Ad Hoc Committee; and (*g*) the informal consultations could be assigned, *inter alia*, to translate into appropriate language the agreements reached in plenary or any other function determined by the Chairman of the Ad Hoc Committee. At its meeting on 7 September, 1999, the Bureau of the Ad Hoc Committee, on the basis of proposals submitted to it by the Secretary, decided that the informal consultations at the fifth session of the Ad Hoc Committee would be devoted to issues related to the texts of the revised draft Protocol against the Smuggling of Migrants by Land, Air and Sea, supplementing the United Nations Convention against Transnational Organized Crime, and the revised draft Protocol to Prevent Trafficking in Persons, especially Women and Children, supplementing the United Nations Convention against Transnational Organized Crime. At the fifth session of the Ad Hoc Committee, informal consultations were held in parallel with the meetings of the plenary of the Ad Hoc Committee from 4-8 October, 1999.

F. *Sixth Session*

50. The Ad Hoc Committee held its sixth session in Vienna from 6-17 December, 1999, during which it held 20 meetings.
51. The sixth session of the Ad Hoc Committee was attended by representatives of 106 States. Also attending the session were observers for entities maintaining permanent observer missions to the United Nations, organisations of the United Nations system, institutes of the United Nations Crime Prevention and Criminal Justice Programme network, inter-governmental organisations and non-governmental organisations.
52. The Ad Hoc Committee discussed Articles 4 *ter,* 17 *bis* and 20-30 of the draft Convention. The Ad Hoc Committee based its work on a revised text of the draft United Nations Convention against Transnational Organized Crime (A/ AC. 254/4/ Rev. 5) and on proposals and contributions submitted by Governments.
53. The Ad Hoc Committee also discussed the additional legal instrument against illegal trafficking in and transporting of migrants, with particular emphasis on Articles 7-19. It based its work on a document containing a revised text of the draft Protocol against the Smuggling of Migrants by Land, Air and Sea, supplementing the United Nations Convention against Transnational Organized Crime (A/ AC. 254/4/Add. l/Rev. 3), and on proposals and contributions submitted by Governments.
54. The Ad Hoc Committee further discussed the additional legal instrument against trafficking in persons, especially women and children, with particular emphasis on Articles 8-18. The Ad Hoc Committee decided to base its work on a restructured version of the revised draft Protocol to Prevent, Suppress and Punish Trafficking in Persons, Especially Women and Children, supplementing the United Nations Convention against Transnational Organized Crime (A/ AC. 254/5/Add. l3), as had been recommended by the informal consultations held during the fifth session of the

Ad Hoc Committee, and on other proposals and contributions submitted by Governments.

G. *Seventh Session*

55. The Ad Hoc Committee held its seventh session in Vienna from 17-2S January, 2000, during which it held 20 meetings.
56. The seventh session of the Ad Hoc Committee was attended by representatives of 109 States. Also attending the session were observers for organisations of the United Nations system, institutes of the United Nations Crime Prevention and Criminal Justice Programme network, inter-governmental organisations and non-governmental organisations.
57. The Ad Hoc Committee discussed Articles 1-3, 5 and 6 of the Draft Convention. The Ad Hoc Committee based its work on a revised text of the draft United Nations Convention against Transnational Organized Crime (A/AC. 25 4/4/ Rev. 6) and on proposals and contributions submitted by Governments.
58. The Ad Hoc Committee discussed the additional legal instrument against illicit manufacturing of and trafficking in firearms, their parts and components and ammunition. It based its work on a document containing a revised text of the draft Protocol against the Illicit Manufacturing of and Trafficking in Firearms. Their Parts and Components and Ammunition, supplementing the United Nations Convention against Transnational Organized Crime (A/ AC. 254/4/Add. 2/Rev. 3), and on proposals and contributions submitted by Governments. The Ad Hoc Committee was informed of a legal opinion provided by the Office of Legal Affairs of the Secretariat regarding the interpretation of General Assembly resolution 54/127. Following a discussion on the matter, the Ad Hoc Committee at its seventh session decided to remove references to explosives from the draft Protocol.
59. At its fourth session, the Ad Hoc Committee had decided that, in future, informal consultations should be organized in order to facilitate the implementation of its mandate.
60. Pursuant to a decision taken at its sixth session, the Ad Hoc

Committee devoted the informal consultations held from I8-21 January to the consideration of the additional international legal instrument against trafficking in persons, especially women and children, and common provisions of that instrument and the additional international legal instrument against illegal trafficking in and transporting of migrants. Pursuant to the same decision, the Ad Hoc Committee devoted the informal consultations held from 24-27 January to the consideration of Articles 4, 4 *bis*, 4 *ter*, 4 *quater*, 7, 7 *bis*, 7 *ter*, 17, 17 *bis*, 18, 18 *bis* and 18 *ter* of the Draft Convention, in preparation for the finalization of those articles by the Ad Hoc Committee at its eighth session.

H. *Eighth Session*

61. The Ad Hoc Committee held its eighth session in Vienna from 21 February-3 March, 2000, during which it held 20 meetings.
62. The eighth session of the Ad Hoc Committee was attended by representatives of 112 States. Also attending the session were observers for organisations of the United Nations system, institutes of the United Nations Crime Prevention and Criminal Justice Programme network, inter-governmental organisations and non-governmental organisations.
63. The Ad Hoc Committee discussed Articles 2, 2 *bis* [sub-para, (*a*) only], 4, 4 *ter*, 4 *quater*, 7, 7 *bis*, 7 *ter*, 17, 17 *bis*, 18, 18 *bis* and 18 *ter* of the draft Convention. Because of lack of time, Article 4 *bis* was not discussed and would, therefore, be deferred to the ninth session of the Ad Hoc Committee. The Ad Hoc Committee based its work on a revised text of the draft United Nations Convention against Transnational Organized Crime (A/AC. 254/4/Rev. 7) and on proposals and contributions submitted by Governments.
64. The Ad Hoc Committee discussed the additional legal instrument against illegal trafficking in and transporting of migrants. It based its work on a document containing a revised text of the draft Protocol against the Smuggling of Migrants by Land, Air and Sea, supplementing the United Nations Convention against Transnational Organized

Crime (A/AC. 254/4/Add. l/Rev. 4), and on proposals and contributions submitted by Governments.

65. The Ad Hoc Committee devoted the informal consultations held during its eighth session, from 22-25 February, to the consideration of the additional international legal instrument against the illicit manufacturing of and trafficking in firearms, their parts and components and ammunition. The Ad Hoc Committee devoted the informal consultations held from 28 February-2 March to the consideration of Articles 9, 10, 10 *bis*, 14, 14 *bis*, 15 and 16 of the Draft Convention, in preparation for the finalization of those articles by the Ad Hoc Committee at its ninth session.

I. *Ninth Session*

66. The Ad Hoc Committee held its ninth session in Vienna from 5-16 June, 2000, during which it held 18 meetings.

67. The ninth session of the Ad Hoc Committee was attended by representatives of 116 States. Also attending the session were observers for organisations of the United Nations system, institutes of the United Nations Crime Prevention and Criminal Justice Programme network, inter-governmental organisations and non-governmental organisations.

68. The Ad Hoc Committee discussed Articles 2, 2 *bis* [sub-para. (*a*) only], 4 *bis*, *9* and paragraphs 1-10 of Article 10 of the Draft Convention. Because of lack of time, paragraphs 11-15 of Article 10 and Articles 10 *bis*, 14, 14 *bis*, 15 and 16 of the draft Convention were not discussed and discussion of them was therefore deferred to the tenth session of the Ad Hoc Committee. The Ad Hoc Committee based its work on a revised text of the draft United Nations Convention against Transnational Organized Crime (A/AC. 254/4/Rev. 8) and on proposals and contributions submitted by Governments.

69. The Ad Hoc Committee discussed the additional legal instrument against trafficking in persons, especially women and children. It based its work on a revised text of the draft Protocol to Prevent, Suppress and Punish Trafficking in Persons, Especially Women and Children, supplementing the United Nations Convention against Transnational

Organized Crime (A/AC. 254/4/Add. 3/Rev. 6), and on proposals and contributions submitted by Governments.

70. The Ad Hoc Committee devoted the informal consultations held during its ninth session, from 6-9 June, to the consideration of Articles 19-30 of the draft Convention, in preparation for the finalization of those articles by the Ad Hoc Committee at its tenth session. The Ad Hoc Committee devoted the informal consultations held from 13-15 June to the consideration of the additional international legal instrument against the illegal trafficking in and transporting of migrants.

J. *Tenth Session*

71. The Ad Hoc Committee held its tenth session in Vienna from 17-28 July, 2000, during which it held 23 meetings.
72. At its ninth session, held in Vienna from 5-16 June, 2000, the Ad Hoc Committee had decided that its tenth session would be devoted to the finalization and approval of the draft United Nations Convention against Transnational Organized Crime for submission to the General Assembly at its fifty-fifth session for adoption in accordance with Assembly resolution 54/126.
73. Also at its ninth session, the Chairman had requested all regional groups to appoint representatives to form a group that would be asked, at the tenth session of the Ad Hoc Committee, to ensure consistency of the text in all official languages of the United Nations.
74. The Secretary recalled that, at the ninth session of the Ad Hoc Committee, the Group of Eastern European States had decided to appoint the representatives of the Russian Federation and Slovakia to the consistency group. He announced the following other appointments to the consistency group: the representatives of Cameroon, Egypt, Morocco, Nigeria and South Africa, appointed by the Group of African States; the representatives of China, India, Japan and Jordan, appointed by the Group of Asian and Pacific States; the representatives of Colombia, Cuba, Guatemala and Mexico, appointed by the Group of Latin American and Caribbean States; and the representatives of France, Italy, Spain and the United States, appointed by

the Group of Western European and Other States. The Secretary also informed the Ad Hoc Committee that the consistency group would be assisted in its work by an editor, by translators from the translation section for each official language and by a member of the secretariat of the Ad Hoc Committee.

75. The Chairman informed the Ad Hoc Committee that he had asked the representative of Mexico to act as coordinator of the consistency group.
76. The tenth session of the Ad Hoc Committee was attended by representatives of 121 States. Also attending the session were observers for organisations of the United Nations system, institutes of the United Nations Crime Prevention and Criminal Justice Programme network, inter-governmental organisations and non-governmental organisations.
77. The Ad Hoc Committee considered and finalized all the articles of the draft Convention. It based its work on a revised text of the draft United Nations Convention against Transnational Organized Crime (A/AC. 254/4/Rev. 9) and on proposals and contributions submitted by Governments.
78. The consistency group held 14 meetings, on 18-27 July, and reviewed all the articles of the draft Convention. Its recommendations were incorporated into the final text of the draft Convention and submitted to the Ad Hoc Committee for consideration.
79. At its 177th meeting, on 28 July, the Ad Hoc Committee approved the draft United Nations Convention against Transnational Organized Crime and decided to submit it to the General Assembly for consideration and action at its fifty-fifth session, in accordance with Assembly resolution 54/126.
80. The Ad Hoc Committee considered a draft resolution submitted by the Chairman, entitled "United Nations Convention against Transnational Organized Crime." (A/AC: 254/L. 224/Rev. 1). The Ad Hoc Committee also had before it proposals for amendments to the draft resolution submitted by Governments, the European Union and the Chairman.

81. At its 177th meeting, on 28 July, the Ad Hoc Committee approved the draft resolution, as orally amended, on the understanding that the text of the draft resolution would be finalized by the Ad Hoc Committee at its eleventh session, in order to take into account the results of that session with respect to the draft protocols, and submitted to the General Assembly for consideration and action at its fifty-fifth session.

82. Also at the 177th meeting, on 28 July, the representative of Turkey stated that his country considered the draft Convention a valuable tool in fighting organized crime, in line with Turkey's consistent determination and support for bilateral and multi-lateral cooperation in combating that phenomenon. For that reason, Turkey had attributed great importance to the development of the draft Convention and had participated actively in the process from its initial stages. Turkey had been confident until the final phase of the negotiation that the Convention would cover all aspects of transnational organized crime. Turkey's experience had demonstrated that there were evident links between terrorist crimes and organized crime. Those links had been established at the World Ministerial Conference on Organized Transnational Crime, held in Naples, Italy, in 1994. Turkey therefore believed that the reflection of those dangerous links in the text of the Convention would better serve that instrument's purposes. Unfortunately, and despite the efforts of several delegations to draw attention to those links through constructive and concrete proposals, the links had been consciously omitted from the final text of the draft Convention. The result was not satisfactory to Turkey, because the Convention would leave loopholes that criminals might exploit. Nevertheless, Turkey did not intend to block consensus on the approval of the draft Convention. Following careful evaluation, its competent authorities would decide whether Turkey would sign the Convention. Prior to concluding his statement, the representative of Turkey thanked the Chairman and the secretariat for all their tireless efforts to conclude the work of the Ad Hoc Committee.

83. Following the adoption of the report, the representative of Lebanon requested that it reflect the reservations expressed by his country regarding Article 7, paragraph 6, on confiscation and seizure, and Article 14, paragraph 8, on mutual legal assistance, of the draft Convention.
84. The Chairman of the Ad Hoc Committee expressed his gratitude to all delegations for displaying throughout the negotiation process a spirit of cooperation and mutual understanding and for working together in the constructive manner that had made the achievement of the ambitious task of the Ad Hoc Committee possible. The Chairman thanked the Rapporteur, the Secretary of the Ad Hoc Committee and the staff of the Centre for International Crime Prevention. He also thanked the interpreters and conference officers for their support to the Ad Hoc Committee. The Chairman further expressed the gratitude of the Ad Hoc Committee to all States that had made voluntary contributions throughout the negotiation process to the United Nations Crime Prevention and Criminal Justice Fund, thus facilitating the work of the Ad Hoc Committee and making possible the attendance of a number of representatives of least developed countries.
85. The representative of Italy informed delegations of the preparations for the High-level Political Signing Conference, to be held in Palermo, Italy, from 12-15 December, 2000, in accordance with General Assembly resolution 54/129. Pursuant to that resolution, consultations on the draft agenda of the Conference would be organized by the Secretariat in Vienna in September.
86. The representative of Uruguay, speaking on behalf of the Group of 77 and China, expressed satisfaction at the completion of the work of the Ad Hoc Committee on the draft Convention. The good will of all delegations had enabled the achievement of general consensus. He was confident that the Convention would enter into force quickly. The Group of 77 and China wished to reiterate the importance of reinforcing technical and economic cooperation internationally, as a means of giving States the possibility to fulfil all the obligations arising from the Convention. Th e representative of Uruguay called upon

the Committee to focus on the completion of the three additional protocols. The Group of 77 and China, as had been stressed on previous occasions, would strive to that end in order to fulfil the mandate given to the Ad Hoc Committee by the General Assembly. Nevertheless, time constraints should not be allowed to compromise the quality of the texts, which should be transparent and universally accepted. Finally, the representative expressed the Group's appreciation to the Chairman, the other members of the Bureau, the consistency group and the secretariat for the support provided to the work of the Ad Hoc Committee.

87. The representative of Mexico, speaking on behalf of the Group of Latin American and Caribbean States, offered the Group's congratulations to the Ad Hoc Committee on the completion of its work on the draft Convention. The Group had once again demonstrated its political will to arrive at compromise solutions, convinced of the importance of reinforcing international cooperation against transnational organized crime. The approval of the draft Convention by consensus demonstrated that the draft text had taken into account the concerns of all States. The Convention represented the most important development of international criminal law since the adoption of the United Nations Convention against Illicit Traffic in Narcotic Drugs and Psychotropic Substances of 1988.[1] The members of the Group hoped that after its adoption by the General Assembly and its signature in Palermo, the Convention would enter into force quickly. The challenge facing the Ad Hoc Committee now was the conclusion of the drafting of the three protocols. The members of the Group were confident that the same spirit of compromise would prevail in achieving that task. The representative of Mexico expressed the gratitude of the members of the Group to the Chairman, the members of the Bureau, the representatives who had chaired more informal meetings, the Centre for International

---

1. Official Records of the United Nations Conference for the Adoption of a Convention against Illicit Traffic in Narcotic Drugs and Psychotropic Substances, Vienna, 25 November–20 December, 1988, Vol. I (United Nations Publication, Sales No, E.94.XI.5).

Crime Prevention and conference service staff, as well as to the Secretary of the Ad Hoc Committee.

88. The representative of Pakistan associated himself with the statement of the representative of Uruguay on behalf of the Group of 77 and China and expressed his deepest appreciation to those delegations who had specific concerns but had displayed a remarkable spirit of accommodation, thus making it possible for the Ad Hoc Committee to approve the draft Convention by consensus.

89. The representative of Egypt wished to place on record his country's position on the work of the Ad Hoc Committee at its tenth session and on the draft Convention. Egypt had participated, with all commitment and responsibility, in all stages of the negotiation process, pursuing the common objective of fighting against a very serious criminal phenomenon affecting, to varying degrees, all countries of the world. Acting on the principle that, in preparing an international convention, the concerns of some were the concerns of all, Egypt had repeatedly called for including in the Convention a clear and express reference to the growing relationship between transnational organized crime and terrorist crimes. That plea was in conformity with various United Nations instruments that had affirmed that fact, including resolution 4 of the Ninth United Nations Congress on the Prevention of Crime and the Treatment of Offenders. Egypt had demonstrated great flexibility regarding the way in which such a reference would be embodied in the Convention and had expected that such flexibility would have been met with a greater degree of understanding, so that the Convention, being of worldwide scope, would reflect the concerns of all States. The representative of Egypt expressed his deep regret at the deliberate omission from the text of the Convention of a serious dimension of transnational organized crime, represented in the link between such crime and terrorism. He was certain that such a lacuna constituted a basic shortcoming in the Convention, which would weaken international cooperation in containing and eliminating the phenomenon of terrorism and might prevent the Convention from becoming an influential element of the international

legal system that served the interests of all. Finally, the representative of Egypt thanked all the delegations, who had spared no effort in reaching compromise formulas that had had a great effect in supporting the work of the Committee.

90. The representative of France, speaking on behalf of the States members of the European Union that are Members of the United Nations, expressed her satisfaction at the approval of the draft Convention by consensus. That was a success belonging to all delegations, who had managed to find formulas to reconcile different aspects of legal systems and to ensure that all concerns were adequately and appropriately reflected in the final text. The representative of France expressed her appreciation to the Chairman, members of the Bureau and the secretariat for the support they had provided to the Ad Hoc Committee. She was confident that the Ad Hoc Committee would be able to comply fully with its mandate by finalizing the three additional protocols at its eleventh session, through the continued collective good will of all States.

91. The representative of the Syrian Arab Republic, speaking on behalf of the Group of Arab States, emphasized the participation of all Arab States in the negotiation process. Such participation and interest were underpinned by the conviction of being engaged and actively contributing to achieving a common goal that was in the interest of the international community. The representative also expressed his appreciation to the Chairman, members of the Bureau and the secretariat for their support.

92. The representative of Thailand, speaking on behalf of the States members of the Association of South-East Asian Nations that are Members of the United Nations, expressed his appreciation to the Chairman for his able leadership, which had made possible the conclusion of the work of the Ad Hoc Committee on the Convention. He also extended his gratitude to the representative of Pakistan for his efforts as Vice-Chairman of the Ad Hoc Committee and to the secretariat of the Committee for the support provided to all delegations. Once implemented, the Convention would enhance existing bilateral or

multi-lateral cooperation and thus bridge the gaps that had to date been exploited by organized criminal groups. The success of the Ad Hoc Committee should motivate all delegations to pursue vigorously the conclusion of the three additional protocols at the eleventh session of the Ad Hoc Committee.

93. The representative of Nigeria, speaking on behalf of the Group of African States, stated that dealing with the global problem of transnational organized crime required structural cooperation, in whose framework those with capacity would render technical assistance and training to those with insufficient expertise and resources. It was the hope of the members of the Group that the provisions of the Convention designed to enhance capacity-building would soon be implemented. This should be without prejudice to existing foreign assistance commitments to the countries concerned.

94. The representative of Indonesia, speaking on behalf of the Group of Asian and Pacific States, thanked the Chairman, the members of the Bureau and the secretariat and called for flexibility, which was necessary in achieving the goal of finalizing the three additional protocols at the eleventh session of the Ad Hoc Committee.

95. The representative of the Islamic Republic of Iran joined previous speakers in expressing the profound appreciation of his delegation to the Chairman, the members of the Bureau and the Chairman of the consistency group. The approved text of the Convention might not fully satisfy all delegations. However, in multi-lateral negotiations on a Convention of such a high magnitude and sensitivity, all delegations were bound to exercise a degree of sacrifice and indulgence to achieve a losty goal. That goal had been achieved thanks to the collective good will and efforts of all delegations. The representative of the Islamic Republic of Iran concluded by thanking the secretariat for the support extended to all delegations in the past two years and expressing his hope that the same level of support would enable the Ad Hoc Committee to fulfil its task of completing the three additional protocols.

96. The representative of Algeria expressed his satisfaction

with the results of the work of the Ad Hoc Committee at its tenth session and the approval of the draft Convention. While sharing the views expressed by Egypt, he called upon all delegations to spare no effort in ensuring the success of the work on the development of a comprehensive convention against terrorism, which was due to begin in New York in September.

97. The representative of South Africa thanked the Chairman and other members of the Bureau for their perseverance and the secretariat for its professionalism. He was convinced that the new Convention would significantly strengthen cooperation against organized criminal groups and looked forward to the successful completion of the three additional protocols at the eleventh session of the Ad Hoc Committee.

K. *Eleventh Session*

98. The Ad Hoc Committee held its eleventh session in Vienna from 2-28 October, 2000, during which it held 52 meetings.
99. The Secretary recalled that the composition of the consistency group was the following: the representatives of Cameroon, Egypt, Morocco, Nigeria and South Africa, appointed by the Group of African States; the representatives of China, India, Japan and Jordan, appointed by the Group of Asian and Pacific States; the representatives of the Russian Federation and Slovakia, appointed by the Group of Eastern European States; the representatives of Colombia, Cuba, Guatemala and Mexico, appointed by the Group of Latin American and Caribbean States; and the representatives of France, Italy, Spain and the United States, appointed by the Group of Western European and Other States. The Secretary also informed the Ad Hoc Committee that the consistency group would continue to be assisted in its work by an editor, by translators from the translation section for each official language and by a member of the secretariat of the Ad Hoc Committee.
100. The Chairman asked the consistency group to review the concordance among the three draft protocols and the draft United Nations Convention against Transnational Organized Crime, as approved by the Ad Hoc Committee at its tenth session, in addition to ensuring the consistency of

the texts of the draft protocols in all the official languages of the United Nations. The Chairman requested the representative of Mexico to continue to act as coordinator of the consistency group.

101. The eleventh session of the Ad Hoc Committee was attended by representatives of 121 States. Also attending the session were observers for organisations of the United Nations system, institutes of the United Nations Crime Prevention and Criminal Justice Programme network, inter-governmental organisations and non-governmental organisations.

102. The Ad Hoc Committee considered and finalized all the articles of the draft Protocol to Prevent, Suppress and Punish Trafficking in Persons, Especially Women and Children, supplementing the United Nations Convention against Transnational Organized Crime. It based its work on a revised text of the draft Protocol (A/AC. 254/4/Add. 3/ Rev. 7) and on proposals and contributions submitted by Governments.

103. The representative of the Islamic Republic of Iran requested that the report of the Ad Hoc Committee on its eleventh session indicate that his country had joined the consensus on Article 3, sub-paragraph (*a*), of the draft Protocol, but had registered a reservation regarding the inclusion of the expression "exploitation of the prostitution of others." That reservation was due to inconsistency with domestic law.

104. The representative of the United Arab Emirates requested that the report of the Ad Hoc Committee on its eleventh session reflect its position on Article 7, paragraph 1, of the draft Protocol, namely, that it considered itself not bound to provide the right of residence referred to at the end of that article.

105. The representative of the United Kingdom of Great Britain and Northern Ireland stated that his country had joined the consensus on Article 3, sub-paragraph (*b*), but that it reserved its right to make an interpretative statement at the time of signing the Protocol.

106. The representative of Japan requested that the report of the Ad Hoc Committee on its eleventh session reflect his view that the *travaux préparatoires* on Article 1 of the draft Protocol

should indicate that there were some provisions of the Convention that would not be applicable to the Protocol. Examples of such provisions, at a minimum, were Article 3 of the Convention, since Article 4 of the Protocol provided otherwise; Article 5 of the Convention, since Article 5, paragraph 2, of the Protocol provided otherwise; Articles 8 and 9 of the Convention, since it was absolutely unnecessary to have these articles apply to the Protocol; and Articles 35-41 of the Convention, since Articles 15-20 of the Protocol provided otherwise.

107. At its 218th meeting, on 23 October, the Ad Hoc Committee approved the draft Protocol to Prevent, Suppress and Punish Trafficking in Persons, Especially Women and Children, supplementing the United Nations Convention against Transnational Organized Crime, and decided to submit it to the General Assembly for consideration and action at its fifty-fifth session, in accordance with resolution 54/126.

108. The Ad Hoc Committee considered and finalized all the articles of the draft Protocol against the Smuggling of Migrants by Land, Sea and Air, supplementing the United Nations Convention against Transnational Organized Crime. It based its work on a revised text of the draft Protocol (A/AC. 254/4/Add. 1/Rev. 6) and on proposals and contributions submitted by Governments.

109. The representative of Azerbaijan requested that the report of the Ad Hoc Committee on its eleventh session indicate that his country reserved its right to make an interpretative statement or reservation regarding Article 5 of the Protocol.

110. The representative of Pakistan requested that the report of the Ad Hoc Committee on its eleventh session reflect that her country had joined the consensus on Article 6, paragraph 1, of the Protocol, but understood that the offences established in accordance with that paragraph implied the involvement of an organized criminal group.

111. The representatives of Denmark and Norway indicated that their countries would make an interpretative statement at the time of signing the Protocol regarding Article 6, paragraph 4, of the Protocol, in connection with a technical matter related to their penal systems.

112. The representative of Turkey requested that the report of the Ad Hoc Committee on its eleventh session reflect his country's understanding that the references to the United Nations Convention on the Law of the Sea[1] in the interpretative notes to article 7 of the Protocol for the *travaux préparatoires* neither prejudiced nor affected the position of Turkey concerning that Convention.
113. The representative of Denmark requested that the report of the Ad Hoc Committee on its eleventh session reflect the position of his country in relation to Article 8, paragraph 2, of the Protocol. According to Danish constitutional law, a State Party wishing to take appropriate measures in accordance with that paragraph with regard to vessels of Danish nationality or registry would have to request authorization from Denmark and could not act of its own accord. Denmark indicated that it would examine such requests on a case-by-case basis.
114. The representative of Canada indicated that his country, according to current practice, did not authorize other States to board vessels of Canadian nationality or registry. However, upon request under the Protocol, Canada undertook not to object to such action, provided that the action taken was consistent with the Protocol.
115. The representative of Spain requested that the report of the Ad Hoc Committee on its eleventh session reflect his country's understanding concerning Article 8, paragraph 6, namely, that the authorities mentioned therein were central authorities.
116. The representative of Bangladesh requested that the report of the Ad Hoc Committee on its eleventh session reflect his country's position on Article 16, paragraph 5. In the view of the representative, that paragraph was overly restrictive. The obligation to inform smuggled migrants about rights of consular access should have been expanded to create a further right to be informed of other rights set forth in this article. The representative also expressed concern that, by

1. Official Records of the Third United Nations Conference on the Law of the Sea, Vol. XVII (United Nations Publication. Sales No. E.84, V.3), document A/CONF.62/122.

referring to the Vienna Convention on Consular Relations,[1] the paragraph would not apply to States Parties to the Protocol that had not ratified or acceded to that Convention.

117. The representative of Japan requested that the report of the Ad Hoc Committee on its eleventh session reflect his view that the *travaux préparatoires* on Article 1 of the Protocol should indicate that there were some provisions of the Convention that would not be applicable to the Protocol. Examples of such provisions, at a minimum, were Article 3 of the Convention, since Article 4 of the Protocol provided otherwise; Article 5 of the Convention, since Article 6, paragraph 2 of the Protocol provided otherwise; Articles 8 and 9 of the Convention, since it was absolutely unnecessary to have these Articles apply to the Protocol; and Articles 35-41 of the Convention, since Articles 20-25 of the Protocol provided otherwise. The representative of Japan also requested that the report of the Ad Hoc Committee on its eleventh session reflect his view that the *travaux préparatoires* should indicate that, in the application of paragraph 3 of Article 15 of the Convention, States Parties should not be obliged to establish their jurisdiction under that provision over the offences established in accordance with Article 6 of the Protocol.

118. At its 222nd meeting, on 24 October, the Ad Hoc Committee approved the draft Protocol against the Smuggling of Migrants by Land, Sea and Air, supplementing the United Nations Convention against Transnational Organized Crime, and decided to submit it to the General Assembly for consideration and action at its fifty-fifth session, in accordance with resolution 54/126.

119. The Ad Hoc Committee considered all the articles of the draft Protocol against the Illicit Manufacturing of and Trafficking in Firearms, Their Parts and Components and Ammunition, supplementing the United Nations Convention against Transnational Organized Crime. It based its work on a revised text of the draft Protocol (A/AC.254/4/Add.2/Rev. 5) and on proposals

1. United Nations, *Treaty Series*, Vol. 596, Nos. 8638-8640.

and contributions submitted by Governments and by the European Commission.

120. In an effort to achieve consensus that would permit the finalization and approval of the draft Protocol, the Ad Hoc Committee extended its eleventh session by holding an additional meeting on 28 October. In spite of the fact that the Ad Hoc Committee came very close to achieving the necessary consensus, it was unable to complete its work in relation to the draft Protocol. Consequently, the Ad Hoc Committee decided to include in the draft resolution it was submitting to the General Assembly at its fifty-fifth session for consideration and action two paragraphs, in which the Assembly would note that the Ad Hoc Committee had not completed its work on the draft Protocol and would request it to finalize such work as soon as possible. In that connection, many delegations emphasized the importance of the finalization of the draft Protocol prior to the Conference on Small Arms and Light Weapons, scheduled for 2001. The Ad Hoc Committee proposed the inclusion of the phrase "as soon as possible" on the understanding that every effort should be made to finalize the draft Protocol by early 2001, but deemed it appropriate to leave to the Assembly the decision of whether to include a more specific deadline.

L. *Matters Calling for Action by the General Assembly at its Fifty-fifth Session*

121. The Ad Hoc Committee recommends to the General Assembly the adoption of the following draft resolution and the United Nations Convention against Transnational Organized Crime and the protocols thereto:

Draft Resolution

United Nations Convention against Transnational Organized Crime

The General Assembly,

Recalling its resolution 53/111 of 9 December, 1998, in which it decided to establish an open-ended inter-governmental Ad Hoc Committee for the purpose of elaborating a comprehensive international convention against transnational organized crime and of discussing the elaboration, as appropriate, of international instruments addressing trafficking in women and children, combating the illicit manufacturing of and trafficking in firearms, their parts and components and ammunition, and illegal trafficking in and transporting of migrants, including by sea,

Recalling also its resolution 54/126 of 17 December, 1999, in which it requested the Ad Hoc Committee on the Elaboration of a Convention against Transnational Organized Crime to continue its work, in accordance with resolutions 53/111 and 53/114 of 9 December, 1998, and to intensify that work in order to complete it in 2000.

Recalling further its resolution 54/129 of 17 December, 1999, in which it accepted with appreciation the offer of the Government of Italy to host a high-level political signing conference in Palermo for the purpose of signing the United Nations Convention against Transnational Organized Crime (Palermo Convention) and the protocols thereto, and requested the Secretary-General to schedule the conference for a period of upto one week before the end of the Millennium Assembly in 2000.

Expressing its appreciation to the Government of Poland for submitting to it at its fifty-first session a first draft of the United Nations Convention against Transnational Organized Crime and for hosting the meeting of the open-ended inter-governmental group of experts established pursuant to resolution 52/85 of 12 December, 1997, held in Warsaw from 2-6 February, 1998.

Expressing its appreciation to the Government of Argentina for hosting the informal preparatory meeting of the Ad Hoc Committee on the Elaboration of a Convention against Transnational Organized Crime, held in Buenos Aires from 31 August - 4 September 1998.

Expressing its appreciation to the Government of Thailand for hosting the Asia-Pacific Ministerial Seminar on Building Capacities for Fighting Transnational Organized Crime, held in Bangkok on 20 and 21 March, 2000.

Deeply concerned by the negative economic and social implications related to organized criminal activities, and convinced of the urgent need to strengthen cooperation to prevent and combat such activities more effectively at the national, regional and international levels.

Noting with deep concern the growing links between transnational organized crime and terrorist crimes, taking into account the Charter of the United Nations and the relevant resolutions of the General Assembly.

Determined to deny safe havens to those who engage in transnational organized crime by prosecuting their crimes wherever they occur and by cooperating at the international level.

Strongly convinced that the United Nations Convention against Transnational Organized Crime will constitute an effective tool and the necessary legal framework for international cooperation in combating, *inter alia*, such criminal activities as money-laundering, corruption, illicit trafficking in endangered species of wild flora and fauna, offences against cultural heritage and the growing links between transnational organized crime and terrorist crimes:

1. *Takes note* of the report of the Ad Hoc Committee on the Elaboration of a Convention against Transnational Organized Crime, which carried out its work at the headquarters of the Office for Drug Control and Crime Prevention of the Secretariat in Vienna, and commends the Ad Hoc Committee for its work;
2. *Adopts* the United Nations Convention against Transnational Organized Crime and the Protocol to Prevent, Suppress and Punish Trafficking in Persons, Especially Women and Children, supplementing the United Nations Convention against Transnational Organized Crime, and the Protocol against the Smuggling of Migrants by Land, Sea and Air, supplementing the United Nations Convention against Transnational Organized Crime annexed to the present resolution, and opens them for signature at the high-level political signing conference to be held in Palermo, Italy, from 12-15 December, 2000 in accordance with resolution 54/129;
3. *Requests* the Secretary-General to prepare summary records of the high-level political signing conference to be held in Palermo in accordance with resolution 54/129;
4. *Notes* that the Ad Hoc Committee has not yet completed its work on the draft Protocol against the Illicit Manufacturing of and Trafficking in Firearms, Their Parts and Components and Ammunition, supplementisng the United Nations Convention against Transnational Organized Crime;

5. *Requests* the Ad Hoc Committee to continue its work in relation to this Protocol, in accordance with resolutions 53/111, 53/114 and 54/126, and to finalize such work as soon as possible;
6. *Calls upon* all States to recognize the links between transnational organized criminal activities and acts of terrorism, taking into account the relevant General Assembly resolutions, and to apply the United Nations Convention against Transnational Organized Crime in combating all forms of criminal activity, as provided therein;
7. *Recommends* that the Ad Hoc Committee established by the General Assembly in its resolution 51/210 of 17 December 1996, which is beginning its deliberations with a view to developing a comprehensive convention on international terrorism, pursuant to Assembly resolution 54/110 of 9 December 1999, should take into consideration the provisions of the United Nations Convention against Transnational Organized Crime;
8. Urges all States and regional economic organizations to sign and ratify the United Nations Convention against Transnational Organized Crime and the protocols thereto as soon as possible in order to ensure the speedy entry into force of the Convention and the protocols thereto;
9. *Decides* that, until the Conference of the Parties to the Convention established pursuant to the United Nations Convention against Transnational Organized Crime decides otherwise, the account referred to in Article 30 of the Convention will be operated within the United Nations Crime Prevention and Criminal Justice Fund, and encourages Member States to begin making adequate voluntary contributions to the above-mentioned account for the provision to developing countries and countries with economies in transition of the technical assistance that they might require for implementation of the Convention and the protocols thereto, including for the preparatory measures needed for that implementation;
10. *Decides also* that the Ad Hoc Committee on the Elaboration of a Convention against Transnational Organized Crime will complete its tasks arising from the elaboration of the

United Nations Convention against Transnational Organized Crime by holding a meeting well before the convening of the first session of the Conference of the Parties to the Convention, in order to prepare the draft text of the rules of procedure for the Conference of the Parties and other rules and mechanisms described in Article 32 of the Convention, which will be communicated to the Conference of the Parties at its first session for consideration and action;

11. *Requests* the Secretary-General to designate the Centre for International Crime Prevention of the Office for Drug Control and Crime Prevention to serve as the secretariat for and under the direction of the Conference of the Parties to the Convention;
12. *Also requests* the Secretary-General to provide the Centre for International Crime Prevention with the resources necessary to enable it to promote in an effective manner the expeditious entry into force of the United Nations Convention against Transnational Organized Crime and to discharge the functions of secretariat of the Conference of the Parties to the Convention and to support the Ad Hoc Committee in its work pursuant to paragraph 10 above.

ANNEXURE I

United Nations Convention against Transnational Organized Crime

Article 1: Statement of Purpose

The purpose of this Convention is to promote cooperation to prevent and combat transnational organized crime more effectively.

Article 2: Use of Terms

For the purposes of this Convention:

(*a*) "Organized criminal group" shall mean a structured group of three or more persons, existing for a period of time and acting in concert with the aim of committing one or more serious crimes or offences established in accordance with this Convention, in order to obtain, directly or indirectly, a financial or other material benefit;

(*b*) "Serious crime" shall mean conduct constituting an offence punishable by a maximum deprivation of liberty of at least four years or a more serious penalty;

(*c*) "Structured group" shall mean a group that is not randomly formed for the immediate commission of an offence and that does not need to have formally defined roles for its members, continuity of its membership or a developed structure;

(*d*) "Property" shall mean assets of every kind, whether corporeal or incorporeal, movable or immovable, tangible or intangible, and legal documents or instruments evidencing title to, or interest in, such assets;

(*e*) "Proceeds of crime" shall mean any property derived from or obtained, directly or indirectly, through the commission of an offence;

(*f*) "Freezing" or "seizure" shall mean temporarily prohibiting the transfer, conversion, disposition or movement of property or temporarily assuming custody or control of property on the basis of an order issued by a court or other competent authority;

(*g*) "Confiscation", which includes forfeiture where applicable, shall mean the permanent deprivation of property by order of a court or other competent authority;

(*h*) "Predicate offence" shall mean any offence as a result of which proceeds have been generated that may become the subject of an offence as defined in Article 6 of this Convention;

(*i*) "Controlled delivery" shall mean the technique of allowing illicit or suspect consignments to pass out of, through or into the territory of one or more States, with the knowledge and under the supervision of their competent authorities, with a view to the investigation of an offence and the identification of persons involved in the commission of the offence;

(*j*) "Regional economic integration organization" shall mean an organization constituted by sovereign States of a given region, to which its member States have transferred competence in respect of matters governed by this Convention and which has been duly authorized, in accordance with its internal procedures, to sign, ratify, accept, approve or accede to it; references to "States Parties" under this Convention shall apply to such organisations within the limits of their competence.

Article 3: *Scope of Application*

1. This Convention shall apply, except as otherwise stated herein, to the prevention, investigation and prosecution of:
   (*a*) the offences established in accordance with Articles 5, 6, 8 and 23 of this Convention; and
   (*b*) serious crime as defined in Article 2 of this Convention; where the offence is transnational in nature and involves an organized criminal group.
2. For the purpose of paragraph 1 of this article, an offence is transnational in nature if:
   (*a*) it is committed in more than one State;
   (*b*) it is committed in one State but a substantial part of its preparation, planning, direction or control takes place in another State;
   (*c*) it is committed in one State but involves an organized criminal group that engages in criminal activities in more than one State; or
   (*d*) it is committed in one State but has substantial effects in another State.

Article 4: *Protection of Sovereignty*

1. States Parties shall carry out their obligations under this Convention in a manner consistent with the principles of sovereign equality and territorial integrity of States and that osf non-intervention in the domestic affairs of other States.
2. Nothing in this Convention entitles a State Party to undertake in the territory of another State the exercise of jurisdiction and performance of functions that are reserved exclusively for the authorities of that other State by its domestic law.

Article 5: *Criminalization of Participation in an Organized Criminal Group*

1. Each State Party shall adopt such legislative and other

measures as may be necessary to establish as criminal offences, when committed intentionally:

(*a*) Either or both of the following as criminal offences distinct from those involving the attempt or completion of the criminal activity:

(*i*) Agreeing with one or more other persons to commit a serious crime for a purpose relating directly or indirectly to the obtaining of a financial or other material benefit and, where required by domestic law, involving an act undertaken by one of the participants in furtherance of the agreement or involving an organized criminal group;

(*ii*) Conduct by a person who, with knowledge of either the aim and general criminal activity of an organized criminal group or its intention to commit the crimes in question, takes an active part in;

(*a*) Criminal activities of the organized criminal group;

(*b*) Other activities of the organized criminal group in the knowledge that his or her participation will contribute to the achievement of the above-described criminal aim;

(*b*) Organizing, directing, aiding, abetting, facilitating or counselling the commission of serious crime involving an organized criminal group.

2. The knowledge, intent, aim, purpose or agreement referred to in paragraph 1 of this article may be inferred from objective factual circumstances.

3. States Parties whose domestic law requires involvement of an organized criminal group for purposes of the offences established in accordance with paragraph 1 (*a*) (*i*) of this article shall ensure that their domestic law covers all serious crimes involving organized criminal groups. Such States Parties, as well as States Parties whose domestic law requires an act in furtherance of the agreement for purposes of the offences established in accordance with paragraph 1 (*a*) (*i*) of this article, shall so inform the Secretary-General of the United Nations at the time of their signature or of deposit of their instrument of ratification, acceptance or approval of or accession to this Convention.

Article 6: Criminalization of the Laddering of Proceeds of Crime

1. Each State Party shall adopt, in accordance with fundamental principles of its domestic law, such legislative and other measures as may be necessary to establish as criminal offences, when committed intentionally:
   (*a*) (*i*) The conversion or transfer of property, knowing that such property is the proceeds of crime, for the purpose of concealing or disguising the illicit origin of the property or of helping any person who is involved in the commission of the predicate offence to evade the legal consequences of his or her action;
   (*ii*) The concealment or disguise of the time nature, source, location, disposition, movement or ownership of or rights with respect to property, knowing that such property is the proceeds of crime;
   (*b*) Subject to the basic concepts of its legal system:
   (*i*) The acquisition, possession or use of property, knowing, at the time of receipt, that such property is the proceeds of crime;
   (*ii*) Participation in, association with or conspiracy to commit, attempts to commit and aiding, abetting, facilitating and counselling the commission of any of the offences established in accordance with this article.
2. For purposes of implementing or applying paragraph 1 of this article:
   (*a*) Each State Party shall seek to apply paragraph 1 of this article to the widest range of predicate offences;
   (*b*) Each State Party shall include as predicate offences all serious crime as defined in Article 2 of this Convention and the offences established in accordance with Articles 5, 8 and 23 of this Convention. In the case of States Parties whose legislation sets out a list of specific predicate offences, tshey shall, at a minimum, include in such list a comprehensive range of offences associated with organized criminal groups;
   (*c*) For the purposes of sub-paragraph (*b*), predicate offences shall include offences committed both within and outside the jurisdiction of the State Party in

question. However, offences committed outside the jurisdiction of a State Party shall constitute predicate offences only when the relevant conduct is a criminal offence under the domestic law of the State where it is committed and would be a criminal offence under the domestic law of the State Party implementing or applying this article had it been committed there;

(*d*) Each State Party shall furnish copies of its laws that give effect to this article and of any subsequent changes to such laws or a description thereof to the Secretary-General of the United Nations;

(*e*) If required by fundamental principles of the domestic law of a State Party, it may be provided that the offences set forth in paragraph 1 of this article do not apply to the persons who committed the predicate offence;

(*f*) Knowledge, intent or purpose required as an element of an offence set forth in paragraph 1 of this article may be inferred from objective factual circumstances.

Article 7: Measures to Combat Money-Laundering

1. Each State Party:

(*a*) shall institute a comprehensive domestic regulatory and supervisory regime for banks and non-bank financial institutions and, where appropriate, other bodies particularly susceptible to money-laundering, within its competence, in order to deter and detect all forms of money-laundering, which regime shall emphasize requirements for customer identification, record-keeping and the reporting of suspicious transactions;

(*b*) shall, without prejudice to Articles 18 and 27 of this Convention, ensure that administrative, regulatory, law enforcement and other authorities dedicated to combating money-laundering (including, where appropriate under domestic law, judicial authorities) have the ability to cooperate and exchange information at the national and international levels within the conditions prescribed by its domestic law and, to that end, shall consider the establishment of a financial intelligence unit to serve as a national centre for the collection, analysis and dissemination of information regarding potential money-laundering.

2. States Parties shall consider implementing feasible measures to detect and monitor the movement of cash and appropriate negotiable instruments across their borders, subject to safeguards to ensure proper use of information and without impeding in any way the movement of legitimate capital. Such measures may include a requirement that individuals and businesses report the cross-border transfer of substantial quantities of cash and appropriate negotiable instruments.
3. In establishing a domestic regulatory and supervisory regime under the terms of this article, and without prejudice to any other article of this Convention, States Parties are called upon to use as a guideline the relevant initiatives of regional, inter-regional and multi-lateral organisations against money-laundering.
4. States Parties shall endeavour to develop and promote global, regional, sub-regional and bilateral cooperation among judicial, law enforcement and financial regulatory authorities in order to combat money-laundering.

Article 8: *Criminalization of Corruption*

1. Each State Party shall adopt such legislative and other measures as may be necessary to establish as criminal offences, when committed intentionally:
   (*a*) The promise, offering or giving to a public official, directly or indirectly, of an undue advantage, for the official himself or herself or another person or entity, in order that the official act or refrain from acting in the exercise of his or her official duties;
   (*b*) The solicitation or acceptance by a public official, directly or indirectly, of an undue advantage, for the official himself or herself or another person or entity, in order that the official act or refrain from acting in the exercise of his or her official duties.
2. Each State Pasrty shall consider adopting such legislative and other measures as may be necessary to establish as criminal offences conduct referred to in paragraph 1 of this article involving a foreign public official or international

civil servant. Likewise, each State Party shall consider establishing as criminal offences other forms of corruption.

3. Each State Party shall also adopt such measures as may be necessary to establish as a criminal offence participation as an accomplice in an offence established in accordance with this article.
4. For the purposes of paragraph 1 of this article and Article 9 of this Convention, "public official" shall mean a public official or a person who provides a public service as defined in the domestic law and as applied in the criminal law of the State Party in which the person in question performs that function.

Article 9: Measures Against Corruption

1. In addition to the measures set forth in Article 8 of this Convention, each State Party shall, to the extent appropriate and consistent with its legal system, adopt legislative, administrative or other effective measures to promote integrity and to prevent, detect and punish the corruption of public officials.
2. Each State Party shall take measures to ensure effective action by its authorities in the prevention, detection and punishment of the corruption of public officials, including providing such authorities with adequate independence to deter the exertion of inappropriate influence on their actions.

Article 10: Liability of Legal Persons

1. Each State Party shall adopt such measures as may be necessary, consistent with its legal principles, to establish the liability of legal persons for participation in serious crimes involving an organized criminal group and for the offences established in accordance with Articles 5, 6, 8 and 23 of this Convention.
2. Subject to the legal principles of the State Party, the liability of legal persons may be criminal, civil or administrative.
3. Such liability shall be without prejudice to the criminal liability of the natural persons who have committed the offences.

4. Each State Party shall, in particular, ensure that legal persons held liable in accordance with this article are subject to effective, proportionate and dissuasive criminal or non-criminal sanctions, including monetary sanctions.

Article 11: *Prosecution, Adjudication and Sanctions*

1. Each State Party shall make the commission of an offence established in accordance with Articles 5, 6, 8 and 23 of this Convention liable to sanctions that take into account the gravity of that offence.
2. Each State Party shall endeavour to ensure that any discretionary legal powers under its domestic law relating to the prosecution of persons for offences covered by this Convention are exercised to maximize the effectiveness of law enforcement measures in respect of those offences and with due regard to the need to deter the commission of such offences.
3. In the case of offences established in accordance with Articles 5, 6, 8 and 23 of this Convention, each State Party shall take appropriate measures, in accordance with its domestic law and with due regard to the rights of the defence, to seek to ensure that conditions imposed in connection with decisions on release pending trial or appeal take into consideration the need to ensure the presence of the defendant at subsequent criminal proceedings.
4. Each State Party shall ensure that its courts or other competent authorities bear in mind the grave nature of the offences covered by this Convention when considering the eventuality of early release or parole of persons convicted of such offences.
5. Each State Party shall, where appropriate, establish under its domestic law a long statute of limitations period in which to commence proceedings for any offence covered by this Convention and a longer period where the alleged offender has evaded the administration of justice.
6. Nothing contained in this Convention shall affect the principle that the description of the offences established in accordance with this Convention and of the applicable legal defences or other legals principles controlling the lawfulness

of conduct is reserved to the domestic law of a State Party and that such offences shall be prosecuted and punished in accordance with that law.

Article 12: *Confiscation and Seizure*

1. States Parties shall adopt, to the greatest extent possible within their domestic legal systems, such measures as may be necessary to enable confiscation of:
   (a) proceeds of crime derived from offences covered by this Convention or property the value of which corresponds to that of such proceeds;
   (*b*) property, equipment or other instrumentalities used in or destined for use in offences covered by this Convention.
2. States Parties shall adopt such measures as may be necessary to enable the identification, tracing, freezing or seizure of any item referred to in paragraph 1 of this article for the purpose of eventual confiscation.
3. If proceeds of crime have been transformed or converted, in part or in full, into other property, such property shall be liable to the measures referred to in this article instead of the proceeds.
4. If proceeds of crime have been intermingled with property acquired from legitimate sources, such property shall, without prejudice to any powers relating to freezing or seizure, be liable to confiscation up to the assessed value of the intermingled proceeds.
5. Income or other benefits derived from proceeds of crime, from property into which proceeds of crime have been transformed or converted or from property with which proceeds of crime have been intermingled shall also be liable to the measures referred to in this article, in the same manner and to the same extent as proceeds of crime.
6. For the purposes of this article and Article 13 of this Convention, each State Party shall empower its courts or other competent autho rities to order that bank, financial or commercial records be made available or be seized. States Parties shall not decline to act under the provisions of this paragraph on the ground of bank secrecy.

7. States Parties may consider the possibility of requiring that an offender demonstrate the lawful origin of alleged proceeds of crime or other property liable to confiscation, to the extent that such a requirement is consistent with the principles of their domestic law and with the nature of the judicial and other proceedings.
8. The provisions of this article shall not be construed to prejudice the rights of *bona fide* third parties.
9. Nothing contained in this article shall affect the principle that the measures to which it refers shall be defined and implemented in accordance with and subject to the provisions of the domestic law of a State Party.

Article 13: *International Cooperation for Purposes of Confiscation*

1. A State Party that has received a request from another State Party having jurisdiction over an offence covered by this Convention for confiscation of proceeds of crime, property, equipment or other instrumentalities referred to in Article 12, paragraph 1, of this Convention situated in its territory shall, to the greatest extent possible within its domestic legal system:
   (*a*) Submit the request to its competent authorities for the purpose of obtaining an order of confiscation and, if such an order is granted, give effect to it; or
   (*b*) Submit to its comspetent authorities, with a view to giving effect to it to the extent requested, an order of confiscation issued by a court in the territory of the requesting State Party in accordance with Article 12, paragraph 1, of this Convention insofar as it relates to proceeds of crime, property, equipment or other instrumentalities referred to in Article 12, paragraph 1, situated in the territory of the requested State Party.
2. Following a request made by another State Party having jurisdiction over an offence covered by this Convention, the requested State Party shall take measures to identify, trace and freeze or seize proceeds of crime, property, equipment or other instrumentalities referred to in Article 12, paragraph 1, of this Convention for the purpose of

eventual confiscation to be ordered either by the requesting State Party or, pursuant to a request under paragraph 1 of this article, by tshe requested State Party.s

3. The provisions of Article 18 of this Convention are applicable, *mutatis mutandis,* to this article. In addition to the information specified in Article 18, paragraph 15, requests made pursuant to this article shall contain:
   (*a*) In the case of a request pertaining to paragraph 1 (*a*) of this article, a description of the property to be confiscated and a statement of the facts relied upon by the requesting State Party sufficient to enable the requested State Party to seek the order under its domestic law;
   (*b*) In the case of a request pertaining to paragraph 1 (*b*) of this article, a legally admissible copy of an order of confiscation upon which the request is based issued by the requesting State Party, a statement of the facts and information as to the extent to which execution of the order is requested;
   (*c*) In the case of a request pertaining to paragraph 2 of this article, a statement of the facts relied upon by the requesting State Party and a description of the actions requested.
4. The decisions or actions provided for in paragraphs 1 and 2 of this article shall be taken by the requested State Party in accordance with and subject to the provisions of its domestic law and its procedural rules or any bilateral or multi-lateral treaty, agreement or arrangement to which it may be sbound in relation to the requesting State Party.
5. Each State Party shall furnish copies of its laws and regulations that give effect to this article and of any subsequent changes to such laws and regulations or a description thereof to the Secretary-General of the United Nations.
6. If a State Party elects to make the taking of the measures referred to in paragraphs 1 and 2 of this article conditional on the existence of a relevant treaty, that State Party shall consider this Convention the necessary and sufficient treaty basis.

7. Cooperation under this article may be refused by a State Party if the offence to which the request relates is not an offence covered by this Convention.
8. The provisions of this article shall not be construed to prejudice the rights of *bona fide* third parties.
9. States Parties shall consider concluding bilateral or multilateral treaties, agreements or arrangements to enhance the effectiveness of international cooperation undertaken pursuant to this article.

Article 14: *Disposal of Confiscated Proceeds of Crime or Property*

1. Proceeds of crime or property confiscated by a State Party pursuant to Article 12 or 13, paragraph 1, of this Convention shall be disposed osf by that State Party in accordance with its domestic law and administrative procedures.
2. When acting on the request made by another State Party in accordance with Article 13 of this Convention, States Parties shall, to the extent permitted by domestic law and if so requested, give priority consideration to returning the confiscated proceeds of crime or property to the requesting State Party so that it can give compensation to the victims of the crime or return such proceeds of crime or property to their legitimate owners.
3. When acting on the request made by another State Party in accordance with Articles 12 and 13 of this Convention, a State Party may give special consideration to concluding agreements or arrangements on:
   (*a*) contributing the value of such proceeds of crime or property or funds derived from the sale of such proceeds of crime or property or a part thereof to the account designated in accordance with Article 30, paragraph 2 (*c*), of this Convention and to inter-governmental bodies specializing in the fight against organized crime;
   (*b*) sharing with other States Parties, on a regular or case-by-case basis, such proceeds of crime or property, or funds derived from the sale of such proceeds of crime or property, in accordance with its domestic law or administrative procedures.

Article 15: *Jurisdiction*

1. Each State Party shall adopt such measures as may be necessary to establish its jurisdiction over the offences established in accordance with Articles 5, 6, 8 and 23 of this Convention when:
   (*a*) the offence is committed in the territory of that State Party; or
   (*b*) the offence is committed on board a vessel that is flying the flag of that State Party or an aircraft that is registered under the laws of that State Party at the time that the offence is committed.
2. Subject to Article 4 of this Convention, a State Party may also establish its jurisdiction over any such offence when:
   (*a*) the offence is committed against a national of that State Party;
   (*b*) the offence is committed by a national of that State Party or a stateless person who has his or her habitual residence in its territory; or
   (*c*) the offence is:
      (*i*) one of those established in accordance with Article 5, paragraph 1, of this Convention and is committed outside its territory with a view to the commission of a serious crime within its territory;
      (*ii*) one of those established in accordance with Article 6, paragraph 1 (*b*) (*ii*), of this Convention and is committed outside its territory with a view to the commission of an offence established in accordance with Article 6, paragraph 1 (*a*) (*i*) or (*ii*) or (*b*) (*i*), of this Convention within its territory.
3. For the purposes of Article 16, paragraph 10, of this Convention, each State Party shall adopt such measures as may be necessary to establish its jurisdiction over the offences covered by this Convention when the alleged offender is present in its territory and it does not extradite such person solely on the ground that he or she is one of its nationals.
4. Each State Party may also adopt such measures as may be necessary to establish its jurisdiction over the offences covered by this Convention when the alleged offender is present in its territory and it does not extradite him or her.

5. If a State Party exercising its jurisdiction under paragraph 1 or 2 of this article has been notified, or has otherwise learned, that one or more other States Parties are conducting an investigation, prosecution or judicial proceeding in respect of the same conduct, the competent authorities of those States Parties shall, as appropriate, consult one another with a view to coordinating their actions.
6. Without prejudice to norms of general international law, this Convention does not exclude the exercise of any criminal jurisdiction established by a State Party in accordance with its domestic law.

Article 16: *Extradition*

1. This article shall apply to the offences covered by this Convention or in cases where an offence referred to in Article 3, paragraph 1 (*a*) or (*b*), involves an organized criminal group and the person who is the subject of the request for extradition is located in the territory of the requested State Party, provided that the offence for which extradition is sought is punishable under the domestic law of both the requesting State Party and the requested State Party.
2. If the request for extradition includes several separate serious crimes, some of which are not covered by this article, the requested State Party may apply this article also in respect of the latter offences.
3. Each of the offences to which this article applies shall be deemed to be included as an extraditable offence in any extradition treaty existing between States Parties. States Parties undertake to include such offences as extraditable offences in every extradition treaty to be concluded between them.
4. If a State Party that makes extradition conditional on the existence of a treaty receives a request for extradition from another State Party with which it has no extradition treaty, it may consider this Convention the legal basis for extradition in respect of any offence to which this article applies.
5. States Parties that make extradition conditional on the existence of a treaty shall:

(*a*) at the time of deposit of their instrument of ratification, acceptance, approval of or accession to this Convention, inform the Secretary-General of the United Nations whether they will take this Convention as the legal basis for cooperation on extradition with other States Parties to this Convention; and

(*b*) if they do not take this Convention as the legal basis for cooperation on extradition, seek, where appropriate, to conclude treaties on extradition with other States Parties to this Convention in order to implement this article.

6. States Parties that do not make extradition conditional on the existence of a treaty shall recognize offences to which this article applies as extraditable offences between themselves.
7. Extradition shall be subject to the conditions provided for by the domestic law of the requested State Party or by applicable extradition treaties, including, *inter alia*, conditions in relation to the minimum penalty requirement for extradition and the grounds upon which the requested State Party may refuse extradition.
8. States Parties shall, subject to their domestic law, endeavour to expedite extradition procedures and to simplify evidentiary requirements relating thereto in respect of any offence to which this article applies.
9. Subject to the provisions of its domestic law and its extradition treaties, the requested State Party may, upon being satisfied that the circumstances so warrant and are urgent and at the request of the requesting State Party, take a person whose extradition is sought and who is present in its territory into custody or take other appropriate measures to ensure his or her presence at extradition proceedings.
10. A State Party in whose territory an alleged offender is found, if it does not extradite such person in respect of an offence to which this article applies solely on the ground that he or she is one of its nationals, shall, at the request of the State Party seeking extradition, be obliged to submit the case without undue delay to its competent authorities for the purpose of prosecution. Those authorities shall take

their decision and conduct their proceedings in the same manner as in the case of any other offence of a grave nature under the domestic law of that State Party. The States Parties concerned shall cooperate with each other, in particular on procedural and evidentiary aspects, to ensure the efficiency of such prosecution.

11. Whenever, a State Party is permitted under its domestic law to extradite or otherwise surrender one of its nationals only upon the condition that the person will be returned to that State Party to serve the sentence imposed as a result of the trial or proceedings for which the extradition or surrender of the person was sought and that State Party and the State Party seeking the extradition of the person agree with this option and other terms that they may deem appropriate, such conditional extradition or surrender shall be sufficient to discharge the obligation set forth in paragraph 10 of this article.
12. If extradition, sought for purposes of enforcing a sentence, is refused because the person sought is a national of the requested State Party, the requested Party shall, if its domestic law so permits and in conformity with the requirements of such law, upon application of the requesting Party, consider the enforcement of the sentence that has been imposed under the domestic law of the requesting Party or the remainder thereof.
13. Any person regarding whom proceedings are being carried out in connection with any of the offences to which this article applies shall be guaranteed fair treatment at all stages of the proceedings, including enjoyment of all the rights and guarantees provided by the domestic law of the State Party in the territory of which that person is present.
14. Nothing in this Convention shall be interpreted as imposing an obligation to extradite if the requested State Party has substantial grounds for believing that the request has been made for the purpose of prosecuting or punishing a person on account of that person's sex, race, religion, nationality, ethnic origin or political opinions or that compliance with the request would cause prejudice to that person's position for any one of these reasons.

15. States Parties may not refuse a request for extradition on the sole ground that the offence is also considered to involve fiscal matters.
16. Before refusing extradition, the requested State Party shall, where appropriate, consult with the requesting State Party to provide it with ample opportunity to present its opinions and to provide information relevant to its allegation.
17. States Parties shall seek to conclude bilateral and multilateral agreements or arrangements to carry out or to enhance the effectiveness of extradition.

Article 17: *Transfer of Sentenced Persons*

States Parties may consider entering into bilateral or multi-lateral agreements or arrangements on the transfer to their territory of persons sentenced to imprisonment or other forms of deprivation of liberty for offences covered by this Convention, in order that they may complete their sentences there.

Article 18: *Mutual Legal Assistance*

1. States Parties shall afford one another the widest measure of mutual legal assistance in investigations, prosecutions and judicial proceedings in relation to the offences covered by this Convention as provided for in Article 3 and shall reciprocally extend to one another similar assistance where the requesting State Party has reasonable grounds to suspect that the offence referred to in Article 3, paragraph 1 (*a*) or (*b*), is transnational in nature, including that victims, witnesses, proceeds, instrumentalities or evidence of such offences are located in the requested State Party and that the offence involves an organized criminal group.
2. Mutual legal assistance shall be afforded to the fullest extent possible under relevant laws, treaties, agreements and arrangements of the requested State Party with respect to investigations, prosecutions and judicial proceedings in relation to the offences for which a legal person may be held liable in accordance with Article 10 of this Convention in the requesting State Party.
3. Mutual legal assistance to be afforded in accordance with this article may be requested for any of the following purposes:

(*a*) Taking evidence or statements from persons;
(*b*) Effecting service of judicial documents;
(*c*) Executing searches and seizures, and freezing;
(*d*) Examining objects and sites;
(*e*) Providing information, evidentiary items and expert evaluations;
(*f*) Providing originals or certified copies of relevant documents and records, including government, bank, financial, corporate or business records;
(*g*) Identifying or tracing proceeds of crime, property, instrumentalities or other things for evidentiary purposes;
(*h*) Facilitating the voluntary appearance of persons in the requesting State Party; and
(*i*) Any other type of assistance that is not contrary to the domestic law of the requested State Party.

4. Without prejudice to domestic law, the competent authorities of a State Party may, without prior request, transmit information relating to criminal matters to a competent authority in another State Party where they believe that such information could assist the authority in undertaking or successfully concluding inquiries and criminal proceedings or could result in a request formulated by the latter State Party pursuant to this Convention.
5. The transmission of information pursuant to paragraph 4 of this article shall be without prejudice to inquiries and criminal proceedings in the State of the competent authorities providing the information. The competent authorities receiving the information shall comply with a request that said information remain confidential, even temporarily, or with restrictions on its use. However, this shall not prevent the receiving State Party from disclosing in its proceedings information that is exculpatory to an accused person. In such a case, the receiving State Party shall notify the transmitting State Party prior to the disclosure and, if so requested, consult with the transmitting State Party. If, in an exceptional case, advance notice is not possible, the receiving State Party shall inform the transmitting State Party of the disclosure without delay.

6. The provisions of this article shall not affect the obligations under any other treaty, bilateral or multi-lateral, that governs or will govern, in whole or in part, mutual legal assistance.
7. Paragraphs 9 to 29 of this article shall apply to requests made pursuant to this article if the States Parties in question are not bound by a treaty of mutual legal assistance. If those States Parties are bound by such a treaty, the corresponding provisions of that treaty shall apply unless the States Parties agree to apply paragraphs 9 to 29 of this article in lieu thereof. States Parties are strongly encouraged to apply these paragraphs if they facilitate cooperation.
8. States Parties shall not decline to render mutual legal assistance pursuant to this article on the ground of bank secrecy.
9. States Parties may decline to render mutual legal assistance pursuant to this article on the ground of absence of dual criminality. However, the requested State Party may, when it deems appropriate, provide assistance, to the extent it decides at its discretion, irrespective of whether the conduct would constitute an offence under the domestic law of the requested State Party.
10. A person who is being detained or is serving a sentence in the territory of one State Party whose presence in another State Party is requested for purposes of identification, testimony or otherwise providing assistance in obtaining evidence for investigations, prosecutions or judicial proceedings in relation to offences covered by this Convention may be transferred if the following conditions are met:
    (*a*) The person freely gives his or her informed consent;
    (*b*) The competent authorities of both States Parties agree, subject to such conditions as those States Parties may deem appropriate.
11. For the purposes of paragraph 10 of this article:
    (*a*) The State Party to which the person is transferred shall have the authority and obligation to keep the person transferred in custody, unless otherwise requested or authorized by the State Party from which the person was transferred;

(*b*) The State Party to which the person is transferred shall without delay implement its obligation to return the person to the custody of the State Party from which the person was transferred as agreed beforehand, or as otherwise agreed, by the competent authorities of both States Parties;

(*c*) The State Party to which the person is transferred shall not require the State Party from which the person was transferred to initiate extradition proceedings for the return of the person; and

(*d*) The person transferred shall receive credit for service of the sentence being served in the State from which he or she was transferred for time spent in the custody of the State Party to which he or she was transferred.

12. Unless the State Party from which a person is to be transferred in accordance with paragraphs 10 and 11 of this article so agrees, that person, whatever his or her nationality, shall not be prosecuted, detained, punished or subjected to any other restriction of his or her personal liberty in the territory of the State to which that person is transferred in respect of acts, omissions or convictions prior to his or her departure from the territory of the State from which he or she was transferred.

13. Each State Party shall designate a central authority that shall have the responsibility and power to receive requests for mutual legal assistance and either to execute them or to transmit them to the competent authorities for execution. Where a State Party has a special region or territory with a separate system of mutual legal assistance, it may designate a distinct central authority that shall have the same function for that region or territory. Central authorities shall ensure the speedy and proper execution or transmission of the requests received. Where the central authority transmits the request to a competent authority for execution, it shall encourage the speedy and proper execution of the request by the competent authority. The Secretary-General of the United Nations shall be notified of the central authority designated for this purpose at the time each State Party deposits its instrument of ratification, acceptance or approval of or accession to this Convention. Requests for

mutual legal assistance and any communication related thereto shall be transmitted to the central authorities designated by the States Parties. This requirement shall be without prejudice to the right of a State Party to require that such requests and communications be addressed to it through diplomatic channels and, in urgent circumstances, where the States Parties agree, through the International Criminal Police Organisation, if possible.

14. Requests shall be made in writing or, where possible, by any means capable of producing a written record, in a language acceptable to the requested State Party, under conditions allowing that State Party to establish authenticity. The Secretary-General of the United Nations shall be notified of the language or languages acceptable to each State Party at the time it deposits its instrument of ratification, acceptance or approval of or accession to this Convention. In urgent circumstances and where agreed by the States Parties, requests may be made orally, but shall be confirmed in writing forthwith.

15. A request for mutual legal assistance shall contain:
    (*a*) the identity of the authority making the request;
    (*b*) the subject matter and nature of the investigation, prosecution or judicial proceeding to which the request relates and the name and functions of the authority conducting the investigation, prosecution or judicial proceeding;
    (*c*) a summary of the relevant facts, except in relation to requests for the purpose of service of judicial documents;
    (*d*) a description of the assistance sought and details of any particular procedure that the requesting State Party wishes to be followed;
    (*e*) where possible, the identity, location and nationality of any person concerned; and
    (*f*) the purpose for which the evidence, information or action is sought.

16. The requested State Party may request additional information when it appears necessary for the execution of the request in accordance with its domestic law or when it can facilitate such execution.

17. A request shall be executed in accordance with the domestic law of the requested State Party and, to the extent not contrary to the domestic law of the requested State Party and where possible, in accordance with the procedures specified in the request.
18. Wherever possible and consistent with fundamental principles of domestic law, when an individual is in the territory of a State Party and has to be heard as a witness or expert by the judicial authorities of another State Party, the first State Party may, at the request of the other, permit the hearing to take place by video conference if it is not possible or desirable for the individual in question to appear in person in the territory of the requesting State Party. States Parties may agree that the hearing shall be conducted by a judicial authority of the requesting State Party and attended by a judicial authority of the requested State Party.
19. The requesting State Party shall not transmit or use information or evidence furnished by the requested State Party for investigations, prosecutions or judicial proceedings other than those stated in the request without the prior consent of the requested State Party. Nothing in this paragraph shall prevent the requesting State Party from disclosing in its proceedings information or evidence that is exculpatory to an accused person. In the latter case, the requesting State Party shall notify the requested State Party prior to the disclosure and, if so requested, consult with the requested State Party. If, in an exceptional case, advance notice is not possible, the requesting State Party shall inform the requested State Party of the disclosure without delay.
20. The requesting State Party may require that the requested State Party keep confidential the fact and substance of the request, except to the extent necessary to execute the request. If the requested State Party cannot comply with the requirement of confidentiality, it shall promptly inform the requesting State Party.
21. Mutual legal assistance maybe refused:
    (*a*) if the request is not made in conformity with the provisions of this article;
    (*b*) if the requested State Party considers that execution of

the request is likely to prejudice its sovereignty, security, *ordre public* or other essential interests;

(*c*) if the authorities of the requested State Party would be prohibited by its domestic law from carrying out the action requested with regard to any similar offence, had it been subject to investigation, prosecution or judicial proceedings under their own jurisdiction; and

(*d*) if it would be contrary to the legal system of the requested State Party relating to mutual legal assistance for the request to be granted.

22. States Parties may not refuse a request for mutual legal assistance on the sole ground that the offence is also considered to involve fiscal matters.
23. Reasons shall be given for any refusal of mutual legal assistance.
24. The requested State Party shall execute the request for mutual legal assistance as soon as possible and shall take as full account as possible of any deadlines suggested by the requesting State Party and for which reasons are given, preferably in the request. The requested State Party shall respond to reasonable requests by the requesting State Party on progress of its handling of the request. The requesting State Party shall promptly inform the requested State Party when the assistance sought is no longer required.
25. Mutual legal assistance may be postponed by the requested State Party on the ground that it interferes with an ongoing investigation, prosecution or judicial proceeding.
26. Before refusing a request pursuant to paragraph 21 of this article or postponing its execution pursuant to paragraph 25 of this article, the requested State Party shall consult with the requesting State Party to consider whether assistance may be granted subject to such terms and conditions as it deems necessary. If the requesting State Party accepts assistance subject to those conditions, it shall comply with the conditions.
27. Without prejudice to the application of paragraph 12 of this article, a witness, expert or other person who, at the request of the requesting State Party, consents to give evidence in a proceeding or to assist in an investigation, prosecution or judicial proceeding in the territory of the requesting State

Party shall not be prosecuted, detained, punished or subjected to any other restriction of his or her personal liberty in that territory in respect of acts, omissions or convictions prior to his or her departure from the territory of the requested State Party. Such safe conduct shall cease when the witness, expert or other person having had, for a period of fifteen consecutive days or for any period agreed upon by the States Parties from the date on which he or she has been officially informed that his or her presence is no longer required by the judicial authorities, an opportunity of leaving, has nevertheless remained voluntarily in the territory of the requesting State Party or, having left it, has returned of his or her own free will.

28. The ordinary costs of executing a request shall be borne by the requested State Party, unless otherwise agreed by the States Parties concerned. If expenses of a substantial or extraordinary nature are or will be required to fulfil the request, the States Parties shall consult to determine the terms and conditions under which the request will be executed, as well as the manner in which the costs shall be borne.

29. The requested State Party:
    (*a*) shall provide to the requesting State Party copies of government records, documents or information in its possession that under its domestic law are available to the general public; and
    (*b*) may, at its discretion, provide to the requesting State Party in whole, in part or subject to such conditions as it deems appropriate, copies of any government records, documents or information in its possession that under its domestic law are not available to the general public.

30. States Parties shall consider, as may be necessary, the possibility of concluding bilateral or multi-lateral agreements or arrangements that would serve the purposes of, give practical effect to or enhance the provisions of this article.

Article 19: *Joint Investigations*

States Parties shall consider concluding bilateral or multi-lateral agreements or arrangements whereby, in relation to matters that are the subject of investigations, prosecutions or judicial proceedings in one or more States, the competent authorities concerned may establish joint investigative bodies. In the absence of such agreements or arrangements, joint investigations may be undertaken by agreement on a case-by-case basis. The States Parties involved shall ensure that the sovereignty of the State Party in whose territory such investigation is to take place is fully respected.

Article 20: *Special Investigative Techniques*

1. If permitted by the basic principles of its domestic legal system, each State Party shall, within its possibilities and under the conditions prescribed by its domestic law, take the necessary measures to allow for the appropriate use of controlled delivery and, where it deems appropriate, for the use of other special investigative techniques, such as electronic or other forms of surveillance and undercover operations, by its competent authorities in its territory for the purpose of effectively combating organized crime.
2. For the purpose of investigating the offences covered by this Convention, States Parties are encouraged to conclude, when necessary, appropriate bilateral or multi-lateral agreements or arrangements for using such special investigative techniques in the context of cooperation at the international level. Such agreements or arrangements shall be concluded and implemented in full compliance with the principle of sovereign equality of States and shall be carried out strictly in accordance with the terms of those agreements or arrangements.
3. In the absence of an agreement or arrangement as set forth in paragraph 2 of this article, decisions to use such special investigative techniques at the international level shall be made on a case-by-case basis and may, when necessary, take into consideration financial arrangements and understandings with respect to the exercise of jurisdiction by the States Parties concerned.
4. Decisions to use controlled delivery at the international level may, with the consent of the States Parties concerned, include methods such as intercepting and allowing the goods to continue intact or be removed or replaced in whole or in part.

Article 21: *Transfer of Criminal Proceedings*

States Parties shall consider the possibility of transferring to one another proceedings for the prosecution of an offence covered by this Convention in cases where such transfer is considered to be in the interests of the proper administration of justice, in particular in cases where several jurisdictions are involved, with a view to concentrating the prosecution.

Article 22: *Establishment of Criminal Record*

Each State Party may adopt such legislative or other measures as may be necessary to take into consideration, under such terms as and for the purpose that it deems appropriate, any previous conviction in another State of an alleged offender for the purpose of using such information in criminal proceedings relating to an offence covered by this Convention.

Article 23: *Criminalization of Obstruction of Justice*

Each State Party shall adopt such legislative and other measures as may be necessary to establish as criminal offences, when committed intentionally:

(*a*) the use of physical force, threats or intimidation or the promise, offering or giving of an undue advantage to induce false testimony or to interfere in the giving of testimony or the production of evidence in a proceeding in relation to the commission of offences covered by this Convention; and

(*b*) the use of physical force, threats or intimidation to interfere with the exercise of official duties by a justice or law enforcement official in relation to the commission of offences covered by this Convention. Nothing in this sub-paragraph shall prejudice the right of States Parties to have legislation that protects other categories of public officials.

Article 24: *Protection of Witnesses*

1. Each State Party shall take appropriate measures within its means to provide effective protection from potential retaliation or intimidation for witnesses in criminal

proceedings who give testimony concerning offences covered by this Convention and, as appropriate, for their relatives and other persons close to them.

2. The measures envisaged in paragraph 1 of this article may include, *inter alia*, without prejudice to the rights of the defendant, including the right to due process:
   (*a*) Establishing procedures for the physical protection of such persons, such as, to the extent necessary and feasible, relocating them and permitting, where appropriate, non-disclosure or limitations on the disclosure of information concerning the identity and whereabouts of such persons; and
   (*b*) Providing evidentiary rules to permit witness testimony to be given in a manner that ensures the safety of the witness, such as permitting testimony to be given through the use of communications technology such as video links or other adequate means.
3. States Parties shall consider entering into agreements or arrangements with other States for the relocation of persons referred to in paragraph 1 of this article.
4. The provisions of this article shall also apply to victims insofar as they are witnesses.

Article 25: *Assistance to and Protection of Victims*

1. Each State Party shall take appropriate measures within its means to provide assistance and protection to victims of offences covered by this Convention, in particular in cases of threat of retaliation or intimidation.
2. Each State Party shall establish appropriate procedures to provide access to compensation and restitution for victims of offences covered by this Convention.
3. Each State Party shall, subject to its domestic law, enable views and concerns of victims to be presented and considered at appropriate stages of criminal proceedings against offenders in a manner not prejudicial to the rights of the defence.

Article 26: *Measures to Enhance Cooperation with Law Enforcement Authorities*

1. Each State Party shall take appropriate measures to

encourage persons who participate or who have participated in organized criminal groups:

(*a*) To supply information useful to competent authorities for investigative and evidentiary purposes on such matters as:

(*i*) The identity, nature, composition, structure, location or activities of organized criminal groups;

(*ii*) Links, including international links, with other organized criminal groups; and

(*iii*) Offences that organized criminal groups have committed or may commit.

(*b*) To provide factual, concrete help to competent authorities that may contribute to depriving organized criminal groups of their resources or of the proceeds of crime.

2. Each State Party shall consider providing for the possibility, in appropriate cases, of mitigating punishment of an accused person who provides substantial cooperation in the investigation or prosecution of an offence covered by this Convention.
3. Each State Party shall consider providing for the possibility, in accordance with fundamental principles of its domestic law, of granting immunity from prosecution to a person who provides substantial cooperation in the investigation or prosecution of an offence covered by this Convention.
4. Protection of such persons shall be as provided for in Article 24 of this Convention.
5. Where a person referred to in paragraph 1 of this article located in one State Party can provide substantial cooperation to the competent authorities of another State Party, the States Parties concerned may consider entering into agreements or arrangements, in accordance with their domestic law, concerning the potential provision by the other State Party of the treatment set forth in paragraphs 2 and 3 of this article.

Article 27: Law Enforcement Cooperation

1. States Parties shall cooperate closely with one another, consistent with their respective domestic legal and administrative systems, to enhance the effectiveness of law

enforcement action to combat the offences covered by this Convention. Each State Party shall, in particular, adopt effective measures:

(*a*) To enhance and, where necessary, to establish channels of communication between their competent authorities, agencies and services in order to facilitate the secure and rapid exchange of information concerning all aspects of the offences covered by this Convention, including, if the States Parties concerned deem it appropriate, links with other criminal activities;

(*b*) To cooperate with other States Parties in conducting inquiries with respect to offences covered by this Convention concerning:

(*i*) The identity, whereabouts and activities of persons suspected of involvement in such offences or the location of other persons concerned;

(*ii*) The movement of proceeds of crime or property derived from the commission of such offences;

(*iii*) The movement of property, equipment or other instrumentalities used or intended for use in the commission of such offences;

(*c*) To provide, when appropriate, necessary items or quantities of substances for analytical or investigative purposes;

(*d*) To facilitate effective coordination between their competent authorities, agencies and services and to promote the exchange of personnel and other experts, including, subject to bilateral agreements or arrangements between the States Parties concerned, the posting of liaison officers;

(*e*) To exchange information with other States Parties on specific means and methods used by organized criminal groups, including, where applicable, routes and conveyances and the use of false identities, altered or false documents or other means of concealing their activities; and

(*f*) To exchange information and coordinate administrative and other measures taken as appropriate for the purpose of early identification of the offences covered by this Convention.

2. With a view to giving effect to this Convention, States Parties shall consider entering into bilateral or multi-lateral agreements or arrangements on direct cooperation between their law enforcement agencies and, where such agreements or arrangements already exist, amending them. In the absence of such agreements or arrangements between the States Parties concerned, the Parties may consider this Convention as the basis for mutual law enforcement cooperation in respect of the offences covered by this Convention. Whenever appropriate, States Parties shall make full use of agreements or arrangements, including international or regional organisations, to enhance the cooperation between their law enforcement agencies.
3. States Parties shall endeavour to cooperate within their means to respond to transnational organized crime committed through the use of modem technology.

Article 28: *Collection, Exchange and Analysis of Information on the Nature of Organized Crime*

1. Each State Party shall consider analysing, in consultation with the scientific and academic communities, trends in organized crime in its territory, the circumstances in which organized crime operates, as well as the professional groups and technologies involved.
2. States Parties shall consider developing and sharing analytical expertise concerning organized criminal activities with each other and through international and regional organisations. For that purpose, common definitions, standards and methodologies should be developed and applied as appropriate.
3. Each State Party shall consider monitoring its policies and actual measures to combat organized crime and making assessments of their effectiveness and efficiency.

Article 29: *Training and Technical Assistance*

1. Each State Party shall, to the extent necessary, initiate, develop or improve specific training programmes for its law enforcement personnel, including prosecutors, investigating magistrates and customs personnel, and other

personnel charged with the prevention, detection and control of the offences covered by this Convention. Such programmes may include secondments and exchanges of staff. Such programmes shall deal, in particular and to the extent permitted by domestic law, with the following:

(*a*) Methods used in the prevention, detection and control of the offences covered by this Convention;

(*b*) Routes and techniques used by persons suspected of involvement in offences covered by this Convention, including in transit States, and appropriate countermeasures;

(*c*) Monitoring of the movement of contraband;

(*d*) Detection and monitoring of the movements of proceeds of crime, property, equipment or other instrumentalities and methods used for the transfer, concealment or disguise of such proceeds, property, equipment or other instrumentalities, as well as methods used in combating money-laundering and other financial crimes;

(*e*) Collection of evidence;

(*f*) Control techniques in free trade zones and free ports;

(*g*) Modern law enforcement equipment and techniques, including electronic surveillance, controlled deliveries and undercover operations;

(*h*) Methods used in combating transnational organized crime committed through the use of computers, telecommunications networks or other forms of modern technology; and

(*i*) Methods used in the protection of victims and witnesses.

2. States Parties shall assist one another in planning and implementing research and training programmes designed to share expertise in the areas referred to in paragraph 1 of this article and to that end shall also, when appropriate, use regional and international conferences and seminars to promote cooperation and to stimulate discussion on problems of mutual concern, including the special problems and needs of transit States.

3. States Parties shall promote training and technical assistance that will facilitate extradition and mutual legal

assistance. Such training and technical assistance may include language training, secondments and exchanges between personnel in central authorities or agencies with relevant responsibilities.

4. In the case of existing bilateral and multi-lateral agreements or arrangements. States Parties shall strengthen, to the extent necessary, efforts to maximize operational and training activities within international and regional organisations and within other relevant bilateral and multi-lateral agreements or arrangements.

Article 30: *Other Measures—Implementation of the Convention through Economic Development and Technical Assistance*

1. States Parties shall take measures conducive to the optimal implementation of this Convention to the extent possible, through international cooperation, taking into account the negative effects of organized crime on society in general, in particular on sustainable development.
2. States Parties shall make concrete efforts to the extent possible and in coordination with each other, as well as with international and regional organisations:
   (*a*) To enhance their cooperation at various levels with developing countries, with a view to strengthening the capacity of the latter to prevent and combat transnational organised crime;
   (*b*) To enhance financial and material assistance to support the efforts of developing countries to fight transnational organized crime effectively and to help them implement this Convention successfully;
   (*c*) To provide technical assistance to developing countries and countries with economies in transition to assist them in meeting their needs for the implementation of this Convention. To that end, States Parties shall endeavour to make adequate and regular voluntary contributions to an account specifically designated for that purpose in a United Nations funding mechanism. States Parties may also give special consideration, in accordance with their domestic law and the provisions of this Convention, to contributing to the

aforementioned account a percentage of the money or of the corresponding value of proceeds of crime or property confiscated in accordance with the provisions of this Convention;

(*d*) To encourage and persuade other States and financial institutions as appropriate to join them in efforts in accordance with this article, in particular by providing more training programmes and modern equipment to developing countries in order to assist them in achieving the objectives of this Convention.

3. To the extent possible, these measures shall be without prejudice to existing foreign assistance commitments or to other financial cooperation arrangements at the bilateral, regional or international level.
4. States Parties may conclude bilateral or multi-lateral agreements or arrangements on material and logistical assistance, taking into consideration the financial arrangements necessary for the means of international cooperation provided for by this Convention to be effective and for the prevention, detection and control of transnational organized crime.

Article 31: *Prevention*

1. States Parties shall endeavour to develop and evaluate national projects and to establish and promote best practices and policies aimed at the prevention of transnational organized crime.
2. States Parties shall endeavour, in accordance with fundamental principles of their domestic law, to reduce existing or future opportunities for organized criminal groups to participate in lawful markets with proceeds of crime, through appropriate legislative, administrative or other measures. These measures should focus on:

(*a*) The strengthening of cooperation between law enforcement agencies or prosecutors and relevant private entities, including industry;

(*b*) The promotion of the development of standards and procedures designed to safeguard the integrity of public and relevant private entities, as well as codes of conduct for relevant professions, in particular lawyers, notaries public, tax consultants and accountants;

(*c*) The prevention of the misuse by organized criminal groups of tender procedures conducted by public authorities and of subsidies and licences granted by public authorities for commercial activity;

(*d*) The prevention of the misuse of legal persons by organized criminal groups; such measures could include:

(*i*) The establishment of public records on legal and natural persons involved in the establishment, management and funding of legal persons;

(*ii*) The introduction of the possibility of disqualifying by court order or any appropriate means for a reasonable period of time persons convicted of offences covered by this Convention from acting as directors of legal persons incorporated within their jurisdiction;

(*iii*) The establishment of national records of persons disqualified from acting as directors of legal persons; and

(*iv*) The exchange of information contained in the records referred to in sub-paragraphs (*d*) (*i*) and (*iii*) of this paragraph with the competent authorities of other States Parties.

3. States Parties shall endeavour to promote the reintegration into society of persons convicted of offences covered by this Convention.
4. States Parties shall endeavour to evaluate periodically existing relevant legal instruments and administrative practices with a view to detecting their vulnerability to misuse by organized criminal groups.
5. States Parties shall endeavour to promote public awareness regarding the existence, causes and gravity of and the threat posed by transnational organized crime. Information may be disseminated where appropriate through the mass media and shall include measures to promote public participation in preventing and combating such crime.
6. Each State Party shall inform the Secretary-General of the United Nations of the name and address of the authority or

authorities that can assist other States Parties in developing measures to prevent transnational organised crime.

7. States Parties shall, as appropriate, collaborate with each other and relevant international and regional organisations in promoting and developing the measures referred to in this article. This includes participation in international projects aimed at the prevention of transnational organized crime, for example by alleviating the circumstances that render socially marginalized groups vulnerable to the action of transnational organized crime.

Article 32: *Conference of the Parties to the Convention*

1. A Conference of the Parties to the Convention is hereby established to improve the capacity of States Parties to combat transnational organized crime and to promote and review the implementation of this Convention.
2. The Secretary-General of the United Nations shall convene the Conference of the Parties not later than one year following the entry into force of this Convention. The Conference of the Parties shall adopt rules of procedure and rules governing the activities set forth in paragraphs 3 and 4 of this article (including rules concerning payment of expenses incurred in carrying out those activities).
3. The Conference of the Parties shall agree upon mechanisms for achieving the objectives mentioned in paragraph 1 of this article, including:
   (*a*) Facilitating activities by States Parties under Articles 29, 30 and 31 of this Convention, including by encouraging the mobilization of voluntary contributions;
   (*b*) Facilitating the exchange of information among States Parties on patterns and trends in transnational organized crime and on successful practices for combating it;
   (*c*) Cooperating with relevant international and regional organisations and non-governmental organisations;
   (*d*) Reviewing periodically the implementation of this Convention; and
   (*e*) Making recommendations to improve this Convention and its implementation.

4. For the purpose of paragraphs 3 (*d*) and (*e*) of this article, the Conference of the Parties shall acquire the necessary knowledge of the measures taken by States Parties in implementing this Convention and the difficulties encountered by them in doing so through information provided by them and through such supplemental review mechanisms as may be established by the Conference of the Parties.
5. Each State Party shall provide the Conference of the Parties with information on its programmes, plans and practices, as well as legislative and administrative measures to implement this Convention, as required by the Conference of the Parties.

Article 33: *Secretariat*

1. The Secretary-General of the United Nations shall provide the necessary secretariat services to the Conference of the Parties to the Convention.
2. The Secretariat shall:
   (*a*) Assist the Conference of the Parties in carrying out the activities set forth in Article 32 of this Convention and make arrangements and provide the necessary services for the sessions of the Conference of the Parties;
   (*b*) Upon request, assist States Parties in providing information to the Conference of the Parties as envisaged in Article 32, paragraph 5, of this Convention; and
   (*c*) Ensure the necessary coordination with the secretariats of relevant international and regional organisations.

Article 34: *Implementation of the Convention*

1. Each State Party shall take the necessary measures, including legislative and administrative measures, in accordance with fundamental principles of its domestic law, to ensure the implementation of its obligations under this Convention.
2. The offences established in accordance with Articles 5, 6, 8 and 23 of this Convention shall be established in the domestic law of each State Party independently of the transnational

nature or the involvement of an organized criminal group as described in Article 3, paragraph 1, of this Convention, except to the extent that Article 5 of this Convention would require the involvement of an organized criminal group.

3. Each State Party may adopt more strict or severe measures than those provided for by this Convention for preventing and combating transnational organized crime.

Article 35: *Settlement of Disputes*

1. States Parties shall endeavour to settle disputes concerning the interpretation or application of this Convention through negotiation.
2. Any dispute between two or more States Parties concerning the interpretation or application of this Convention that cannot be settled through negotiation within a reasonable time shall, at the request of one of those States Parties, be submitted to arbitration. If, six months after the date of the request for arbitration, those States Parties are unable to agree on the organization of the arbitration, anyone of those States Parties may refer the dispute to the International Court of Justice by request in accordance with the Statute of the Court.
3. Each State Party may, at the time of signature, ratification, acceptance or approval of or accession to this Convention, declare that it does not consider itself bound by paragraph 2 of this article. The other States Parties shall not be bound by paragraph 2 of this article with respect to any State Party that has made such a reservation.
4. Any State Party that has made a reservation in accordance with paragraph 3 of this article may at any time withdraw that reservation by notification to the Secretary-General of the United Nations.

Article 36: *Signature, Ratification, Acceptance, Approval and Accession*

1. This Convention shall be open to all States for signature from 12 to 15 December, 2000 in Palermo, Italy, and thereafter at United Nations Headquarters in New York until 12 December, 2002.

2. This Convention shall also be open for signature by regional economic integration organisations provided that at least one member State of such organisation has signed this Convention in accordance with paragraph 1 of this article.
3. This Convention is subject to ratification, acceptance or approval. Instruments of ratification, acceptance or approval shall be deposited with the Secretary-General of the United Nations. A regional economic integration organisation may deposit its instrument of ratification, acceptance or approval if at least one of its member States has done likewise. In that instrument of ratification, acceptance or approval, such organisation shall declare the extent of its competence with respect to the matters governed by this Convention. Such organisation shall also inform the depositary of any relevant modification in the extent of its competence.
4. This Convention is open for accession by any State or any regional economic integration organisation of which at least one member State is a Party to this Convention. Instruments of accession shall be deposited with the Secretary-General of the United Nations. At the time of its accession, a regional economic integration organisation shall declare the extent of its competence with respect to matters governed by this Convention. Such organisation shall also inform the depositary of any relevant modification in the extent of its competence.

Article 37: Relation with Protocols

1. This Convention may be supplemented by one or more protocols.
2. In order to become a Party to a protocol, a State or a regional economic integration organisation must also be a Party to this Convention.
3. A State Party to this Convention is not bound by a protocol unless it becomes a Party to the protocol in accordance with the provisions thereof.
4. Any protocol to this Convention shall be interpreted together with this Convention, taking into account the purpose of that protocol.

Article 38: *Entry into Force*

1. This Convention shall enter into force on the ninetieth day after the date of deposit of the fortieth instrument of ratification, acceptance, approval or accession. For the purpose of this paragraph, any instrument deposited by a regional economic integration organisation shall not be counted as additional to those deposited by member States of such organisation.
2. For each State or regional economic integration organization ratifying, accepting, approving or acceding to this Convention after the deposit of the fortieth instrument of such action, this Convention shall enter into force on the thirtieth day after the date of deposit by such State or organization of the relevant instrument.

Article 39: *Amendment*

1. After the expiry of five years from the entry into force of this Convention, a State Party may propose an amendment and file it with the Secretary-General of the United Nations, who shall thereupon communicate the proposed amendment to the States Parties and to the Conference of the Parties to the Convention for the purpose of considering and deciding on the proposal. The Conference of the Parties shall make every effort to achieve consensus on each amendment. If all efforts at consensus have been exhausted and no agreement has been reached, the amendment shall, as a last resort, require for its adoption a two-thirds majority vote of the States Parties present and voting at the meeting of the Conference of the Parties.
2. Regional economic integration organisations, in matters within their competence, shall exercise their right to vote under this article with a number of votes equal to the number of their member States that are Parties to this Convention. Such organisations shall not exercise their right to vote if their member States exercise theirs and *vice versa*.
3. An amendment adopted in accordance with paragraph 1 of this article is subject to ratification, acceptance or approval by States Parties.

4. An amendment adopted in accordance with paragraph 1 of this article shall enter into force in respect of a State Party ninety days after the date of the deposit with the Secretary-General of the United Nations of an instrument of ratification, acceptance or approval of such amendment.
5. When an amendment enters into force, it shall be binding on those States Parties which have expressed their consent to be bound by it. Other States Parties shall still be bound by the provisions of this Convention and any earlier amendments that they have ratified, accepted or approved.

Article 40: *Denunciation*

1. A State Party may denounce this Convention by written notification to the Secretary-General of the United Nations. Such denunciation shall become effective one year after the date of receipt of the notification by the Secretary-General.
2. A regional economic integration organisation shall cease to be a Party to this Convention when all of its member States have denounced it.
3. Denunciation of this Convention in accordance with paragraph 1 of this article shall entail the denunciation of any protocols thereto.

Article 41: *Depositary and Languages*

1. The Secretary-General of the United Nations is designated depositary of this Convention.
2. The original of this Convention, of which the Arabic, Chinese, English, French, Russian and Spanish texts are equally authentic, shall be deposited with the Secretary-General of the United Nations.

In Witness Whereof, the undersigned plenipotentiaries, being duly authorized thereto by their respective Governments, have signed this Convention.

ANNEXURE II

Protocol to Prevent, Suppress and Punish Trafficking in Persons, Especially Women and Children, Supplementing the United Nations Convention against Transnational Organized Crime

Preamble

The States Parties to this Protocol

Declaring that effective action to prevent and combat trafficking in persons, especially women and children, requires a comprehensive international approach in the countries of origin, transit and destination that includes measures to prevent such trafficking, to punish the traffickers and to protect the victims of such trafficking, including by protecting their internationally recognized human rights.

Taking into account the fact that, despite the existence of a variety of international instruments containing rules and practical measures to combat the exploitation of persons, especially women and children, there is no universal instrument that addresses all aspects of trafficking in persons.

Concerned that, in the absence of such an instrument, persons who are vulnerable to trafficking will not be sufficiently protected.

Recalling General Assembly resolution 53/111 of 9 December, 1998, in which the Assembly decided to establish an open-ended inter-governmental Ad Hoc Committee for the purpose of elaborating a comprehensive international convention against transnational organized crime and of discussing the elaboration of, *inter alia*, an international instrument addressing trafficking in women and children.

Convinced that supplementing the United Nations Convention against Transnational Organized Crime with an international instrument for the prevention, suppression and punishment of trafficking in persons, especially women and children, will be useful in preventing and combating that crime.

Have agreed as follows:

I. *General Provisions*

Article 1: *Relation with the United Nations Convention against Transnational Organized Crime*

1. This Protocol supplements the United Nations Convention

against Transnational Organized Crime. It shall be interpreted together with the Convention.

2. The provisions of the Convention shall apply, *mutatis mutandis*, to this Protocol unless otherwise provided herein.
3. The offences established in accordance with Article 5 of this Protocol shall be regarded as offences established in accordance with the Convention.

Article 2: Statement of Purpose

The purposes of this Protocol are:

(*a*) to prevent and combat trafficking in persons, paying particular attention to women and children;
(*b*) to protect and assist the victims of such trafficking, with full respect for their human rights; and
(*c*) to promote cooperation among States Parties in order to meet those objectives.

Article 3: Use of Terms

For the purposes of this Protocol:

(*a*) "Trafficking in persons" shall mean the recruitment, transportation, transfer, harbouring or receipt of persons, by means of the threat or use of force or other forms of coercion, of abduction, of fraud, of deception, of the abuse of power or of a position of vulnerability or of the giving or receiving of payments or benefits to achieve the consent of a person having control over another person, for the purpose of exploitation. Exploitation shall include, at a minimum, the exploitation of the prostitution of others or other forms of sexual exploitation, forced labour or services, slavery or practices similar to slavery, servitude or the removal of organs;
(*b*) The consent of a victim of trafficking in persons to the intended exploitation set forth in sub-paragraph (*a*) of this article shall be irrelevant where any of the means set forth in sub-paragraph (*a*) have been used;
(*c*) The recruitment, transportation, transfer, harbouring or

receipt of a child for the purpose of exploitation shall be considered "trafficking in persons" even if this does not involve any of the means set forth in sub-paragraph (*a*) of this article; and

(*d*) "Child" shall mean any person under eighteen years of age.

Article 4: *Scope of Application*

This Protocol shall apply, except as otherwise stated herein, to the prevention, investigation and prosecution of the offences established in accordance with Article 5 of this Protocol, where those offences are transnational in nature and involve an organized criminal group, as well as to the protection of victims of such offences.

Article 5: *Criminalization*

1. Each State Party shall adopt such legislative and other measures as may be necessary to establish as criminal offences the conduct set forth in Article 3 of this Protocol, when committed intentionally.
2. Each State Party shall also adopt such legislative and other measures as may be necessary to establish as criminal offences:
   (*a*) Subject to the basic concepts of its legal system, attempting to commit an offence established in accordance with paragraph 1 of this article;
   (*b*) Participating as an accomplice in an offence established in accordance with paragraph 1 of this article; and
   (*c*) Organizing or directing other persons to commit an offence established in accordance with paragraph 1 of this article.

II. ***Protection of Victims of Trafficking in Persons***

Article 6: *Assistance to and Protection of Victims of Trafficking in Persons*

1. In appropriate cases and to the extent possible under its domestic law, each State Party shall protect the privacy and identity of victims of trafficking in persons, including,

inter alia, by making legal proceedings relating to such trafficking confidential.

2. Each State Party shall ensure that its domestic legal or administrative system contains measures that provide to victims of trafficking in persons, in appropriate cases:
   (*a*) Information on relevant court and administrative proceedings; and
   (*b*) Assistance to enable their views and concerns to be presented and considered at appropriate stages of criminal proceedings against offenders, in a manner not prejudicial to the rights of the defence.
3. Each State Party shall consider implementing measures to provide for the physical, psychological and social recovery of victims of trafficking in persons, including, in appropriate cases, in cooperation with non-governmental organisations, other relevant organisations and other elements of civil society, and, in particular, the provision of:
   (*a*) Appropriate housing;
   (*b*) Counselling and information, in particular as regards their legal rights, in a language that the victims of trafficking in persons can understand;
   (*c*) Medical, psychological and material assistance; and
   (*d*) Employment, educational and training opportunities.
4. Each State Party shall take into account, in applying the provisions of this article, the age, gender and special needs of victims of trafficking in persons, in particular the special needs of children, including appropriate housing, education and care.
5. Each State Party shall endeavour to provide for the physical safety of victims of trafficking in persons while they are within its territory.
6. Each State Party shall ensure that its domestic legal system contains measures that offer victims of trafficking in persons the possibility of obtaining compensation for damage suffered.

Article 7: Status of Victims of Trafficking in Persons in Receiving States

1. In addition to taking measures pursuant to Article 6 of this Protocol, each State Party shall consider adopting

legislative or other appropriate measures that permit victims of trafficking in persons to remain in its territory, temporarily or permanently, in appropriate cases.

2. In implementing the provision contained in paragraph 1 of this article, each State Party shall give appropriate consideration to humanitarian and compassionate factors.

Article 8: *Repatriation of Victims of Trafficking in Persons*

1. The State Party of which a victim of trafficking in persons is a national or in which the person had the right of permanent residence at the time of entry into the territory of the receiving State Party shall facilitate and accept, with due regard for the safety of that person, the return of that person without undue or unreasonable delay.
2. When a State Party returns a victim of trafficking in persons to a State Party of which that person is a national or in which he or she had, at the time of entry into the territory of the receiving State Party, the right of permanent residence, such return shall be with due regard for the safety of that person and for the status of any legal proceedings related to the fact that the person is a victim of trafficking and shall preferably be voluntary.
3. At the request of a receiving State Party, a requested State Party shall, without undue or unreasonable delay, verify whether a person who is a victim of trafficking in persons is its national or had the right of permanent residence in its territory at the time of entry into the territory of the receiving State Party.
4. In order to facilitate the return of a victim of trafficking in persons who is without proper documentation, the State Party of which that person is a national or in which he or she had the right of permanent residence at the time of entry into the territory of the receiving State Party shall agree to issue, at the request of the receiving State Party, such travel documents or other authorization as may be necessary to enable the person to travel to and re-enter its territory.
5. This article shall be without prejudice to any right afforded to victims of trafficking in persons by any domestic law of the receiving State Party.

6. This article shall be without prejudice to any applicable bilateral or multi-lateral agreement or arrangement that governs, in whole or in part, the return of victims of trafficking in persons.

III. *Prevention, Cooperation and Other Measures*

Article 9: *Prevention of Trafficking in Persons*

1. States Parties shall establish comprehensive policies, programmes and other measures:
   (*a*) To prevent and combat trafficking in persons; and
   (*b*) To protect victims of trafficking in persons, especially women and children, from re-victimization.
2. States Parties shall endeavour to undertake measures such as research, information and mass media campaigns and social and economic initiatives to prevent and combat trafficking in persons.
3. Policies, programmes and other measures established in accordance with this article shall, as appropriate, include cooperation with non-governmental organisations, other relevant organisations and other elements of civil society.
4. States Parties shall take or strengthen measures, including through bilateral or multi-lateral cooperation, to alleviate the factors that make persons, especially women and children, vulnerable to trafficking, such as poverty, under-development and lack of equal opportunity.
5. States Parties shall adopt or strengthen legislative or other measures, such as educational, social or cultural measures, including through bilateral and multi-lateral cooperation, to discourage the demand that fosters all forms of exploitation of persons, especially women and children, that leads to trafficking.

Article 10: *Information Exchange and Training*

1. Law enforcement, immigration or other relevant authorities of States Parties shall, as appropriate, cooperate with one another by exchanging information, in accordance with their domestic law, to enable them to determine:
   (*a*) Whether individuals crossing or attempting to cross an international border with travel documents

belonging to other persons or without travel documents are perpetrators or victims of trafficking in persons;

(*b*) The types of travel document that individuals have used or attempted to use to cross an international border for the purpose of trafficking in persons; and

(*c*) The means and methods used by organized criminal groups for the purpose of trafficking in persons, including the recruitment and transportation of victims, routes and links between and among individuals and groups engaged in such trafficking, and possible measures for detecting them.

2. States Parties shall provide or strengthen training for law enforcement, immigration and other relevant officials in the prevention of trafficking in persons. The training should focus on methods used in preventing such trafficking, prosecuting the traffickers and protecting the rights of the victims, including protecting the victims from the traffickers. The training should also take into account the need to consider human rights and child-and gender-sensitive issues and it should encourage cooperation with non-governmental organisations, other relevant organisations and other elements of civil society.
3. A State Party that receives information shall comply with any request by the State Party that transmitted the information that places restrictions on its use.

Article 11: *Border Measures*

1. Without prejudice to international commitments in relation to the free movement of people. States Parties shall strengthen, to the extent possible, such border controls as may be necessary to prevent and detect trafficking in persons.
2. Each State Party shall adopt legislative or other appropriate measures to prevent, to the extent possible, means of transport operated by commercial carriers from being used in the commission of offences established in accordance with Article 5 of this Protocol.
3. Where appropriate, and without prejudice to applicable international conventions, such measures shall include establishing the obligation of commercial carriers,

including any transportation company or the owner or operator of any means of transport, to ascertain that all passengers are in possession of the travel documents required for entry into the receiving State.

4. Each State Party shall take the necessary measures, in accordance with its domestic law, to provide for sanctions in cases of violation of the obligation set forth in paragraph 3 of this article.
5. Each State Party shall consider taking measures that permit, in accordance with its domestic law, the denial of entry or revocation of visas of persons implicated in the commission of offences established in accordance with this Protocol.
6. Without prejudice to Article 27 of the Convention, States Parties shall consider strengthening cooperation among border control agencies by, *inter alia*, establishing and maintaining direct channels of communication.

Article 12: *Security and Control of Documents*

Each State Party shall take such measures as may be necessary, within available means:

(*a*) To ensure that travel or identity documents issued by it are of such quality that they cannot easily be misused and cannot readily be falsified or unlawfully altered, replicated or issued; and

(*b*) To ensure the integrity and security of travel or identity documents issued by or on behalf of the State Party and to prevent their unlawful creation, issuance and use.

Article 13: *Legitimacy and Validity of Documents*

At the request of another State Party, a State Party shall, in accordance with its domestic law, verify within a reasonable time the legitimacy and validity of travel or identity documents issued or purported to have been issued in its name and suspected of being used for trafficking in persons.

IV. ***Final Provisions***

Article 14: *Saving Clause*

1. Nothing in this Protocol shall affect the rights, obligations

and responsibilities of States and individuals under international law, including international humanitarian law and international human rights law and, in particular, where applicable, the 1951 Convention[1] and the 1967 Protocol[2] relating to the Status of Refugees and the principle of non-refoulement as contained therein.

2. The measures set forth in this Protocol shall be interpreted and applied in a way that is not discriminatory to persons on the ground that they are victims of trafficking in persons. The interpretation and application of those measures shall be consistent with internationally recognized principles of non-discrimination.

Article 15: *Settlement of Disputes*

1. States Parties shall endeavour to settle disputes concerning the interpretation or application of this Protocol through negotiation.
2. Any dispute between two or more States Parties concerning the interpretation or application of this Protocol that cannot be settled through negotiation within a reasonable time shall, at the request of one of those States Parties, be submitted to arbitration. If, six months after the date of the request for arbitration, those States Parties are unable to agree on the organisation of the arbitration, any one of those States Parties may refer the dispute to the International Court of Justice by request in accordance with the Statute of the Court.
3. Each State Party may, at the time of signature, ratification, acceptance or approval of or accession to this Protocol, declare that it does not consider itself bound by paragraph 2 of this article. The other States Parties shall not be bound by paragraph 2 of this article with respect to any State Party that has made such a reservation.
4. Any State Party that has made a reservation in accordance with paragraph 3 of this article may at any time withdraw that reservation by notification to the Secretary-General of the United Nations.

---

1. United Nations, *Treaty Series*, Vol. 189, No. 2545.
2. *Ibid.*, Vol. 606, No. 8791.

Article 16: *Signature, Ratification, Acceptance, Approval and Accession*

1. This Protocol shall be open to all States for signature from 12-15 December, 2000 in Palermo, Italy, and thereafter at United Nations Headquarters in New York until 12 December, 2002.
2. This Protocol shall also be open for signature by regional economic integration organisations provided that at least one member State of such organisation has signed this Protocol in accordance with paragraph 1 of this article.
3. This Protocol is subject to ratification, acceptance or approval. Instruments of ratification, acceptance or approval shall be deposited with the Secretary-General of the United Nations. A regional economic integration organisation may deposit its instrument of ratification, acceptance or approval if at least one of its member States has done likewise. In that instrument of ratification, acceptance or approval, such organisation shall declare the extent of its competence with respect to the matters governed by this Protocol. Such organisation shall also inform the depositary of any relevant modification in the extent of its competence.
4. This Protocol is open for accession by any State or any regional economic integration organisation of which at least one member State is a Party to this Protocol. Instruments of accession shall be deposited with the Secretary-General of the United Nations. At the time of its accession, a regional economic integration organisation shall declare the extent of its competence with respect to matters governed by this Protocol. Such organisation shall also inform the depositary of any relevant modification in the extent of its competence.

Article 17: *Entry into Force*

1. This Protocol shall enter into force on the ninetieth day after the date of deposit of the fortieth instrument of ratification, acceptance, approval or accession, except that it shall not enter into force before the entry into force of the Convention. For the purpose of this paragraph, any instrument deposited by a regional economic integration organisation shall not

be counted as additional to those deposited by member States of such organisation.

2. For each State or regional economic integration organisation ratifying, accepting, approving or acceding to this Protocol after the deposit of the fortieth instrument of such action, this Protocol shall enter into force on the thirtieth day after the date of deposit by such State or organisation of the relevant instrument or on the date this Protocol enters into force pursuant to paragraph 1 of this article, whichever is the later.

Article 18: *Amendment*

1. After the expiry of five years from the entry into force of this Protocol, a State Party to the Protocol may propose an amendment and file it with the Secretary-General of the United Nations, who shall thereupon communicate the proposed amendment to the States Parties and to the Conference of the Parties to the Convention for the purpose of considering and deciding on the proposal. The States Parties to this Protocol meeting at the Conference of the Parties shall make every effort to achieve consensus on each amendment. If all efforts at consensus have been exhausted and no agreement has been reached, the amendment shall, as a last resort, require for its adoption a two-thirds majority vote of the States Parties to this Protocol present and voting at the meeting of the Conference of the Parties.
2. Regional economic integration organisations, in matters within their competence, shall exercise their right to vote under this article with a number of votes equal to the number of their member States that are Parties to this Protocol. Such organizations shall not exercise their right to vote if their member States exercise theirs and *vice versa*.
3. An amendment adopted in accordance with paragraph 1 of this article is subject to ratification, acceptance or approval by States Parties.
4. An amendment adopted in accordance with paragraph 1 of this article shall enter into force in respect of a State Party ninety days after the date of the deposit with the Secretary-General of the United Nations of an instrument of ratification, acceptance or approval of such amendment.

5. When an amendment enters into force, it shall be binding on those States Parties which have expressed their consent to be bound by it. Other States Parties shall still be bound by the provisions of this Protocol and any earlier amendments that they have ratified, accepted or approved.

Article 19: *Denunciation*

1. A State Party may denounce this Protocol by written notification to the Secretary-General of the United Nations. Such denunciation shall become effective one year after the date of receipt of the notification by the Secretary-General.
2. A regional economic integration organisation shall cease to be a Party to this Protocol when all of its member States have denounced it.

Article 20: *Depositary and Languages*

1. The Secretary-General of the United Nations is designated depositary of this Protocol.
2. The original of this Protocol, of which the Arabic, Chinese, English, French, Russian and Spanish texts are equally authentic, shall be deposited with the Secretary-General of the United Nations.

In Witness Whereof, the undersigned plenipotentiaries, being duly authorized thereto by their respective Governments, have signed this Protocol.

ANNEXURE III

Protocol against the Smuggling of Migrants by Land, Sea and Air, Supplementing the United Nations Convention against Transnational Organized Crime

Preamble

The States Parties to this Protocol,

Declaring that effective action to prevent and combat the smuggling of migrants by land, sea and air requires a comprehensive international approach, including cooperation, the exchange of information and other appropriate measures, including socio-economic measures, at the national, regional and international levels.

Recalling General Assembly resolution 54/212 of 22 December, 1999, in which the Assembly urged Member States and the United Nations system to strengthen international cooperation in the area of international migration and development in order to address the root causes of migration, especially those related to poverty, and to maximize the benefits of international migration to those concerned, and encouraged, where relevant, inter-regional, regional and sub-regional mechanisms to continue to address the question of migration and development.

Convinced of the need to provide migrants with humane treatment and full protection of their rights.

Taking into account the fact that, despite work undertaken in other international forums, there is no universal instrument that addresses all aspects of smuggling of migrants and other related issues.

Concerned at the significant increase in the activities of organized criminal groups in smuggling of migrants and other related criminal activities set forth in this Protocol, which bring great harm to the States concerned.

Also concerned that the smuggling of migrants can endanger the lives or security of the migrants involved.

Recalling General Assembly resolution 53/111 of 9 December, 1998, in which the Assembly decided to establish an open-ended inter-governmental Ad Hoc Committee for the purpose of elaborating a comprehensive international convention against transnational organized crime and of discussing the elaboration of, *inter alia*, an international instrument addressing illegal trafficking in and transporting of migrants, including by sea.

Convinced that supplementing the United Nations Convention against Transnational Organized Crime with an international instrument against the smuggling of migrants by land, sea and air will be useful in preventing and combating that crime.

Have agreed as follows:

I. *General Provisions*

Article 1: *Relation with the United Nations Convention against Transnational Organized Crime*

1. This Protocol supplements the United Nations Convention against Transnational Organized Crime. It shall be interpreted together with the Convention.

2. The provisions of the Convention shall apply, *mutatis mutandis*, to this Protocol unless otherwise provided herein.
3. The offences established in accordance with Article 6 of this Protocol shall be regarded as offences established in accordance with the Convention.

Article 2: Statement of Purpose

The purpose of this Protocol is to prevent and combat the smuggling of migrants, as well as to promote cooperation among States Parties to that end, while protecting the rights of smuggled migrants.

Article 3: Use of Terms

For the purposes of this Protocol:

(*a*) "Smuggling of migrants" shall mean the procurement, in order to obtain, directly or indirectly, a financial or other material benefit, of the illegal entry of a person into a State Party of which the person is not a national or a permanent resident;

(*b*) "Illegal entry" shall mean crossing borders without complying with the necessary requirements for legal entry into the receiving State;

(*c*) "Fraudulent travel or identity document" shall mean any travel or identity document:

- (*i*) That has been falsely made or altered in some material way by anyone other than a person or agency lawfully authorized to make or issue the travel or identity document on behalf of a State; or
- (*ii*) That has been improperly issued or obtained through misrepresentation, corruption or duress or in any other unlawful manner; or
- (*iii*) That is being used by a person other than the rightful holder; and

(*d*) "Vessel" shall mean any type of water craft, including non-displacement craft and seaplanes, used or capable of being used as a means of transportation on water, except a warship, naval auxiliary or other vessel owned or operated by a Government and used, for the time being, only on government non-commercial service.

Article 4: Scope of Application

This Protocol shall apply, except as otherwise stated herein, to the prevention, investigation and prosecution of the offences established in accordance with Article 6 of this Protocol, where the offences are transnational in nature and involve an organized criminal group, as well as to the protection of the rights of persons who have been the object of such offences.

Article 5: Criminal Liability of Migrants

Migrants shall not become liable to criminal prosecution under this Protocol for the fact of having been the object of conduct set forth in Article 6 of this Protocol.

Article 6: Criminalization

1. Each State Party shall adopt such legislative and other measures as may be necessary to establish as criminal offences, when committed intentionally and in order to obtain, directly or indirectly, a financial or other material benefit:
   (*a*) The smuggling of migrants;
   (*b*) When committed for the purpose of enabling the smuggling of migrants:
      (*i*) Producing a fraudulent travel or identity document; and
      (*ii*) Procuring, providing or possessing such a document;
   (*c*) Enabling a person who is not a national or a permanent resident to remain in the State concerned without complying with the necessary requirements for legally remaining in the State by the means mentioned in sub-paragraph (*b*) of this paragraph or any other illegal means.
2. Each State Party shall also adopt such legislative and other measures as may be necessary to establish as criminal offences:
   (*a*) Subject to the basic concepts of its legal system, attempting to commit an offence established in accordance with paragraph 1 of this article;

   (*b*) Participating as an accomplice in an offence established in accordance with paragraph 1 (*a*), (*b*) (*i*) or (*c*) of this article and, subject to the basic concepts of its legal system, participating as an accomplice in an offence established in accordance with paragraph 1 (*b*) (*ii*) of this article; and
   (*c*) Organizing or directing other persons to commit an offence established in accordance with paragraph 1 of this article.
3. Each State Party shall adopt such legislative and other measures as may be necessary to establish as aggravating circumstances to the offences established in accordance with paragraph 1 (*a*), (*b*) (*i*) and (*c*) of this article and, subject to the basic concepts of its legal system, to the offences established in accordance with paragraph 2 (*b*) and (*c*) of this article, circumstances:
   (*a*) That endanger, or are likely to endanger, the lives or safety of the migrants concerned; or
   (*b*) That entail inhuman or degrading treatment, including for exploitation, of such migrants.
4. Nothing in this Protocol shall prevent a State Party from taking measures against a person whose conduct constitutes an offence under its domestic law.

II. *Smuggling of Migrants by Sea*

Article 7: Cooperation

States Parties shall cooperate to the fullest extent possible to prevent and suppress the smuggling of migrants by sea, in accordance with the international law of the sea.

Article 8: Measures against the Smuggling of Migrants by Sea

1. A State Party that has reasonable grounds to suspect that a vessel that is flying its flag or claiming its registry, that is without nationality or that, though flying a foreign flag or refusing to show a flag, is in reality of the nationality of the State Party concerned is engaged in the smuggling of migrants by sea may request the assistance of other States Parties in suppressing the use of the vessel for that purpose.

The States Parties so requested shall render such assistance to the extent possible within their means.

2. A State Party that has reasonable grounds to suspect that a vessel exercising freedom of navigation in accordance with international law and flying the flag or displaying the marks of registry of another State Party is engaged in the smuggling of migrants by sea may so notify the flag State, request confirmation of registry and, if confirmed, request authorization from the flag State to take appropriate measures with regard to that vessel. The flag State may authorize the requesting State, *inter alia*:
   (*a*) To board the vessel;
   (*b*) To search the vessel; and
   (*c*) If evidence is found that the vessel is engaged in the smuggling of migrants by sea, to take appropriate measures with respect to the vessel and persons and cargo on board, as authorized by the flag State.
3. A State Party that has taken any measure in accordance with paragraph 2 of this article shall promptly inform the flag State concerned of the results of that measure.
4. A State Party shall respond expeditiously to a request from another State Party to determine whether a vessel that is claiming its registry or flying its flag is entitled to do so and to a request for authorization made in accordance with paragraph 2 of this article.
5. A flag State may, consistent with Article 7 of this Protocol, subject its authorization to conditions to be agreed by it and the requesting State, including conditions relating to responsibility and the extent of effective measures to be taken. A State Party shall take no additional measures without the express authorization of the flag State, except those necessary to relieve imminent danger to the lives of persons or those which derive from relevant bilateral or multi-lateral agreements.
6. Each State Party shall designate an authority or, where necessary, authorities to receive and respond to requests for assistance, for confirmation of registry or of the right of a vessel to fly its flag and for authorization to take appropriate measures. Such designation shall be notified

through the Secretary-General to all other States Parties within one month of the designation.

7. A State Party that has reasonable grounds to suspect that a vessel is engaged in the smuggling of migrants by sea and is without nationality or may be assimilated to a vessel without nationality may board and search the vessel. If evidence confirming the suspicion is found, that State Party shall take appropriate measures in accordance with relevant domestic and international law.

Article 9: *Safeguard Clauses*

1. Where a State Party takes measures against a vessel in accordance with Article 8 of this Protocol, it shall:
   (*a*) ensure the safety and humane treatment of the persons on board;
   (*b*) take due account of the need not to endanger the security of the vessel or its cargo;
   (*c*) take due account of the need not to prejudice the commercial or legal interests of the flag State or any other interested State; and
   (*d*) ensure, within available means, that any measure taken with regard to the vessel is environmentally sound.
2. Where the grounds for measures taken pursuant to Article 8 of this Protocol prove to be unfounded, the vessel shall be compensated for any loss or damage that may have been sustained, provided that the vessel has not committed any act justifying the measures taken.
3. Any measure taken, adopted or implemented in accordance with this chapter shall take due account of the need not to interfere with or to affect:
   (*a*) The rights and obligations and the exercise of jurisdiction of coastal States in accordance with the international law of the sea; or
   (*b*) The authority of the flag State to exercise jurisdiction and control in administrative, technical and social matters involving the vessel.
4. Any measure taken at sea pursuant to this chapter shall be carried out only by warships or military aircraft, or by other

ships or aircraft clearly marked and identifiable as being on government service and authorized to that effect.

III. *Prevention, Cooperation and other Measures*

Article 10: *Information*

1. Without prejudice to Articles 27 and 28 of the Convention, States Parties, in particular those with common borders or located on routes along which migrants are smuggled, shall, for the purpose of achieving the objectives of this Protocol, exchange among themselves, consistent with their respective domestic legal and administrative systems, relevant information on matters such as:
   (*a*) Embarkation and destination points, as well as routes, carriers and means of transportation, known to be or suspected of being used by an organized criminal group engaged in conduct set forth in Article 6 of this Protocol;
   (*b*) The identity and methods of organisations or organized criminal groups known to be or suspected of being engaged in conduct set forth in Article 6 of this Protocol;
   (*c*) The authenticity and proper form of travel documents issued by a State Party and the theft or related misuse of blank travel or identity documents;
   (*d*) Means and methods of concealment and transportation of persons, the unlawful alteration, reproduction or acquisition or other misuse of travel or identity documents used in conduct set forth in Article 6 of this Protocol and ways of detecting them;
   (*e*) Legislative experiences and practices and measures to prevent and combat the conduct set forth in Article 6 of this Protocol; and
   (*f*) Scientific and technological information useful to law enforcement, so as to enhance each other's ability to prevent, detect and investigate the conduct set forth in Article 6 of this Protocol and to prosecute those involved.
2. A State Party that receives information shall comply with any request by the State Party that transmitted the information that places restrictions on its use.

Article 11: *Border Measures*

1. Without prejudice to international commitments in relation to the free movement of people. States Parties shall strengthen, to the extent possible, such border controls as may be necessary to prevent and detect the smuggling of migrants.
2. Each State Party shall adopt legislative or other appropriate measures to prevent, to the extent possible, means of transport operated by commercial carriers from being used in the commission of the offence established in accordance with Article 6, paragraph 1 (*a*), of this Protocol.
3. Where appropriate, and without prejudice to applicable international conventions, such measures shall include establishing the obligation of commercial carriers, including any transportation company or the owner or operator of any means of transport, to ascertain that all passengers are in possession of the travel documents required for entry into the receiving State.
4. Each State Party shall take the necessary measures, in accordance with its domestic law, to provide for sanctions in cases of violation of the obligation set forth in paragraph 3 of this article.
5. Each State Party shall consider taking measures that permit, in accordance with its domestic law, the denial of entry or revocation of visas of persons implicated in the commission of offences established in accordance with this Protocol.
6. Without prejudice to Article 27 of the Convention, States Parties shall consider strengthening cooperation among border control agencies by, *inter alia*, establishing and maintaining direct channels of communication.

Article 12: *Security and Control of Documents*

Each State Party shall take such measures as may be necessary, within available means:

(*a*) to ensure that travel or identity documents issued by it are of such quality that they cannot easily be misused and cannot readily be falsified or unlawfully altered, replicated or issued; and (*b*) to ensure the integrity and security of travel or identity documents issued by or on behalf of the State Party and to prevent their unlawful creation, issuance and use.

Article 13: *Legitimacy and Validity of Documents*

At the request of another State Party, a State Party shall, in accordance with its domestic law, verify within a reasonable time the legitimacy and validity of travel or identity documents issued or purported to have been issued in its name and suspected of being used for purposes of conduct set forth in Article 6 of this Protocol.

Article 14: *Training and Technical Cooperation*

1. States Parties shall provide or strengthen specialized training for immigration and other relevant officials in preventing the conduct set forth in Article 6 of this Protocol and in the humane treatment of migrants who have been the object of such conduct, while respecting their rights as set forth in this Protocol.
2. States Parties shall cooperate with each other and with competent international organisations, non-governmental organisations, other relevant organisations and other elements of civil society as appropriate to ensure that there is adequate personnel training in their territories to prevent, combat and eradicate the conduct set forth in Article 6 of this Protocol and to protect the rights of migrants who have been the object of such conduct. Such training shall include:
   (*a*) Improving the security and quality of travel documents;
   (*b*) Recognizing and detecting fraudulent travel or identity documents;
   (*c*) Gathering criminal intelligence, relating in particular to the identification of organized criminal groups known to be or suspected of being engaged in conduct set forth in Article 6 of this Protocol, the methods used to transport smuggled migrants, the misuse of travel or identity documents for purposes of conduct set forth in Article 6 and the means of concealment used in the smuggling of migrants;
   (*d*) Improving procedures for detecting smuggled persons

at conventional and non-conventional points of entry and exit; and

(*e*) The humane treatment of migrants and the protection of their rights as set forth in this Protocol.

3. States Parties with relevant expertise shall consider providing technical assistance to States that are frequently countries of origin or transit for persons who have been the object of conduct set forth in Article 6 of this Protocol. States Parties shall make every effort to provide the necessary resources, such as vehicles, computer systems and document readers, to combat the conduct set forth in Article 6.

Article 15: *Other Prevention Measures*

1. Each State Party shall take measures to ensure that it provides or strengthens information programmes to increase public awareness of the fact that the conduct set forth in Article 6 of this Protocol is a criminal activity frequently perpetrated by organized criminal groups for profit and that it poses serious risks to the migrants concerned.
2. In accordance with Article 31 of the Convention, States Parties shall cooperate in the field of public information for the purpose of preventing potential migrants from falling victim to organized criminal groups.
3. Each State Party shall promote or strengthen, as appropriate, development programmes and cooperation at the national, regional and international levels, taking into account the socio-economic realities of migration and paying special attention to economically and socially depressed areas, in order to combat the root socio-economic causes of the smuggling of migrants, such as poverty and under-development.

Article 16: *Protection and Assistance Measures*

1. In implementing this Protocol, each State Party shall take, consistent with its obligations under international law, all appropriate measures, including legislation if necessary, to preserve and protect the rights of persons who have been the object of conduct set forth in Article 6 of this Protocol as accorded under applicable international law, in particular

the right to life and the right not to be subjected to torture or other cruel, inhuman or degrading treatment or punishment.

2. Each State Party shall take appropriate measures to afford migrants appropriate protection against violence that may be inflicted upon them, whether by individuals or groups, by reason of being the object of conduct set forth in Article 6 of this Protocol.
3. Each State Party shall afford appropriate assistance to migrants whose lives or safety are endangered by reason of being the object of conduct set forth in Article 6 of this Protocol.
4. In applying the provisions of this article, States Parties shall take into account the special needs of women and children.
5. In the case of the detention of a person who has been the object of conduct set forth in Article 6 of this Protocol, each State Party shall comply with its obligations under the Vienna Convention on Consular Relations,[1] where applicable, including that of informing the person concerned without delay about the provisions concerning notification to and communication with consular officers.

Article 17: *Agreements and Arrangements*

States Parties shall consider the conclusion of bilateral or regional agreements or operational arrangements or understandings aimed at:

(*a*) Establishing the most appropriate and effective measures to prevent and combat the conduct set forth in Article 6 of this Protocol; or

(*b*) Enhancing the provisions of this Protocol among themselves.

Article 18: *Return of Smuggled Migrants*

1. Each State Party agrees to facilitate and accept, without undue or unreasonable delay, the return of a person who has been the object of conduct set forth in Article 6 of this Protocol and who is its national or who has the right of permanent residence in its territory at the time of return.

1. United Nations, *Treaty Series*, Vol. 596, Nos. 8638-8640.

2. Each State Party shall consider the possibility of facilitating and accepting the return of a person who has been the object of conduct set forth in Article 6 of this Protocol and who had the right of permanent residence in its territory at the time of entry into the receiving State in accordance with its domestic law.
3. At the request of the receiving State Party, a requested State Party shall, without undue or unreasonable delay, verify whether a person who has been the object of conduct set forth in Article 6 of this Protocol is its national or has the right of permanent residence in its territory.
4. In order to facilitate the return of a person who has been the object of conduct set forth in Article 6 of this Protocol and is without proper documentation, the State Party of which that person is a national or in which he or she has the right of permanent residence shall agree to issue, at the request of the receiving State Party, such travel documents or other authorization as may be necessary to enable the person to travel to and re-enter its territory.
5. Each State Party involved with the return of a person who has been the object of conduct set forth in Article 6 of this Protocol shall take all appropriate measures to carry out the return in an orderly manner and with due regard for the safety and dignity of the person.
6. States Parties may cooperate with relevant international organisations in the implementation of this article.
7. This article shall be without prejudice to any right afforded to persons who have been the object of conduct set forth in Article 6 of this Protocol by any domestic law of the receiving State Party.
8. SThis article shall not affect the obligations entered into under any other applicable treaty, bilateral or multi-lateral, or any other applicable operational agreement or arrangement that governs, in whole or in part, the return of persons who have been the object of conduct set forth in Article 6 of this Protocol.

IV. *Final Provisions*

Article 19: *Saving Clause*

1. Nothing in this Protocol shall affect the other rights,

obligations and responsibilities of States and individuals under international law, including international humanitarian law and international human rights law and, in particular, where applicable, the 1951 Convention[1] and the 1967 Protocol[2] relating to the Status of Refugees and the principle of non-refoulement as contained therein.

2. The measures set forth in this Protocol shall be interpreted and applied in a way that is not discriminatory to persons on the ground that they are the object of conduct set forth in Article 6 of this Protocol. The interpretation and application of those measures shall be consistent with internationally recognized principles of non-discrimination.

Article 20: *Settlement of Disputes*

1. States Parties shall endeavour to settle disputes concerning the interpretation or application of this Protocol through negotiation.
2. Any dispute between two or more States Parties concerning the interpretation or application of this Protocol that cannot be settled through negotiation within a reasonable time shall, at the request of one of those States Parties, be submitted to arbitration. If, six months after the date of the request for arbitration, those States Parties are unable to agree on the organisation of the arbitration, any one of those States Parties may refer the dispute to the International Court of Justice by request in accordance with the Statute of the Court.
3. Each State Party may, at the time of signature, ratification, acceptance or approval of or accession to this Protocol, declare that it does not consider itself bound by paragraph 2 of this article. The other States Parties shall not be bound by paragraph 2 of this article with respect to any State Party that has made such a reservation.
4. Any State Party that has made a reservation in accordance with paragraph 3 of this article may at any time withdraw that reservation by notification to the Secretary-General of the United Nations.

---

1. United Nations. *Treaty Series*, Vol. 189, No. 2545.
2. *Ibid.*, Vol. 606, No. 8791.

Article 21: *Signature, Ratification, Acceptance, Approval and Accession*

1. This Protocol shall be open to all States for signature from 12-15 December, 2000 in Palermo, Italy, and thereafter at United Nations Headquarters in New York until 12 December 2002.
2. This Protocol shall also be open for signature by regional economic integration organisations provided that at least one member State of such organisation has signed this Protocol in accordance with paragraph 1 of this article.
3. This Protocol is subject to ratification, acceptance or approval. Instruments of ratification, acceptance or approval shall be deposited with the Secretary-General of the United Nations. A regional economic integration organisation may deposit its instrument of ratification, acceptance or approval if at least one of its member States has done likewise. In that instrument of ratification, acceptance or approval, such organisation shall declare the extent of its competence with respect to the matters governed by this Protocol. Such organisation shall also inform the depositary of any relevant modification in the extent of its competence.
4. This Protocol is open for accession by any State or any regional economic integration organisation of which at least one member State is a Party to this Protocol. Instruments of accession shall be deposited with the Secretary-General of the United Nations. At the time of its accession, a regional economic integration organisation shall declare the extent of its competence with respect to matters governed by this Protocol. Such organisation shall also inform the depositary of any relevant modification in the extent of its competence.

Article 22: *Entry into Force*

1. This Protocol shall enter into force on the ninetieth day after the date of deposit of the fortieth instrument of ratification, acceptance, approval or accession, except that it shall not enter into force before the entry into force of the Convention. For the purpose of this paragraph, any instrument deposited by a regional economic integration organisation shall not be counted as additional to those deposited by member States of such organisation.

2. For each State or regional economic integration organisation ratifying, accepting, approving or acceding to this Protocol after the deposit of the fortieth instrument of such action, this Protocol shall enter into force on the thirtieth day after the date of deposit by such State or organisation of the relevant instrument or on the date this Protocol enters into force pursuant to paragraph 1 of this article, whichever is the later.

Article 23: *Amendment*

1. After the expiry of five years from the entry into force of this Protocol, a State Party to the Protocol may propose an amendment and file it with the Secretary-General of the United Nations, who shall thereupon communicate the proposed amendment to the States Parties and to the Conference of the Parties to the Convention for the purpose of considering and deciding on the proposal. The States Parties to this Protocol meeting at the Conference of the Parties shall make every effort to achieve consensus on each amendment. If all efforts at consensus have been exhausted and no agreement has been reached, the amendment shall, as a last resort, require for its adoption a two-thirds majority vote of the States Parties to this Protocol present and voting at the meeting of the Conference of the Parties.
2. Regional economic integration organisations, in matters within their competence, shall exercise their right to vote under this article with a number of votes equal to the number of their member States that are Parties to this Protocol. Such organisations shall not exercise their right to vote if their member States exercise theirs and *vice versa*.
3. An amendment adopted in accordance with paragraph 1 of this article is subject to ratification, acceptance or approval by States Parties.
4. An amendment adopted in accordance with paragraph 1 of this article shall enter into force in respect of a State Party ninety days after the date of the deposit with the Secretary-General of the United Nations of an instrument of ratification, acceptance or approval of such amendment.
5. When an amendment enters into force, it shall be binding on those States Parties which have expressed their consent

to be bound by it. Other States Parties shall still be bound by the provisions of this Protocol and any earlier amendments that they have ratified, accepted or approved.

Article 24: *Denunciation*

1. A State Party may denounce this Protocol by written notification to the Secretary-General of the United Nations. Such denunciation shall become effective one year after the date of receipt of the notification by the Secretary-General.
2. A regional economic integration organisation shall cease to be a Party to this Protocol when all of its member States have denounced it.

Article 25: *Depositary and Languages*

1. The Secretary-General of the United Nations is designated depositary of this Protocol.
2. The original of this Protocol, of which the Arabic, Chinese, English, French, Russian and Spanish texts are equally authentic, shall be deposited with the Secretary-General of the United Nations.

In Witness Whereof, the undersigned plenipotentiaries, being duly authorized thereto by their respective Governments, have signed this Protocol.

GENERAL ASSEMBLY

Fifty-fifth Session
Agenda Item 105
Crime Prevention and Criminal Justice

Report of the Ad Hoc Committee on the Elaboration of a Convention against Transnational Organized Crime on the work of its first to eleventh sessions.

Addendum

Interpretative notes for the official records ***(travaux préparatoires)*** *of the negotiation of the United Nations Convention against Transnational Organized Crime and the Protocols thereto.*

Introduction

1. The present document contains interpretative notes that were discussed by the Ad Hoc Committee on the Elaboration of a Convention against Transnational Organized Crime throughout the process of negotiation of the draft Convention. These notes will be included in the official records of the negotiation process, which the Secretariat will prepare in accordance with standard practice. The Ad Hoc Committee was informed by the Secretariat in document A/AC.254/33 of the nature of the official records of the negotiation and of the practice regarding their drafting and compilation. The present document is submitted to the General Assembly for information purposes only. The Ad Hoc Committee took no formal action on these notes and none is expected of the Assembly at its fifty-fifth session.

Interpretative Notes

A. ***Interpretative notes for the official records*** **(travaux préparatoires)** ***of the negotiation of the United Nations Convention against Transnational Organized Crime***

Article 2: Use of Terms

Sub-paragraph (a)

2. The *travaux préparatoires* should indicate that the inclusion of a specific number of persons would not prejudice the rights of States Parties pursuant to Article 34, paragraph 3.
3. The *travaux préparatoires* should indicate that the words "in order to obtain, directly or indirectly, a financial or other material benefit" should be understood broadly, to include, for example, crimes in which the predominant motivation may be sexual gratification, such as the receipt or trade of materials by members of child pornography rings, the trading of children by members of paedophile rings or cost-sharing among ring members.

Sub-paragraph (c)

4. The *travaux préparatoires* should indicate that the term "structured group" is to be used in a broad sense so as to include both groups with hierarchical or other elaborate

structure and non-hierarchical groups where the roles of the members of the group need not be formally defined.

Sub-paragraph (j)

5. The *travaux préparatoires* should indicate that the terms "freezing" or "seizure" as defined in Article 2, sub-paragraph (*f*), can be found in Articles 12 and 13 of the United Nations Convention against Transnational Organized Crime. The term "search and seizure" appearing in Article 18 should not be confused with "seizure" in Article 2. "Search and seizure" refers to the use of intrusive compulsory measures by law enforcement authorities to obtain evidence for purposes of a criminal case. The term "freezing" in Article 18 is used to cover the concept defined as "freezing" or "seizure" in Article 2 and should be understood more broadly to include not only property but also evidence.

Sub-paragraph (g)

6. The *travaux préparatoires* should indicate that when the domestic law of a State Party requires the order of a court for confiscation, that court will be considered the only competent authority for the purposes of this definition.

Article 3: Scope of Application

7. During the negotiation of the Convention, the Ad Hoc Committee noted with deep concern the growing links between transnational organized crime and terrorist crimes, taking into account the Charter of the United Nations and the relevant resolutions of the General Assembly. All States participating in the negotiations expressed their determination to deny safe havens to those who engaged in transnational organized crime by prosecuting their crimes wherever they occurred and by cooperating at the international level. The Ad Hoc Committee was also strongly convinced that the Convention would constitute an effective tool and the necessary legal framework for international cooperation in combating, *inter alia*, such criminal activities as money-laundering, corruption, illicit trafficking in endangered species of wild flora and fauna, offences against cultural heritage, and the growing links between

transnational organized crime and terrorist crimes. Finally, the Ad Hoc Committee was of the view that the Ad Hoc Committee established by the General Assembly in its resolution 51/210 of 17 December, 1996, which was then beginning its deliberations with a view to the development of a comprehensive convention on international terrorism, pursuant to Assembly resolution 54/110 of 9 December, 1999, should take into consideration the provisions of the Convention.

Paragraph 2 (d)

8. The *travaux préparatoires* should indicate that the term "substantial effects" is intended to cover situations where an offence has had a substantial consequential adverse effect on another State Party, for example where the currency of one State Party is counterfeited in another State Party and the organized criminal group has put the counterfeit currency into global circulation.

Article 5: Criminalization of Participation in an Organized Criminal Group

9. The *travaux préparatoires* should indicate that the "other measures" mentioned in Articles 5, 6, 8 and 23 are additional to legislative measures and presuppose the existence of a law.

Article 6: Criminalization of the Laundering of the Proceeds of Crime

10. The *travaux préparatoires* should indicate that the terms "laundering of proceeds of crime" and "money-laundering" are understood to be equivalent.

Paragraphs 1 (a) and (b)

11. The *travaux préparatoires* should show that the terms "concealing or disguising" and "concealment or disguise" should be understood to include preventing the discovery of the illicit origins of property.

Paragraph 2 (b)

12. The *travaux préparatoires* should include a note to the effect that the words "associated with organized criminal groups are intended to indicate criminal activity of the type in which organized criminal groups engage.

Paragraph 2 (e)

13. In the *travaux préparatoires* it should be stated that sub-paragraph (*e*) takes into account legal principles of several States where prosecution or punishment of the same person for both the predicate offence and the money-laundering offence is not permitted. Those States confirmed that they did not refuse extradition, mutual legal assistance or cooperation for purposes of confiscation solely because the request was based on a money-laundering offence the predicate offence of which was committed by the same person.

Article 7: Measures to Combat Money-Laundering

Paragraph 1 (a)

14. The *travaux préparatoires* should indicate that the words "other bodies" may be understood to include intermediaries, which in some jurisdictions may include stock broking firms, other securities dealers, currency exchange bureau or currency brokers.
15. The *travaux préparatoires* should indicate that the words "suspicious transactions" may be understood to include unusual transactions that, by reason of their amount, characteristics and frequency, are inconsistent with the customer's business activity, exceed the normally accepted parameters of the market or have no clear legal basis and could constitute or be connected with unlawful activities in general.

Paragraph 1 (b)

16. The *travaux préparatoires* should indicate that the establishment of a financial intelligence unit called for by this sub-paragraph is intended for cases where such a mechanism does not yet exist.

Paragraph 3

17. The *travaux préparatoires* should indicate that, during the negotiations, the words "relevant initiatives of regional, inter-regional and multi-lateral organisations" were understood to refer in particular to the forty recommendations of the Financial Action Task Force on Money-Laundering, as revised in 1996, and, in addition, to

other existing initiatives of regional, inter-regional and multi-lateral organisations against money-laundering, such as the Caribbean Financial Action Task Force, the Commonwealth, the Council of Europe, the Eastern and Southern African Anti-Money-Laundering Group, the European Union and the Organisation of American States.

Article 8: Criminalization of Corruption

Paragraph 1

18. The *travaux préparatoires* should indicate that the obligation under this article was not intended to include the actions of a person who acted under such a degree of duress or undue influence as to constitute a complete defence to the crime.

Paragraph 4

19. The *travaux préparatoires* should indicate that the concept of a person who provides a public service applies to particular legal systems and that the incorporation of the concept into the definition is intended to facilitate cooperation between States Parties with that concept in their legal systems.

Article 11: Prosecution, Adjudication and Sanctions

Paragraph 4

20. The *travaux préparatoires* should indicate that paragraph 4 would not oblige States Parties to provide for early release or parole of imprisoned persons if their legal systems did not provide for early release or parole.

Article 12: Confiscation and Seizure

21. The *travaux préparatoires* should indicate that interpretation of Article 12 should take into account the principle in international law that property belonging to a foreign State and used for non-commercial purposes may not be confiscated except with the consent of the foreign State. Furthermore, the *travaux préparatoires* should indicate that it is not the intention of the Convention to restrict the rules that apply to diplomatic or State immunity, including that of international organisations.

Paragraph 1 (b)

22. The *travaux préparatoires* should indicate that the words

"used in or destined for use in" are meant to signify an intention of such a nature that it may be viewed as tantamount to an attempt to commit a crime.

Paragraph 5

23. The *travaux préparatoires* should indicate that the words "other benefits" are intended to encompass material benefits, as well as legal rights and interests of an enforceable nature, that are subject to confiscation.

Article 13: *International Cooperation for Purposes of Confiscation*

24. The *travaux préparatoires* should indicate that references in this article to Article 12, paragraph 1, should be understood to include reference to Article 12, paragraphs 3-5.

Article 14: *Disposal of Confiscated Proceeds of Crime or Property*

25. The *travaux préparatoires* should indicate that, when feasible, States Parties would examine whether it would be appropriate, in conformity with individual guarantees embodied in their domestic law, to use confiscated assets to cover the costs of assistance provided pursuant to Article 24, paragraph 2.

Article 15: *Jurisdiction*

Paragraph 2 (a)

26. The *travaux préparatoires* should reflect the understanding that States Parties should take into consideration the need to extend possible protection that might stem from the establishment of jurisdiction to stateless persons who might be habitual or permanent residents in their countries.

Paragraph 5

27. The *travaux préparatoires* should indicate that an example of how useful coordination between States Parties would be was the need to ensure that time-sensitive evidence was not lost.

Article 16: *Extradition*

Paragraph 2

28. The *travaux préparatoires* should indicate that the purpose

of paragraph 2 is to serve as an instrument for States Parties wishing to avail themselves of the facility it provides. It is not intended to broaden the scope of the article unduly.

Paragraph 8

29. The *travaux préparatoires* should indicate that this paragraph should not be interpreted as prejudicing in any way the fundamental legal rights of the defendant.
30. The *travaux préparatoires* should indicate that one example of implementation of this paragraph would be speedy and simplified procedures of extradition, subject to the domestic law of the requested State Party for the surrender of persons sought for the purpose of extradition, subject to the agreement of the requested State Party and the consent of the person in question. The consent, which should be expressed voluntarily and in full awareness of the consequences, should be understood as being in relation to the simplified procedures and not to the extradition itself.

Paragraph 10

31. The *travaux préparatoires* should reflect the general understanding that States Parties should also take into consideration the need to eliminate safe havens for offenders who commit heinous crimes in circumstances not covered by paragraph 10. Several States indicated that such cases should be reduced and several States stated that the principle of *aut dedere aut judlcare* should be followed.

Paragraph 12

32. The *travaux préparatoires* should indicate that the action referred to in paragraph 12 would be taken without prejudice to the principle of double jeopardy *(ne bis in idem).*

Paragraph 14

33. The *travaux préparatoires* should indicate that the term "sex" refers to male and female.
34. The *travaux préparatoires* should indicate that, at the informal consultations held during the eighth session of the Ad Hoc Committee, the delegation of Italy proposed the insertion after paragraph 8 of the following provision:

    "Without prejudice to the use of other grounds for refusal, the requested State may refuse to extradite on the ground that a decision has been issued in absentia only if it is not proved that the case has been tried with the same guarantees as when a defendant is present and he or she, having knowledge of the trial, has deliberately avoided being arrested or has deliberately failed to appear at the trial. However, when such proof is not given, extradition may not be refused if the requesting State gives assurance, deemed satisfactory by the requested State, that the person whose extradition is sought shall be entitled to anew trial protecting his or her rights of defence."

In the discussion that followed, several delegations expressed serious concerns about whether this provision would be compatible with the fundamental principles of their respective legal systems. The delegation of Italy withdrew its proposal at the ninth session of the Ad Hoc Committee on the understanding that, when considering a request for extradition pursuant to a sentence issued in absentia, the requested State Party would take into due consideration whether or not the person whose extradition was sought had been sentenced following a fair trial, for example, whether or not the defendant had been assured the same guarantees as he or she would have enjoyed had he or she been present at the trial and had voluntarily escaped from justice or failed to appear at the trial, or whether or not he or she was entitled to a new trial.

Paragraph 16

35. The *travaux préparatoires* should indicate that the words "where appropriate" in Article 16, paragraph 16, are to be understood and interpreted in the spirit of full cooperation and should not affect, to the extent possible, the obligatory nature of the paragraph. The requested State Party shall, when applying this paragraph, give full consideration to the need to bring offenders to justice through extradition cooperation.

Article 18: *Mutual Legal Assistance*

Paragraph 2

36. The *travaux préparatoires* should indicate that the term "judicial proceedings" in Article 18, paragraph 2, refers to the matter for which mutual legal assistance is requested and is not intended to be perceived as in any way prejudicing the independence of the judiciary.

Paragraph 5

37. The *travaux préparatoires* should indicate that (*a*) when a State Party is considering whether to spontaneously provide information of a particularly sensitive nature or is considering placing strict restrictions on the use of information thus provided, it is considered advisable for the State Party concerned to consult with the potential receiving State beforehand; (*b*) when a State Party that receives information under this provision already has similar information in its possession, it is not obliged to comply with any restrictions imposed by the transmitting State.

Paragraph 8

38. The *travaux préparatoires* should indicate that this paragraph is not inconsistent with paragraphs 17 and 21 of this article.

Paragraph 10 (b)

39. The *travaux préparatoires* should indicate that, among the conditions to be determined by States Parties for the transfer of a person. States Parties may agree that the requested State Party may be present at witness testimony conducted in the territory of the requesting State Party.

Paragraph 13

40. The *travaux préparatoires* should indicate that a central authority may be different at different stages of the proceedings for which mutual legal assistance is requested. Further, the *travaux préparatoires* should indicate that this paragraph is not intended to create an impediment to countries having a central authority as regards receiving requests or to a different central authority as regards making requests.

Paragraph 18

41. The *travaux préparatoires* should indicate that the delegation of Italy made a proposal on the matter covered by this paragraph. During the debate on the proposal, it was pointed out that the following part of it, not reflected in the text of the Convention, could be used by States Parties as guidelines for the implementation of Article 18, paragraph 18:

"(*a*) The judicial authority of the requested State Party shall be responsible for the identification of the person to be heard and shall, on conclusion of the hearing, draw up minutes indicating the date and place of the hearing and any oath taken. The hearing shall be conducted without any physical or mental pressure on the person questioned;

"(*b*) If the judicial authority of the requested State considers that during the hearing the fundamental principles of the law of that State are infringed, he or she has the authority to interrupt or, if possible, to take the necessary measures to continue the hearing in accordance with those principles;

"(*c*) The person to be heard and the judicial authority of the requested State shall be assisted by an interpreter as necessary;

"(*d*) The person to be heard may claim the right not to testify as provided for by the domestic law of the requested State or of the requesting State; the domestic law of the requested State applies to perjury;

"(*e*) All the costs of the video conference shall be borne by the requesting State Party, which may also provide as necessary for technical equipment."

Paragraph 21 (*d*)

42. The *travaux préparatoires* should indicate that the provision of paragraph 21 (*d*) of this article is not intended to encourage refusal of mutual assistance for any reason, but is understood as raising the threshold to more essential principles of domestic law of the requested State. The *travaux préparatoires* should also indicate that the proposed clauses on grounds for refusal relating to the prosecution or punishment of a person on account of that person's sex, race, religion, nationality or political opinions, as well as the political offence exception, were deleted because it was understood that they were sufficiently covered by the words "essential interests" in paragraph 21 (*b*).

Paragraph 28

43. The *travaux préparatoires* should indicate that many of the costs arising in connection with compliance with requests under Article 18, paragraphs 10, 11 and 18, would generally be considered extraordinary in nature. Further, the *travaux préparatoires* should indicate the understanding that developing countries may encounter difficulties in meeting even some ordinary costs and should be provided with

appropriate assistance to enable them to meet the requirements of this article.

Article 20: Special Investigative Techniques

Paragraph 1

44. The *travaux préparatoires* should indicate that this paragraph does not imply an obligation on States Parties to make provisions for the use of all the forms of special investigative technique noted.

Article 22: Establishment of Criminal Record

45. The *travaux préparatoires* should indicate that the term "conviction" should be understood to refer to a conviction no longer subject to any appeal.

Article 23: Criminalization of Obstruction of Justice

Sub-paragraph (a)

46. The *travaux préparatoires* should indicate that the term "proceeding" is intended to cover all official governmental proceedings, which may include the pro-trial stage of a case.
47. The *travaux préparatoires* should indicate that it was understood that some countries may not cover cases where a person has the right not to give evidence and an undue advantage is provided for the exercise of that right.

Article 25: Assistance to and Protection of Victims

48. The *travaux préparatoires* should indicate that, while the purpose of this article is to concentrate on the physical protection of victims, the Ad Hoc Committee was cognizant of the need for protection of the rights of individuals as accorded under applicable international law.

Article 26: Measures to Enhance Cooperation with Law Enforcement Authorities

Paragraph 2

49. The *travaux préparatoires* should indicate that the term "mitigating punishment" might include not only prescribed but also *de facto* mitigation of punishment.

Article 27: Law Enforcement Cooperation

Paragraph 1

50. The *travaux préparatoires* should indicate that the words "consistent with their respective domestic legal and administrative systems" provide States Parties with flexibility regarding the extent and manner of cooperation. For example, this formulation enables States Parties to deny cooperation where it would be contrary to their domestic laws or policies to provide the assistance requested.

Paragraph 1 (a)

51. The *travaux préparatoires* should indicate that States Parties will make their own determination as to how best to ensure the secure and rapid exchange of information. Many delegations endorsed the use of direct communication between their different domestic law enforcement agencies and foreign counterparts. However, States Parties that feel it more advisable to establish a central point of contact to ensure efficiency would not be precluded from doing so.

Paragraph 3

52. The *travaux préparatoires* should indicate that the forms of modern technology referred to in Article 27, paragraph 3, include computers and telecommunications networks.

Article 28: Collection, Exchange and Analysis of Information on the Nature of Organized Crime

Paragraph 2

53. The *travaux préparatoires* should indicate that the mention of international and regional organisations is intended to refer to all relevant organisations, including the International Criminal Police Organisation (Interpol), the Customs Cooperation Council (also called the World Customs Organisation) and the European Police Office (Europe).

Article 29: Training and Technical Assistance

Paragraph 4

54. The *travaux préparatoires* should indicate that the mention of international and regional organisations is intended to

refer to all relevant organisations, including Interpol, the World Customs Organisation and Europol.

Article 31: *Prevention*

Paragraph 3

55. The *travaux préparatoires* should indicate that, in line with constitutional principles of equality, there is no distinction intended between persons convicted of offences covered by the Convention and persons convicted of other offences.

Article 32: *Conference of the Parties to the Convention*

Paragraph 2

56. The *travaux préparatoires* should indicate that, in developing rules concerning payment of its expenses, the Conference of the Parties to the Convention should ensure that voluntary contributions are considered a source of funding.

Paragraph 3

57. The *travaux préparatoires* should state that, in discharging its tasks, the Conference of the Parties should give due regard to the need to preserve the confidentiality of certain information, given the nature of the fight against transnational organized crime.

Paragraph 5

58. The *travaux préparatoires* should show that the Conference of the Parties should take into account the need to foresee some regularity in the provision of the information required. The *travaux préparatoires* should also indicate that the term "administrative measures" is understood to be broad and to include information about the extent to which legislation, policies and other relevant measures have been implemented.

Article 34: *Implementation of the Convention*

Paragraph 2

59. The *travaux préparatoires* should state that the purpose of this paragraph is, without altering the scope of application of the Convention as described in Article 3, to indicate unequivocally that the transnational element and the

involvement of an organized criminal group are not to be considered elements of those offences for Criminalization purposes. The paragraph is intended to indicate to States Parties that, when implementing the Convention, they do not have to include in their Criminalization of laundering of criminal proceeds (Article 6), corruption (Article 8) or obstruction of justice (Article 23) the elements of transnational and involvement of an organized criminal group, nor in the Criminalization in an organized criminal group (Article 5) the element of transnationality. This provision is furthermore intended to ensure clarity for States Parties in connection with their compliance with the Criminalization articles of the Convention and is not intended to have any impact on the interpretation of the cooperation articles of the Convention (Articles 16, 18 and 27).

Article 35: *Settlement of Disputes*

Paragraph 1

60. The *travaux préparatoires* should state that the term "negotiation" is to be understood in a broad sense to indicate an encouragement to States to exhaust all avenues of peaceful settlement of disputes, including conciliation, mediation and recourse to regional bodies.

Article 36: *Signature, Ratification, Acceptance, Approval and Accession*

61. The *travaux préparatoires* should indicate that, while the Convention has no specific provision on reservations, it is understood that the Vienna Convention on the Law of Treaties of 1969 applies regarding reservations.

B. *Interpretative notes for the official records* **(travaux préparatoires)** *of the negotiation of the Protocol to Prevent, Suppress and Punish Trafficking in Persons, Especially Women and Children, Supplementing the United Nations Convention against Transnational Organized Crime*

Chapter* I. *General Provisions

Article 1: *Relation with the United Nations Convention against Transnational Organized Crime*

Paragraph 2

62. The *travaux préparatoires* should indicate that this paragraph was adopted on the understanding that the words "*mutatis mutandis*" meant "with such modifications as circumstances require" or "with the necessary modifications." Provisions of the United Nations Convention against Transnational Organized Crime that are applied to the Protocol under this article would consequently be modified or interpreted so as to have the same essential meaning or effect in the Protocol as in the Convention.

Article 3: Use of Terms

Sub-paragraph (*a*)

63. The *travaux préparatoires* should indicate that the reference to the abuse of a position of vulnerability is understood to refer to any situation in which the person involved has no real and acceptable alternative but to submit to the abuse involved.
64. The *travaux préparatoires* should indicate that the Protocol addresses the exploitation of the prostitution of others and other forms of sexual exploitation only in the context of trafficking in persons. The terms "exploitation of the prostitution of others" or "other forms of sexual exploitation" are not defined in the Protocol, which is therefore without prejudice to how States Parties address prostitution in their respective domestic laws.
65. The *travaux préparatoires* should indicate that the removal of organs from children with the consent of a parent or guardian for legitimate medical or therapeutic reasons should not be considered exploitation.
66. The *travaux préparatoires* should indicate that where illegal adoption amounts to a practice similar to slavery as defined in Article 1, paragraph (*d*), of the Supplementary Convention on the Abolition of Slavery, the Slave Trade, and Institutions

and Practices Similar to Slavery, it will also fall within the scope of the Protocol.

Sub-paragraph (b)

67. The *travaux. préparatoires* should indicate that this sub-paragraph should not be interpreted as restricting the application of mutual legal assistance in accordance with Article 18 of the Convention.

68. The *travaux préparatoires* should indicate that sub-paragraph (*b*) should not be interpreted as imposing any restriction on the right of accused persons to a full defence and to the presumption of innocence. They should also indicate that it should not be interpreted as imposing on the victim the burden of proof. As in any criminal case, the burden of proof is on the State or public prosecutor, in accordance with domestic law. Further, the *travaux préparatoires* will refer to Article 11, paragraph 6, of the Convention, which preserves applicable legal defences and other related principles of the domestic law of States Parties.

Article 5: *Criminalization*

69. The *travaux préparatoires* should indicate that the "other measures" mentioned here are additional to legislative measures and pre-suppose the existence of a law.

Paragraph 2

70. The *travaux préparatoires* should indicate that references to attempting to commit the offences established under domestic law in accordance with this sub-paragraph are understood in some countries to include both acts perpetrated in preparation for a criminal offence and those carried out in an unsuccessful attempt to commit the offence, where those acts are also culpable or punishable under domestic law.

Chapter* II. *Protection of Victims of Trafficking in Persons

Article 6: *Assistance to and Protection of Victims of Trafficking in Persons*

Paragraph 3

71. The *travaux préparatoires* should indicate that the type of

assistance set forth in this paragraph is applicable to both the receiving State and the State of origin of the victims of trafficking in persons, but only as regards victims who are in their respective territory. Paragraph 3 is applicable to the receiving State until the victim of trafficking in persons has returned to his or her State of origin and to the State of origin thereafter.

Article 8: Repatriation of Victims of Trafficking in Persons

Paragraph 1

72. The *travaux préparatoires* should indicate that the words "permanent residence" in this paragraph mean long-term residence, but not necessarily indefinite residence. The paragraph should be understood as being without prejudice to any domestic legislation regarding either the granting of the right of residence or the duration of residence.

Paragraph 2

73. The *travaux préparatoires* should indicate that the words "and shall preferably be voluntary" are understood not to place any obligation on the State Party returning the victims.

Paragraph 3

74. The *travaux préparatoires* should indicate the understanding of the Ad Hoc Committee that a return under this article shall not be undertaken before the nationality or right of permanent residence of the person whose return is sought has been duly verified.

Paragraph 4

75. The *travaux préparatoires* should indicate that the words "travel documents" include any type of document required for entering or leaving a State under its domestic law.

Paragraph 6

76. The *travaux préparatoires* should indicate that the references to agreements or arrangements in this paragraph include both agreements that deal specifically with the subject-matter of the Protocol and more general re-admission agreements that include provisions dealing with illegal migration.

77. The *travaux préparatoires* should indicate that this paragraph should be understood as being without prejudice to any other obligations under customary international law regarding the return of migrants.

Chapter III. *Prevention, Cooperation and other Measures*

Article 10: *Information Exchange and Training*

Paragraph 1

78. The *travaux préparatoires* should indicate that the term "travel documents" includes any type of document required for entering or leaving a State under its domestic law.

Article 11: *Border Measures*

Paragraph 2

79. The *travaux préparatoires* should indicate that victims of trafficking in persons may enter a State legally only to face subsequent exploitation, whereas in cases of smuggling of migrants, illegal means of entry are more generally used. This may make it more difficult for common carriers to apply preventive measures in trafficking cases than in smuggling cases and legislative or other measures taken in accordance with this paragraph should take this into account.

Paragraph 4

80. The *travaux préparatoires* should indicate that measures and sanctions applied in accordance with this paragraph should take into account other international obligations of the State Party concerned. It should also be noted that this article requires States Parties to impose an obligation on common carriers only to ascertain whether or not passengers have the necessary documents in their possession and not to make any judgement or assessment of the validity or authenticity of the documents. It should further be noted that this paragraph does not unduly limit the discretion of States Parties not to hold carriers liable for transporting undocumented refugees.

Article 12: *Security and Control of Documents*

81. The *travaux préparatoires* should indicate that the term "travel

documents" includes any type of document required for entering or leaving a State under its domestic law and that the term "identity documents" includes any document commonly used to establish the identity of a person in a State under the laws or procedures of that State.

82. The *travaux préparatoires* should indicate that the words "falsified or unlawfully altered, replicated or issued" should be interpreted as including not only the creation of false documents, but also the alteration of legitimate documents and the filling in of stolen blank documents. They should also indicate that the intention was to include both documents that had been forged and genuine documents that had been validly issued but were being used by a person other than the lawful holder.

Article 13: *Legitimacy and Validity of Documents*

83. The *travaux préparatoires* should indicate that the term "travel documents" includes any type of document required for entering or leaving a State under its domestic law and that the term "identity documents" includes any document commonly used to establish the identity of a person in a State under the laws or procedures of that State.

Chapter* IV: *Final Provisions

Article 14: Saving Clause

Paragraph 1

84. The *travaux préparatoires* should indicate that the Protocol does not cover the status of refugees.

85. The *travaux préparatoires* should indicate that this Protocol is without prejudice to the existing rights, obligations or responsibilities of States Parties under other international instruments, such as those referred to in this paragraph. Rights, obligations and responsibilities under another instrument are determined by the terms of that instrument and whether the State concerned is a party to it, not by this Protocol. Therefore, any State that becomes a party to this Protocol but is not a party to another international instrument referred to in the Protocol would not become subject to any right, obligation or responsibility under that instrument.

Article 16: *Signature, Ratification, Acceptance, Approval and Accession*

86. The *travaux préparatoires* should indicate that, while the Protocol has no specific provisions or reservations, it is understood that the Vienna Convention on the Law of Treaties of 1969 applies regarding reservations.

C. ***Interpretative notes for the official records* (travaux préparatoires) *of the negotiation of the Protocol against Smuggling of Migrants by Land, Sea and Air, supplementing the United Nations Convention against Transnational Organized Crime.***

Chapter* I. *General Provisions

Article 1: *Relation with the United Nations Convention against Transnational Organized Crime*

Paragraph 2

87. The *travaux préparatoires* should indicate that this paragraph was adopted on the understanding that the words "*mutatis mutandis*" meant "with such modifications as circumstances require" or "with the necessary modifications." Provisions of the Convention that are applied to the Protocol under this article would consequently be modified or interpreted so as to have the same essential meaning or effect in the Protocol as in the Convention.

Article 3: *Use of Terms*

Sub-paragraph (*a*)

88. The *travaux préparatoires* should indicate that the reference to "a financial or other material benefit" as an element of the definition in sub-paragraph (*a*) was included in order to emphasize that the intention was to include the activities of organized criminal groups acting for profit, but to exclude the activities of those who provided support to migrants for humanitarian reasons or on the basis of close family ties. It was not the intention of the Protocol to criminalize the activities of family members or support groups such as religious or non-governmental organisations.

Sub-paragraph (*c*)

89. The *travaux préparatoires* should indicate that the term "travel document" includes any type of document required for entering or leaving a State under its domestic law and that the term "identity document" includes any document commonly used to establish the identity of a person in a State under the laws or procedures of that State.

90. The *travaux préparatoires* should indicate that the words "falsely made or altered" should be interpreted as including not only the creation of false documents, but also the alteration of legitimate documents and the filling in of stolen blank documents. They should also indicate that the intention was to include both documents that had been forged and genuine documents that had been validly issued but were being used by a person other than the lawful holder.

Article 6: Criminalization

91. The *travaux préparatoires* should indicate that the "other measures" mentioned here are additional to legislative measures and pre-suppose the existence of a law.

Paragraph 1

92. The *travaux préparatoires* should indicate that the offences set forth in Article 6 should be seen as being part of the activities of organized criminal groups. In this article, the Protocol follows the precedent of the Convention (Article 34, para, 2). The *travaux préparatoires* should also indicate that the reference to "a financial or other material benefit" as an element of the offences set forth in paragraph 1 was included in order to emphasize that the intention was to include the activities of organized criminal groups acting for profit, but to exclude the activities of those who provided support to migrants for humanitarian reasons or on the basis of close family ties. It was not the intention of the Protocol to criminalize the activities of family members or support groups such as religious or non-governmental organisations.

93. The *travaux préparatoires* should indicate that paragraph 1 (*b*) was adopted on the understanding that sub-paragraph (*ii*) would only apply when the possession in question was for the purpose of smuggling migrants as set forth in

sub-paragraph (*a*). Thus, a migrant who possessed a fraudulent document to enable his or her own smuggling would not be included.

94. The *travaux préparatoires* should indicate that the words "any other illegal means" in paragraph 1 (*c*) refer to illegal means as defined under domestic law.

Paragraph 2

95. The *travaux préparatoires* should indicate that references to attempting to commit the offences established under domestic law in accordance with paragraph 2 (*a*) are understood in some countries to include both acts perpetrated in preparation for a criminal offence and those carried out in an unsuccessful attempt to commit the offence, where those acts are also culpable or punishable under domestic law.

Paragraph 3

96. The *travaux préparatoires* should indicate that the words "inhuman or degrading treatment" in sub-paragraph (*b*) were intended, without prejudice to the scope and application of the Protocol to Prevent, Suppress and Punish Trafficking in Persons, Especially Women and Children, supplementing the United Nations Convention against Transnational Organized Crime, to include certain forms of exploitation.

Paragraph 4

97. The *travaux préparatoires* should indicate that in this paragraph the word "measures" should be interpreted broadly to include both criminal and administrative sanctions.

Chapter II: *Smuggling of Migrants by Sea*

98. The *travaux préparatoires* should indicate that it is understood that the measures set forth in chapter of the Protocol cannot be taken in the territorial sea of another State except with the permission or authorization of the coastal State concerned. This principle is well established in the law of the sea and did not need to be restated in the Protocol. The *travaux préparatoires* should also indicate that the international law of the sea includes the United Nations Convention on the Law of the Sea as well as other relevant

international instruments. References to the United Nations Convention on the Law of the Sea do not prejudice or affect in any way the position of any State in relation to that Convention.

Article 7: Cooperation

99. The *travaux préparatoires* should indicate that this Protocol is without prejudice to the existing rights, obligations or responsibilities of States Parties under other international instruments, such as those referred to in this article. Rights, obligations and responsibilities under another instrument are determined by the terms of that instrument and whether the State concerned is a party to it, not by this Protocol. Therefore, any State that becomes a party to this Protocol but is not a party to another international instrument referred to in the Protocol would not become subject to any right, obligation or responsibility under that other instrument.

Article 8: Measures against the Smuggling of Migrants by Sea

100. The *travaux préparatoires* should indicate that the word "engaged" in paragraphs 1, 2 and 7 of this article and in paragraph 1 of Article 10 should be understood broadly as including vessels "engaged" both directly and indirectly in the smuggling of migrants. Of particular concern was the inclusion of both vessels actually found to be carrying smuggled migrants and vessels ("mother ships") that transport smuggled migrants on open ocean voyages but are sometimes not apprehended until after the migrants have been transferred to smaller local vessels for landing purposes.

Appendix

Expert Group Report on Other Monitoring Programmes

A. OECD CONVENTION ON BRIBERY OF FOREIGN PUBLIC OFFICIALS IN INTERNATIONAL BUSINESS TRANSACTIONS (OECD CONVENTION)

OECD Convention Monitoring

Started: 1999.
Number of countries: 36.
Organisation: OECD Working Group on Bribery; Lead examiners; Secretariat.
Methodology: Self-assessment and peer review with lead examiners and plenary discussion.
Scope of review: Phase 1 legislation; Phase 2 enforcement.
Rate of monitoring for Phase 1: 35 countries reviewed in 2 years. One additional review still to be done.
Rate of monitoring for Phase 2: Approximately 6 per year, all 36 countries reviewed by 2007.
Number of Working Group meetings per year: 5.
In-country visits: Yes for Phase 2.
Civil society participation: Yes.
Follow-up: Yes. Phase 2 bis (Japan) and Reports on Progress.
Technical assistance: No.
Reports published: Country report with recommendations.
Current staffing (estimate): About 10 persons.
Estimated cost: Approximately € 1.5 million.

Strengths

The OECD reviews are effective due to a combination of the following factors:

Organisation

- Adequate funding until 2007; commitment for continued funding thereafter will be needed.
- Strong secretariat and overall professionalism.
- Working Group on Bribery with strong chairman meets five times annually.

Methodology

- Well-designed questionnaires.
- Well-organised country visits.
- Active civil society and private sector participation.
- Record of criticizing even powerful governments, such as UK and Japan.
- Review produces detailed published reports with recommendations.
- Process of follow-up on reports and recommendations, especially regarding countries found to perform inadequately.

Transparency

- Publish explanation of review process, schedule and questionnaires.
- Reports on country reviews published, including on website.
- Steps have been taken to synthesize the lengthy complicated reports for a wider public.

Weaknesses

Some weaknesses of the OECD process relate primarily to the methodology and are:

- Country reports are lengthy and legalistic; efforts have been made recently to make them more accessible.

- Occasional lack of cooperation by reviewed country in agreeing on people/organisations to be interviewed.
- Uneven quality of peer reviewers.

B. GRECO: COUNCIL OF EUROPE CONVENTIONS ON CORRUPTION AND OTHER INSTRUMENTS

GRECO Monitoring

Started: 2000.
Number of countries: 39.
Organisation: GRECO Plenary; Evaluation Team; Secretariat.
Methodology: Peer review with evaluation teams and plenary discussion; questionnaire, responses and other inputs.
Scope of review: Each evaluation phase on given themes and specific provisions.
Rate of monitoring for 1st evaluation/compliance round: 8-13 countries per year; 34 countries in 3 years.
Rate of monitoring for 2nd evaluation round: 7-18 countries per year; 39 countries in 3 years.
Number of Plenary meetings per year: 3-5
In country visits: Yes.
Civil society participation: Yes.
Follow-up: Compliance reports. Thereafter, "addenda" which are additional reports if non-compliance.
Technical assistance: Yes.
Reports published: Evaluation and compliance reports, with government agreement.
Current staffing (estimate): 10 persons employed at the secretariat
Estimated cost: Overall budget of € 1,660,000 for 2005

Strengths

Organisation

- Adequate funding.
- Strong secretariat and high level of professionalism.
- GRECO plenary with strong chairman meets 3-5 times annually.
- EU accession requirements for Central European countries provided an effective lever.

- Associated technical assistance programme.

Methodology

- Well-designed questionnaires.
- Well-organised country visits.
- A compliance process which follows-up on the implementation of the recommendations made in the evaluation process.
- Some civil society participation.
- Scrupulous equal treatment of all countries and willingness to recommend improvements.
- Systemic audit with wide coverage.
- Review produces detailed reports with recommendations.

Transparency

- Publishes explanation of review process, schedule and questionnaires.
- Evaluation and compliance reports are always published, subject however to agreement of country reviewed.

Weaknesses

There has been criticism of GRECO on the following grounds:

- Too much focus on formal provisions, insufficient focus on some questions of real impact.
- Country visits are largely official, with evaluated countries not always providing the civil servants with the best information.
- Civil society participation could be strengthened; it is not required in the rules, but has become a standard part of country reviews.
- Agreement of countries is required for publication of reports.

C. INTER-AMERICAN CONVENTION AGAINST CORRUPTION (OAS CONVENTION)

OAS Convention Monitoring

Started: 2001.
Number of countries; 28 (of 33 signatories).
Organisation: Conference of States Parties; Committee of Experts; expert sub-group; Secretariat.
Methodology: Self-assessment and peer review with expert sub-groups and committee discussion.
Scope of review: Each review phase covers selected articles of the Convention.
Rate of monitoring: Currently 10 countries per year; 28 countries in 5 years.
Number of Committee of Experts meetings per year: 2
In-country visits: No.
Civil society participation: Yes.
Follow-up: Yes starting in 2006.
Technical assistance: In theory, Yes, in practice, No.
Reports punished: Country report with recommendations, civil society reports.
Current staffing (estimate): 6 professionals devoting approximately 30 per cent of their time to monitoring.
Estimated cost: Budget of US $350,000 for 2005.

The OAS Convention follow-up process got off to a very slow start because there was no reference to monitoring in the Convention. This meant that it had to be introduced afterwards, which required four years of effort. Monitoring did not fit readily into the OAS' traditional role of providing help when requested by member governments. As a result of pressure by civil society and several governments, monitoring got under way. The monitoring process is still evolving and still needs strengthening, including increased funding.

Strengths

Methodology

- Well-designed questionnaire.
- Expert teams review country and work with secretariat on draft report to working group.

- Strong civil society participation.
- Useful plenary discussion of draft reports.
- Review produces detailed reports with recommendations.

Transparency

- Publish explanation of review process, schedule and questionnaires.
- Arrangements for website publication of government and civil society responses to the questionnaire, but publication of government responses subject to government agreement, not always given.
- Arrangements for publication of country reports, with conclusions and recommendations. Until recently this was subject to government agreement but this is no longer the case.

Weaknesses

- Inadequate funding; the funding comes primarily from a single country.
- Slow pace of reviews.
- Lack of country visits.
- Too few experts with relevant professional experience.

D. ADB-OECD ACTION PLAN FOR ASIA-PACIFIC

Monitoring of the Anti-Corruption Action Plan

Started: 2002.
Number of countries: Currently 25.
Organisation: Steering Group; Advisory Group; Secretariat.
Methodology: Self-assessment and peer review discussion.
Scope of review: Stocktaking of measures, institutions, legislation; thematic reviews.
Rate of monitoring for stocktaking report: Horizontal study of 25 countries.
Rate of monitoring thematic review: Horizontal study of 21 countries in 1 year.
Number of Steering Group Meetings per year: 2.
In country visits: No.

(*Contd.*)

Civil society participation: Participate in seminars, conferences and in Advisory Group.
Follow-up: Yes, continuous self-reporting on progress in Steering Group and regular updates of Stocktaking and on recommendations to thematic reviews.
Technical assistance: Yes.
Reports published: Self-assessment and stocktaking reports.
Current staffing (estimate): 3.5 persons.
Estimated cost: Annual budget of approximately US$350,000.

The approach to corruption in the Asia-Pacific region thus far has been via a non-binding instrument and an evolving soft review process. Countries that have endorsed the Anti-Corruption Action Plan for Asia-Pacific assess and review progress in their efforts to implement the Action Plan in various ways, including self-assessment and mutual reviews that are supported by horizontal analytical studies. The mechanisms for review of anti-corruption policies and frameworks aim foremost at guiding the national and regional anti-corruption agenda by identifying of legal and institutional weaknesses and priorities for future reform. A report that takes stock of the legal and institutional frameworks to fight corruption assists the countries in detecting needs for reform. (Second round completed in 2005.) Thematic reviews addressing issues that the endorsing countries have identified as common priorities add to these mechanisms. The first such review was launched in 2004 on public procurement and is expected to be completed in 2006.

Strengths

Methodology

- Evolutionary approach, requested and designed by the states concerned.
- Process of dialogue about country performance and action to be taken.
- Process mainly involves officials directly involved in anti-corruption activities.
- Thematic reviews are carried out by the countries with support from the Secretariat; these reviews are discussed in the Group and include recommendations.
- Follow-up is ensured through continuous update of reports and regular discussion in the framework of the Steering Group meetings.

- Independent experts provide expertise that flows into the analysis; countries appreciate this as a form of technical assistance.

Transparency

- Explanation of process published on website.
- Country plans and reports prepared by national governments are published on the website.
- As of recently a comprehensive summary of Steering Group meetings is published on website, subject to clarifications by governments.

Weaknesses

- Instrument is non-binding.
- Lack of country visits.
- Limited discussion in public reports of actual practice.
- Thus far no recommendations to countries, but this is planned.

E. NEPAD: AFRICAN PEER REVIEW MECHANISM

NEPAD Monitoring (APRM)

Started: 2004.
Number of countries: 23.
Monitoring bodies: APR Forum; Panel of Eminent Persons (7 persons); Secretariat.
Methodology: Self-assessment, expert panel and peer review.
Scope of review: Reviews cover 91 indicators.
Rate of monitoring: Each country reviewed every 2-4 years; 2 countries reviewed so far.
Number of APR Panel meetings per year: Approximately 6.
In country visits: Yes.
Reports published: Country reports and action plans.
Follow-up: Not yet known.
Technical assistance: In theory, yes, in practice not yet clear.
Civil society participation: Yes.
Current staffing (estimate): 6 coordinators and 6 personal assistants at the APRM Secretariat.
Estimated cost: At beginning of peer review process each state was to pledge a minimum of US$100,000.

The NEPAD African Peer Review Mechanism (APRM) only began to function in 2005 and thus it is too early for a meaningful evaluation. By way of a preliminary assessment, the APRM appears to have the following features:

Strengths

Organisation

The process foresees an important role for the APRM Secretariat, including preparation of a background document on the reviewed country. The plenary review body is composed of heads of state, which may provide political support, but this is a two-edged sword.

Methodology

- Indicators in addition to questionnaire.
- Government consultation with stakeholder is required prior to self-evaluation.
- Country visits are made by expert reviewers.
- Review produces detailed report with recommendations.
- A national action plan to address deficiencies is prepared by the reviewed government.

Transparency

- It is planned to publish the final reports.

Weaknesses

- Lack of financial and technical resources. The APRM Secretariat is understaffed.

F. FINANCIAL ACTION TASK FORCE (FATF) RECOMMENDATIONS

FATF Monitoring
Started: 1992. *Number of countries:* 31. *Monitoring bodies:* FATF; Secretariat.

(*Contd.*)

Methodology: Self-assessment, peer review with expert teams and plenary discussion.
Scope of review: 47 Recommendations.
Rate of monitoring for 1st evaluation round: 27 countries in 3 years.
Rate of monitoring for 2nd evaluation round: 28 countries in 3 years.
Rate monitoring for 3rd evaluation round: 16 countries in 3 years.
Number of Plenary meetings per year: 3.
In country visits: Yes.
Follow-up: Yes.
Technical assistance: Yes.
Civil society participation: No.
Reports punished: Mutual evaluation report, with government agreement.
Current staffing (estimate): Not available.
Estimated cost: Not available.

The FATF monitoring system for its "Forty Recommendations on Anti-Money-Laundering" began in 1992 and served as a model for the OECD Convention review process. Seven further recommendations have been added.

Strengths

Organisation

- Supported by a small professionally staffed secretariat.
- Plenary review body.
- Cooperates with a number of regional anti-money-laundering groups.

Methodology

- Well-designed questionnaire.
- Country visits by expert teams. These include meetings with bank and other private sector groups which often provide views sharply different from government representatives.
- Peer review process covers most of the principal international financial centres.
- Governments report not only on measures taken but results attained.

- Evaluations focus on whether the system work, not just on whether there are laws, regulations on the books.
- Provides for follow-up measures to address members not sufficiently in compliance; the follow-up process exerts pressure effectively.
- Supports a number of regional anti-money-laundering groups.

Transparency

- In 2005 FATF began publishing country reports, subject to agreement of national governments.

Weaknesses

- It has not been very transparent until recently including lack of publication of country reports.
- Some claim that the standards applied are not high enough and are not consistently applied.

G. STABILITY PACT ANTI-CORRUPTION INITIATIVE (SPAI) COMMITMENTS

SPAI Monitoring

Started: 2003.
Number of countries; 8 in South-Eastern Europe.
Monitoring bodies: Steering Group; Secretariat.
Methodology: Self-assessment, mutual evaluation (twinning) and external review.
Scope of review: Simultaneous submission of complete progress reports.
Rate of monitoring: 8 countries twice a year.
Number of steering group meetings per year: 2.
In country visits: No.
Civil society participation: Observers at Steering Group Meetings
Reports published: Reports by Steering Group.
Follow-up: Periodic reviews on 6 month basis.
Technical assistance: Yes.
Current staffing (estimate): 4 professionals at secretariat devoting 30-40 per cent of their time to monitoring.
Estimated cost: Approximately € 35,000 spent on monitoring each year.

The SPAI (Stability Pact Anti-corruption Initiative—an arm of the Brussels based international Organisation Stability Pact) is a soft monitoring system for South-Eastern Europe in place since 2004, which involves self-assessment and a degree of mutual evaluation. It is interesting to note that SPAI already monitors UNCAC ratification and implementation in its region. The process is still in its early stage, so it is difficult to adequately assess its performances at this time.

Strengths

Organisation

- It is managed by a regional secretariat office (the RSLO—Regional Secretariat Liaison Office), staffed with people from the region.
- Leverage for compliance through development assistance and EU accession.

Methodology

- Method of twinning countries, for mutual review of compliance.
- Compliance matrix tracking measures introduced can potentially give a useful overview of performance.
- Periodic reviews on a six-monthly basis by the Steering Group, the governing body of SPAI including all Member States.

Weaknesses

- Steering Group recommendations, based on country reports and peer evaluations, are not sufficiently critical.
- Steering Group recommendations are not tailored to individual countries.
- Member countries are overwhelmed by monitoring activities from EU and GRECO and devote scarce resources to SPAI monitoring system.

H. UN CONVENTION AGAINST TRANSNATIONAL ORGANIZED CRIME (UNTOC CONVENTION)

UNTOC Monitoring

Started: Not yet established.
Number of countries: 118.
Monitoring bodies: Conference of States Parties; Secretariat.
Methodology: Factual responses, secretariat analytical and assessment report, plenary discussion and follow-up questioning.
Scope of review: Questionnaires on selected topics, based on programme of work of the Conference of Parties.
Rate of monitoring: Planned to cover all countries each year in the first two years, then every second year.
Number of meetings per year: One meeting per year in the first two years, then one every second year.
In *country visits:* None discussed thus far. May have in-country visits for evaluation of technical assistance needs as follow-up to assessments.
Civil society participation: Not yet established.
Follow-up: Some initial steps.
Technical assistance: Yes.
Reports published: Secretariat overview report.
Current staffing (estimate): Potentially 7-9 persons employed in Crimes Convention Section.
Estimated cost: Not yet known

The UNTOC Convention entered into force in September 2003 and the Conference of the Parties has met twice since then, once in 2004 and once in 2005. The review process is in development so it is too early to make observations on how it works.

Developments under the UNTOC Convention are of interest in providing lessons for UNCAC monitoring, given the UN framework, the similar membership, the inclusion of many similar provisions on international cooperation, and the fact that UNODC in Vienna also provides its secretariat. However, the provisions in UNTOC on monitoring are far less extensive than those in UNCAC.

The UNTOC process began developing its working methods without an early preparatory process and thus without the opportunity for States to exchange views in advance and identify issues to be analysed in-depth. Thus, the Conference of Parties has taken longer than expected to determine how to organise its work As part of a programme to build a knowledge base about the status of implementation of the Convention and its Protocols, it instructed the Secretariat to collect information on the basis of questionnaires that it reviewed and approved. The rate of responses to this questionnaire was low but allowed identification of a number of compliance issues. An important development in the UNTOC framework was the decision by the Conference of the Parties to set-up an open-ended interim working group to advise and assist it in the implementation of its mandate on technical assistance. Building on its request for an assessment of the challenges in implementing the Convention and its Protocols, the Conference of Parties decided that the working group should perform the following functions:

(*i*) Review needs for technical assistance.
(*ii*) Provide guidance on priorities.
(*iii*) Take into consideration information on technical assistance activities of the secretariat, as well as of States, and on projects and priorities of States, other entities of the United Nations system and international organisations.
(*iv*) Facilitate mobilisation of potential resources.

The Conference requested the secretariat to develop project proposals to address the needs identified. It was also presented with a secretariat report on the relationship between the Parties to the UNTOC Convention and the Commission on Crime Prevention and Criminal Justice and also with the future Conference of the States Parties to the UNCAC. This concluded that policy coordination might be desirable and that a review of the institutional relationships between the bodies should be considered.

I. UN CONVENTION ON THE RIGHTS OF THE CHILD

Monitoring of the UN Convention on the Rights of the Child

Started: 1991.
Number of countries: 192.
Organisation: Committee on Rights of the Child (18 experts); Secretariat.
Methodology: Reporting and technical assistance.
Scope of review: Every report covers all the articles of the convention.

(*Contd.*)

Rate of monitoring: 27 countries per year (estimate) for the Convention; 4 per Optional Protocol.
Number of Committee meetings per year: 3.
In-country visits: Very rare.
Civil society participation: Yes.
Follow-up: Yes.
Technical assistance: Yes.
Reports published: Country reports with recommendations.
Current staffing (estimate): 8 (but only 3 working full-time).
Estimated cost: US $695,900 for 2004-05.

Strengths

Organisation

- A small professional secretariat.
- Regular funding.

Methodology

- A continuous review process on a 5-year cycle.
- Constructive dialogue: the Committee avoids a confrontational approach.
- Participation of non-governmental actors and other UN agencies in the reporting process and other monitoring mechanisms.
- Cooperation between the various stakeholders (government, UN agencies, NGOs) encouraged through the monitoring process.
- Needs for technical assistance are identified during the monitoring process.

Transparency

- Website explaining the monitoring process and on which the reports and other documents are published.
- Mainly public meetings.
- Summary records of those meetings.
- Published country reports.

Weaknesses

- Backlog due to workload and inadequate staff.

- Wide range of issues covered by the Convention can make it a burden to report on for some countries with little capacity.
- Lack of country visits: no fact-finding missions and very rarely visits to follow-up on the concluding observations.
- Vagueness of the concluding observations.

J. UN CONVENTION AGAINST TORTURE AND OTHER CRUEL, INHUMAN OR DEGRADING TREATMENT OR PUNISHMENT[1]

UNCAT Monitoring

Started: 1988.
Number of countries: 141.
Organisation: Committee against Torture (10 elected experts); Secretariat.
Methodology: Reporting and (if accepted by each specific State Party) individual communications, inter-state complaints and inquiries.
Scope of review: Every report covers all the articles of the Convention. The rest of mechanisms, if they may be used, give to the Committee considerably broad monitoring powers.
Rate of monitoring: Approximately 12 States per year.
Number of Sessions per year: 2.
In-country visits: Allowed upon general acceptance of the States, but not used in practice
Civil society participation: Yes.
Follow-up: Yes.
Reports punished: Annual Report to the General Assembly; country reports on countries; final views in individual communications.
Current staffing: 5 (networking full-time on the CAT).
Estimated cost: Not available.

Strengths

Methodology

- Regular and relatively frequent (every 4 years) individualised scrutiny coupled with requests for further information in the meantime. This brings about a continuous monitoring process.

1. UN General Assembly, A/RES/39/46 of 10 December 1984.

- Complete review of policies and practices of each State party, which tends to be more and more in-depth.
- Possibility to use a fairly wide range of monitoring methods.
- Minimum monitoring level applicably to all State parties in the same manner and on an equal footing.
- Methodology of constructive dialogue, which helps States to adopt a more cooperative attitude.
- Improving follow-up mechanisms.
- Participation of civil society.

Transparency

- Report review sessions are public, summary records of such sessions and final observations/recommendations are made public, as well as final decisions in the framework of individual communications.

Weaknesses

- Significant backlog.
- Lack of means to effectively make States fulfil their reporting obligations.
- Obligation to submit exhaustive reports may become a burden for some countries, especially those with limited resources.
- Poor funding and understating of the CAT secretariat.
- Under-exploitation of several mechanisms provided for in the Convention.
- Lack of means to oblige actual implementation of its recommendations by State parties.

K. INTERNATIONAL COVENANT ON CIVIL AND POLITICAL RIGHTS AND ITS PROTOCOLS

Monitoring by the Human Rights Committee

Started: 1977.
Number of countries: 156 (as of May 8, 2006).
Organisation: Human Rights Committee; Secretariat.

(Contd.)

Methodology: Examination of State reports and individual communications through the 18-member Human Rights Committee.
Scope of review of State reports: Initial and periodic reports should cover all the articles of the Covenant.
Annual rate of monitoring: Approximately 15 State reports and 30 decisions on the merits of individual communications.
Number of sessions per year: Three.
In-country visits: No.
Civil society participation: Yes.
Follow-up: Yes.
Reports published: Country reports with concluding recommendations; decisions on individual communications.
Current staffing (estimate): Not available.
Estimated cost: US $681,600 for 2004-05.

Strengths

Organisation

- Regular funding.
- Election of members by States parties.

Methodology

- Continuous process of examination of State reports on 4-5 year cycle and of individual communications at every session.
- Constructive, non-adversarial dialogue with States parties on their reports.
- Participation of civil society in examination of State reports, individual communications, and drafting of general comments.
- Special review procedure for State reports.
- Follow-up procedure for concluding observations and for decisions on the merits of individual communications.

Transparency

- Website explaining the examination of State reports and individual communications and the drafting of general comments.

- Website on which State reports, concluding observations, views, summary records, and other relevant documents are published.
- Constructive dialogue held in public.

Weaknesses

Methodology

- Range of issues to be covered can impose a burden on States with few resources.
- No country visits.
- No technical assistance provided by the Human Rights Committee.
- No enforcement mechanism.

Transparency

- Discussion of internal matters, concluding observations, and consideration of individual communications are carried out in private.
- Meetings with specialised agencies and other UN organs that wish to provide State-related information are held in private.

L. SPECIAL PROCEDURES OF THE UNITED NATIONS COMMISSION ON HUMAN RIGHTS

Special Procedures, Rapporteurs, Working Groups, etc.
Started: 1967.
Number of Countries: Universal, UN Charter-based.
Methodology: Independent experts are given thematic and country-based mandates; currently, there are 42 different special procedures, 28 of which are thematic, 13 of which are country-based, and one of which is the 1503 procedure.
Scope of review: Each special procedure mandate holder reviews human rights abuses related to his or her theme or country.
In-country visits: Each special procedure mandate holder goes on one to two country visits annually.
Civil Society participation: Yes.

(*Contd.*)

Follow-up: There are no formal mechanisms to ensure that states follow-up on recommendations.
Reports Published: Annual reports to the Commission of Human Rights (now transferred to the HRC).
Current Staffing: Varying OHCHR staff members assigned to each mandate holder.
Estimated Cost: US $3,985,623 in the year 2005-06.

Strengths

Organisational

- Efficiently organised thematically and by countries.
- Regular funding.
- Allocation of staff to assist special rapporteur.

Methodology

- More effective way of ensuring state accountability to human rights protection.
- Integration of the NGO perspective.
- Annual reports to the Commission of Human Rights (now the Human Rights Council).
- Specific recommendations highlighted.

Transparency

- Special rapporteur issues an annual report that documents activities and conclusions annually.
- OHCHR website provides information on all of the special procedures reports, as well as standing requests for country visits.
- OHCHR website also contains individual sections on all of the special procedures, which provides in-depth information on activities, how to file complaints, and actions taken by special rapporteurs regarding specific human rights situations.

Weaknesses

- There is no mechanism to ensure state responsiveness to recommendations made by special rapporteurs.

- There is no mechanism to ensure that states respond to communications received and to requests for state visits.
- There is an overlap between different mandates.
- Unclear regulations on the creation of new mandates.
- Unclear regulations on the termination of existing mandates.

Bibliography

Articles & Reports

"2005 Global Corruption Report", Transparency International, 2005. *The report focuses on corruption in construction and post-conflict reconstruction Available online for ordering or downloading (by chapter) at http:/ wwwqlobalcorruptionreportorg/download html#download.*

"Advancing Democracy", Paula, J. Dobriansky *National Interest*, Fall 2004, 8 pages. *Under Secretary of State for Global Affairs Paula Dobriansky describes several initiatives the Bush administration has undertaken to support democracy worldwide.*

"Building a Strong Local Government Ethics Programme", Michael W. Manske, H. George Frederickson *PM Public Management*, June 2004, 5 pages. *The author discusses a comprehensive ethics programme which rests on four pillars: the code of ethics, the ethics education programme, the oversight of the ethics commission, and the office of the ethics administrator. Each pillar plays an equal and important in each programme, and each depends upon the others for reinforcement and support.*

"Collaborative Governance Practices and Democracy", David, E. Booher, *National Civic Review*, Winter 2004, 15 pages. *Collaborative approaches to governance can resolve seemingly intractable public policy conundrums; produce successful policy outcomes; and increase the capacity of communities, organizations, and individuals to work together.*

"Combating Corruption: Look Before You Leap", James, B. Jacobs. *National Forum/Phi Kappa Phi Journal*, Winter 2004, 5 pages. *Jacobs posits that democracy can succeed even in nations fraught with widespread government corruption. The real challenge for every society, every government, and every people is managing it.*

"Corruption and Democracy", Matt Welch, *Columbia Journalism Review,* September/October 2003, 7 pages. *An ideal vision of how community and communication can preserve scholastic journalism.*

"Faces and Phases of Transparency Reform in Local Government", Eric, E. Otenyo and Nancy, S. Lind, *International Journal of Public Administration,* 2004, 21 pages. *The authors draw on public and official perceptions to discuss the discontinuities between various interpretations of transparency in local government jurisdictions. The article seeks to establish a theoretical understanding of transparency in public administration literature.*

"Good Governance: The Pliability of a Policy Concept", Martin, R. Doornbos, *TRAMES: A Journal of the Humanities and Social Sciences,* 2004, 16 pages. *This article traces the evolution of the concept of 'Good Governance', launched as a guiding policy metaphor in international aid circles at the end of the Cold War.*

"The IMF and Democratic Governance", Devesh Kapur and Moises Naim, *Journal of Democracy,* January, 2005, 14 pages. *Like many other world-governance bodies, the International Monetary Fund is a necessarily non-democratic organisation that cannot help but have an impact on democracy's prospects in poorer countries.*

"Legal Framework for the New Governance: Processes for Citizen Participation in the Work of Government", Lisa Blomgren Bingham, *et al., National Civic Review,* Spring 2005, 8 pages. *How do existing government rules and administrative procedures encourage citizen participation in quasi-legislative and quasi-judicial settings?*

"Modes of Governance and Their Evaluation", Christen Knill, *TRAMES: A Journal of the Humanities & Social Sciences,* 2004 20 pages. *This paper seeks to address a distinction between different ideal type patterns of governance that are characterized by a specific division of competencies between state and society. The appropriateness of different patterns is assessed by taking account of institutional and problem structures as well as normative criteria for the evaluation of governance success.*

"Open-Door or Closed-Door? Transparency in Domestic and International Bargaining", David Stasavage *International Organization,* Fall 2004, 37 pages. *This article develops a game-*

theoretic model that provides four hypotheses about the relative benefits of open-door versus closed-door bargaining, and about the preferences of different actors with regard to this type of transparency.

"Report to Congress Pursuant to the International Anti-corruption and Good Governance Act (Public Law 106-309)" Department of State Anti-corruption Initiatives Website, http://www.state.gov/g/inl/rls/rpt/c6696.htm, updated June 2005, *Congress passed the International Anti-corruption and Good Governance Act of 2000 (IAGGA) (Public Law 106-309) on October 5, 2000. The purpose of this legislation is "to ensure that United States assistance programmes promote good governance by assisting other countries to combat corruption throughout society and to improve transparency and accountability at all levels of government and throughout the private sector." The report, due every two years, gives an outline of the act, summarizes the US government international anti-corruption initiatives, and examines selected US government anti-corruption assistance programmes.*

"Strengthening Governance: Ranking Countries Would Help" Robert, I. Rotberg *Washington Quarterly*, Winter 2004-05, 11 pages. *As the threat of nation-state failure and the problem of governance quality in the developing world become increasingly daunting and well-documented, the need to improve governance grows consistently more urgent. The author suggests that creating an effective, impartial good-governance ranking system and advisory service will help meet this critical challenge.*

"Sweetheart Deals", Alan Greenblatt *Governing*, December, 2004, 6 pages. *To save money and increase government efficiency, the public sector increasingly relies on the services and specialized expertise of private companies. But allegations of favouritism and collusion in the awarding of government contracts have prompted closer scrutiny of the government contract process. Greenblatt cites examples of both problems and reform from around the country.*

"Transparency in Government", A publication of the US Department of State, December, 1999, 20 pages. *Discusses the importance of opening government deliberations and rule-making processes to the public and of making government documents available to concerned citizens. Available on the Internet at http://usinfo. state. gov/products/pubs/transgov/.*

Recommended Websites

The Carter Center, URL: http://www.cartercenter.orq *Founded in 1982 by former US President Jimmy Carter and his wife, Rosalynn, the Atlanta-based Center has helped to improve the quality of life for people in more than 65 countries. The site featuring transparency programmes in several developing countries and anti-corruption initiatives.*

Center for International Private Enterprise (CIPE), URL: http://www.cipe.org *CIPE) is an independent, non-profit affiliate of the US Chamber of Commerce. As one of the four core institutes of the National Endowment for Democracy, CIPE promotes democratic and market-oriented economic reform by working directly with the private sector in developing countries. Featuring articles, speeches, and invaluable resources on strengthening corporate governance as well as resources, toolkits, and articles on combating corruption worldwide.*

The Committee of Sponsoring Organisations of the Treadway Commission (COSO), IIR1 : *http://www.coso.org/ The COSO "Treadway Commission" is a volunteer private sector organization consisting of the five major financial professional associations dedicated to improving the quality of financial reporting through business ethics, effective internal controls, and corporate governance. The five associations are the American Accounting Association (AAA); the American Institute of Certified Public Accountants(AICPA); the Financial Executives Institute (FEI); the Institute of Internal Auditors (IIA): and the Institute of Management Accountants (IMA).*

Ethics Resource Center (ERC), URL: http://www.ethics.org/ *ERC) is a non-profit, non-partisan educational organization whose vision is a world where individuals and organisations act with integrity. The mission of the Ethics Resource Center is to strengthen ethical leadership worldwide by providing leading-edge expertise and services through research, education and partnerships.*

Fighting Corruption — US Agency for International Development (USAID), URL: http://www.usaid.gov/our work/democracy and governance/technical areas/anti-corruption/. *USAID's efforts and programmes on international anti-corruption Handbook on Fighting Corruption is available for download.*

Good Governance Programme, International Trade Administration, US Department of Commerce, URL: http://ira.adoc.gov/goodgover nance/. *The Good Governance Programme works to increase market access and ensure a level playing field for US companies in emerging markets by promoting transparency through Business Ethics and Anti-Corruption, Acc ountability in Corporate Governance, Fairness in Commercial Dispute Resolution, and Protection of Intellectual Property Rights.*

The Office of The National Counter Corruption Commission, Royal Thai Government, URL: http://www.nccc.thaigov.net/nccc/lphp. *Thai laws and complaints on corruption and good governance Information available in English and Thai.*

Public Sector Governance—The World Bank URL: http://wwwl.worldbank.org/publicsector/index.c.fm. *The Public Sector Group's objectives are based on the view that the Bank must focus more of its efforts on building efficient and accountable public sector institutions —rather than simply providing discrete policy advise. Latest news, reports and publications are provided.*

Transparency International USA (TI-USA), URL: http://www.transparency-usa.org/. *TI-USA is the US chapter of Transparency International (TI), the Berlin-based non-profit, non-partisan organisation founded in 1993 to curb corruption in international transactions. Through its network of chapters in over 80 countries, TI encourages governments to implement effective anti-corruption laws and policies, promotes reform through international organisations and raises public awareness.*

US Office of Government Ethics (OGE) URL: http://www.usoge.gov/. *Information on ethics, latest developments in ethics, ethics programmes, and informational and educational materials.*

US Securities and Exchange Commission (SEC), URL: http://www.sec.gov. *Information about SEC enforcement actions, Complaint Center, and further information for accountants and auditors.*

US Department of State Anti-corruption Initiatives, URL: http://www.state.gov/g/inl/corr/. *Press releases, fact sheets, reports and remarks focusing on the US anti-corruption and good governance initiatives. Links to useful resources on the subjects are provided.*

US Department of Justice, Fraud Section, URL: http://www.usdojgov/criminal/fraudhtml. *Comprehensive information on the FCPA, legislative history of FCPA, 1998 amendments, opinion procedures, and international agreements.*

US Department of State International Information Programme: Bribery and Corruption, URL: http://usinfo.state.gov/ei/economic issues/bribery and corruption.html. Featuring updated news and information on US policy and measures against bribery and corruption. Reports, electronic journals and US government publications are available for download. Links to useful Internet resources are provided.

Index